STUDY AS WORSHIP

STUDIES IN JUDAISM
IN LATE ANTIQUITY

EDITED BY

JACOB NEUSNER

VOLUME TWENTY-SIX

BENEDICT THOMAS VIVIANO, O.P.

STUDY AS WORSHIP

LEIDEN

E. J. BRILL

1978

STUDY AS WORSHIP

ABOTH AND THE NEW TESTAMENT

BY

BENEDICT THOMAS VIVIANO, O.P.

LEIDEN
E. J. BRILL
1978

ISBN 90 04 05775 7

Sicut enim a perfecta scientia procul sumus, levioris culpae arbitramur saltem parum, quam omnino nihil dicere.

Jerome

Parentibus primitias

TABLE OF CONTENTS

INTRODUCTION

The subject of study as worship, that is, the religious value of study of Scripture and the postbiblical tradition, has not yet been the object of a full-length monograph. This is true whether one considers the rabbinic attitude or that of the New Testament. Of course the theme of study has long been recognized to have been of central significance in ancient Judaism, and each of the standard modern syntheses of rabbinic thought, those of Schechter, [1] Bousset-Gressmann, [2] Foot Moore [3] and J. Bonsirven, [4] devote a chapter or more to it. The situation is similar with respect to the New Testament. Since its various books do not directly address themselves to the question of the religious value of sacred study, it has not often been directly discussed by exegetes. With these facts in mind, it would seem natural and desirable that someone fill in the gap.

Yet on the other hand, the materials for such a monograph have, for the most part, always lain ready to hand and have not been neglected. On the rabbinic side the chief source is the Mishnah tractate Aboth, and it has been the object of innumerable commentaries. On the New Testament side questions like Jesus' attitude toward the Torah and the nature of discipleship have often been discussed, and even the theme of wisdom in the Gospels and Paul is belatedly receiving its due recognition. But up till now no one, it seems, has made a systematic effort to interpret Aboth primarily with a view to its affinities and disagreements with the New Testament. Charles Taylor made a start in 1897 but barely scratched the surface. This should suffice as a justification for the present work, imperfect as it may be.

From a personal point of view, I may say that this theme has interested me since many years ago I read the church historian John

---

[1] Solomon Schechter, *Aspects of Rabbinic Theology* (New York: Schocken, 1961; 1st ed. 1909), pp. 116-169.

[2] W. Bousset and H. Gressmann, *Die Religion des Judentums im späthellenistischen Zeitalter*, 4th ed. (Tübingen: Mohr, 1966), pp. 119-141 (Das Gesetz), 162-171 (Die Theologen), 181-182 (Jugendunterricht).

[3] G. F. Moore, *Judaism in the First Centuries of the Christian Era* (Cambridge, Mass.: Harvard U.P., 1927), vol. 2, pp. 239-247.

[4] J. Bonsirven, *Le Judaïsme palestinien au temps de Jésus-Christ* (Paris: Beauchesne, 1934), vol. 2, pp. 247-303 (La révélation—La Tora), esp. pp. 282-300 (Étude de la Loi): *idem, Palestinian Judaism in the Time of Jesus Christ* (New York: Holt, 1964), pp. 79-97.

Tracy Ellis' essay *American Catholics and the Intellectual Life,* [5] a
work which provoked an enormous reaction [6] and challenged American
Catholics to make their due contribution to the culture of their new
homeland and this on the basis of their religious heritage. The problem
was not merely a Catholic one, as the Columbia historian Richard
Hofstadter demonstrated in his outstanding work *Anti-Intellectualism
in American Life.* [7] Moreover, as a member of the Dominican order
I was committed by vow to the "assiduous study of sacred truth" as one
of the four principal means of sanctification and of the pursuit of the
goal of preaching the gospel. But the question could be asked: what
was the theological, the biblical, basis for such an evaluation of study?
With rare exceptions, [8] the answers were generally of a pragmatic
order, e.g., to answer objections. These then were some of the elements
in my personal involvement with the topic.

The method employed has been a simple one. The first chapter
contains a long series of notes on selected texts from the oldest strata
of Aboth (chapters one to four), besides M. Kiddushin 1:10 and the
talmudic developments of this pasage. These notes concentrate on the
original meaning of the sayings, their internal relations, and their
parallels in the New Testament. The discussion of other matters is
kept to a minimum. The second chapter investigates the roots of the
Aboth ideology in the Old Testament and in the intertestamental
literature, including Qumran, Philo and Josephus. The third chapter
examines the correspondences and divergences within the Synoptic
Gospels to the Aboth ideal. To keep the study within reasonable
bounds has meant having to renounce full consideration of the contributions of Paul and John. These may be reserved for a later study.

I would like here to thank all those who have helped in the writing
of this work, and they are many, but especially Professor W. D. Davies,
a wise master, as whose assistant I was privileged to serve for two
years, and the professors at the École biblique in Jerusalem, particularly

---

[5] Originally given as an address in St. Louis on 14 May 1955, then published as
an article in *Thought* (Fordham) 30 (1955): 351-388, finally as a book (Chicago:
Heritage, 1956).

[6] The periodical literature has been collected by F. L. Christ and G. E. Sherry,
editors of *American Catholics and the Intellectual Ideal* (New York: Appleton-
Century-Crofts, 1961). Andrew Greeley replied to Ellis in *Religion and Career*
(New York: Sheed and Ward, 1963).

[7] New York: Vintage, 1963. Pulitzer Prize, 1964.

[8] E.g., Thomas Aquinas, *Summa theologiae*, II-II, q. 188, a. 5. This may be regarded
as the Christian scholastic equivalent of Aboth. A modern work in the same spirit is
that of A. D. Sertillanges, *The Intellectual Life* (Westminster: Newman, 1956).

Father Jerome Murphy-O'Connor, who taught me to do my own work, especially the work of literary analysis.

For help with the cost of publication I would like to thank my parents, the Jack Adler Foundation of St. Louis, and Mr. E. J. Nusrala.

Benedict Thomas Viviano, O.P.

Dubuque, October, 1975

CHAPTER ONE

ABOTH AND THE IDEAL OF TORAH-STUDY AS WORSHIP

The tractate Aboth is of special importance, both because of its enormous influence on the Judaism of all subsequent ages, and because, more clearly than any other Mishnah treatise, it expresses the inner values of the Pharisaic-rabbinic religious movement with which Christianity must always be in dialogue. Pharisaic Judaism, partly prior to Christianity, partly in conscious opposition to Christianity, [1] developed a "Torah-ontology," the functional equivalent of our Christology. The earthly locus of the most intense presence of God, the Shekinah, is for rabbinic Judaism the Torah (as well as the ark in which the Torah scrolls are kept), whereas for Christianity it is the person of Jesus Christ primarily, and then secondarily the hearts of Spirit-filled believers. This Torah-ontology receives its classical expression in Aboth.

The basic message of Aboth is that Jewish man was created to study Torah. Torah study is his reason for being and his highest joy. It is an intrinsically salvific activity and indeed a precondition of serious progress in holiness and piety (2:6); one's place in heaven is in a measure determined by it: "He that has a knowledge of Scripture and Mishnah and right conduct will not soon fall into sin.... But he that has no knowledge of Scripture and Mishnah and right conduct has no part in the habitable world," M. Kiddushin 1:10. Most of the sayings in Aboth reinforce this message and in this message the thematic unity of the tractate is to be found, insofar as one can speak of thematic unity in a composite collection of sayings.

Dating and historicity. Aboth, together with the other tractates of the Mishnah, grew gradually over the century and a half which stretched from the synod or academy of Jamnia (circa A.D. 80) to the final redaction of its contents by Rabbi Judah ha-Nasi (between 200 and 220). The first four chapters are commonly considered the oldest and

---

1 Arnold Ehrhardt, "The birth of the synagogue and R. Akiba," *The Framework of the New Testament Stories* (Manchester: U.P., 1964), pp. 103-131 (= S.T. 12 [1958]: 86-111); W. D. Davies, *The Setting of the Sermon on the Mount* (Cambridge: U.P., 1964), chapter three, the section on Jamnia, pp. 256-315.

none of the authorities cited in them lived after Rabbi. The oldest
stratum of all runs 1:1-15; 2:8-14. The fifth chapter contains numerical
sayings which are mostly anonymous, while the few sayings with
personal attributions refer only to Tannaitic authors. The sixth chapter is
commonly agreed to have been added much later, during the early
medieval period, when Aboth was introduced into the synagogue
service. Chapters five and six lie outside of our purview.

If we could trust the personal attributions at the beginnings of
sayings, it would follow that most of the material in Aboth is older
than the final redaction around 200. Some sayings would predate the
birth of Jesus (1:1-11), others would have been uttered during his
lifetime (e.g., those ascribed to Hillel and Shammai), others during
the period of the formation of the Gospels and the other New Testament books. There are, to be sure, accretions to the original sayings
(e.g., scriptural proof texts), interpolations into the original order of
sayings (e.g., 1:16-18 and 2:1-4 seem to interrupt the Hillel and Shammai collection), and indeed a different stage of the redaction of the
tractate as a whole has come down to us preserved in Aboth de Rabbi
Nathan, itself extant in two recensions, A and B. [2]

The question remains: can we trust the personal attributions? Until
fairly recently scholars both Christian and Jewish tended to assume
that when a rabbinic text begins "Hillel said" what follows really was
said by Hillel, just as, until the advent of form criticism, people
generally assumed that when the Synoptic Gospels said "and Jesus
said" Jesus really did say what followed. In respect of historical skepticism Jewish scholarship lags somewhat behind Christian, but recently
Professor Jacob Neusner has endeavored to introduce healthy doses of
skepticism into the matter of rabbinic claims to authenticity of utterance.
When however we turn to his treatment of the Aboth sayings, [3] we
find that on the whole he accepts the substantial historicity of most
of the ascriptions, especially those ascribed to Johanan ben Zakkai
and the *Tannaim* who came after him. We may turn then to the Aboth
sayings with some confidence in the legitimacy of their use as comparative material for a better understanding of the New Testament.

Literary forms. Aboth stands in the tradition of Israel's proverbial

---

[2] Louis Finkelstein, "Introductory study to Pirke Abot," JBL 57 (1938): 13-50,
gives further details of overall literary analysis and of the relationship between Aboth
and Aboth de Rabbi Nathan. A. Guttmann, "Abot," JQR 41 (1951): 181-193, argues
that Aboth was not originally part of the Mishnah and was added around 300 C.E.
[3] Scattered throughout his three-volume work *Rabbinic Traditions about the
Pharisees before 70* (Leiden: Brill, 1971).

wisdom literature, and may be seen as the end of the line which begins with Proverbs and passes through ben Sira. [4] The basic formal pattern of the sayings in Aboth is triadic. The pattern can work itself out in different ways. An introductory phrase followed by three nouns (as in 1:2), or by three sentences (1:1b), or simply "he said" followed by three sayings are the most common structures. Sometimes two of the three are more closely related to one another than they are to the third member, which then takes on the character of an appendage, added merely to achieve the triadic pattern. Sometimes each member, sometimes the final member, is supplied with scriptural support. Sometimes, especially in the later sayings, the pattern is ignored, or disintegrates because overloaded. In chapter five a numerical concern provides the structural element. When the triadic pattern is disturbed, we may suspect contamination, but each case must be judged on its own merits.

Text. Most of the Mishnah has never been critically edited. The closest to a critical edition we possess is the Hanoch Albeck edition. [5] The best readings are generally found in the Kaufmann manuscript, usually printed in the back of the Giessener Mischna fascicles. But Aboth early received preferential treatment, above all in the fastidious edition of Charles Taylor, recently reprinted, but also in the H. L. Strack edition, so that we may feel reasonably confident that we have a reliable text and enough collation of variants to enable us to form a judgment on the text to be followed. Textual difficulties will be discussed as they come up. On the other hand, the numbering of the paragraphs varies considerably from edition to edition, making references sometimes confusing.

We will comment on the Albeck text and follow his numbering of mishnayoth, which correspond to the English translation of Aboth by Herbert Danby, except in chapter three where Albeck joins Danby's nos. 7 and 8 into one mishnah, giving a total of eighteen mishnayoth in the chapter as against Danby's nineteen. In chapter two Albeck divides mishnayoth five to seven differently from Danby. In commenting on chapter two then we follow Danby's division and numbering as more logical, in chapter three Albeck's.

The author has had before him at all times the commentaries on Aboth of Charles Taylor, Marti-Beer, R. T. Herford, as well as the

---

[4] James M. Robinson, "*Logoi sophon*: on the *Gattung* of Q," *The Future of our Religious Past* (Bultmann Fs.), ed. J. M. Robinson (London: SCM, 1971), pp. 84-130.

[5] Jerusalem: Bialik Institute, 1953, 6 volumes (in Hebrew).

Jewish commentators excerpted and translated by Judah Goldin, and those translated in full in the great Surenhusius edition of the Mishnah, and especially the Aboth de Rabbi Nathan as printed in the Talmud and in the Goldin translation. [6] But they have been referred to explicitly but rarely, except for Aboth de Rabbi Nathan, since they are pre-supposed, especially the historical information which they contain on the individual tradents. They have been of greatest help in noticing New Testament parallels which might otherwise have escaped notice.

1:1

א   מֹשֶׁה קִבֵּל תּוֹרָה מִסִּינַי וּמְסָרָהּ לִיהוֹשֻׁעַ, וִיהוֹשֻׁעַ לִזְקֵנִים, וּזְקֵנִים לִנְבִיאִים, וּנְבִיאִים
מְסָרוּהָ לְאַנְשֵׁי כְנֶסֶת הַגְּדוֹלָה. הֵם אָמְרוּ שְׁלֹשָׁה דְבָרִים: הֱווּ מְתוּנִים בַּדִּין, וְהַעֲמִידוּ
תַלְמִידִים הַרְבֵּה, וַעֲשׂוּ סְיָג לַתּוֹרָה.

1   Moses received the Law from Sinai and committed it to Joshua, and Joshua to the elders, and the elders to the Prophets; and the Prophets committed it to the men of the Great Synagogue. They said three things: Be deliberate in judgment, raise up many disciples, and make a fence around the Law.

The first mishnah of Aboth begins with the programmatic assertion of a chain of tradition which, the Pharisaic party claimed, began at Sinai. Sinai here stands for God himself. What is at issue is the claim that the Pharisaic tradition participates in the revelation made to Moses at Sinai and hence that it too possesses normative, because ultimately divine, authority. By Law (Torah) here is meant not only the Penta-teuch or the totality of biblical revelation, but also the oral Torah (*Torah shel be-ʿal pe*). This oral Torah consisted of the peculiarly Pharisaic tradition of *halacha* (legal rules) and *hagadda* (homiletic stories), themselves an amalgam of biblical interpretation and Pale-stinian customary law. The oral Torah eventually came to be written down and is embodied in a series of books of which the earliest, and, at least from a juridic point of view, the most noteworthy is the Mishnah of which Aboth forms a part.

---

[6] Taylor, *Sayings of the Jewish Fathers* (Cambridge, 1897-1900; repr. Amsterdam: Philo, 1970); Karl Marti and Georg Beer, *Abot* (Giessen: Töpelmann, 1972); Her-ford, *The Ethics of the Talmud* (1925; New York: Schocken, 1966); Goldin, *The Living Talmud, The Wisdom of the Fathers* (Chicago: University of Chicago, 1957); Willem Surenhusius, *Mischna sive totius hebraeorum juris ... systema, cum clarissi-morum rabbinorum Maimonides et Bartenorae commentariis integris* (Amsterdam, 1698-1703, 6 vols., fol.); J. Goldin, trans., *The Fathers according to Rabbi Nathan* (Yale Judaica Series, 10; New Haven: Yale U.P., 1955).

The language of receiving (*qibbel*) and committing (*masarah*)
Torah is the technical language of transmission of traditions through
compressed formulation and memorization, from which words like
Cabbala, Massorah, and, in New Testament Greek, *paradosis* are
derived. [7]

The chain of tradition in Aboth contains fourteen intermediary
generations and runs through the whole of the first chapter. In this
respect it reminds us both of the discussion of various generations
in M. Sanhedrin 10 and also of Mt 1:2-17, where the genealogy of
Jesus is presented in the stylized pattern of three sets of fourteen
generations each. [8] But the novel feature of the Pharisaic chain of tradition is that it did not proceed by way of natural filiation but rather
by way of professorial lineage or academic filiation. The true analogues
to this chain then are not the biblical genealogies but rather the lists
of the scholarchs or successors (*diadochoi*) of the Greek philosophical
schools drawn up by Sotion around 200 B.C., [9] and the lists of bishops
as successors of the apostles as presented in Irenaeus and Eusebius. [10]

It is noteworthy that the chain goes from Moses and Joshua through
the elders (?) to the Prophets and the men of the Great Synagogue
without ever stopping at the priests (*cahanim*). Such an omission is
strange and requires an explanation. It can hardly be accidental. It
probably reflects an anti-Sadducean, anti-Zadokite bias on the part
of the Pharisees, who also regarded themselves evidently as the direct
heirs of the prophets, though some Pharisees were priests, especially
after A.D. 70. The priesthood was hereditary in Israel and hence con-
flicted partially with the rabbinic ideal of an aristocracy of learning. [11]

---

[7] Cf. St. Paul's language in 1 Cor 11:23; 15:3; Gal 1:14; Mk 7:3, 5, 8, 9, and 13
and the Matthean parallels; on the role of tradition in the rabbis and in the New
Testament see Birger Gerhardsson, *Memory and Manuscript* (Lund: Gleerup, 1961).

[8] On the relation between the chain of tradition in Aboth and the genealogy in
Matthew, see M. D. Johnson, *The Purpose of the Biblical Genealogies* (SNTS, MS,
8; Cambridge: University Press, 1969).

[9] E. Bickermann, "La chaine de la tradition pharisienne," RB 59 (1952): 44-54.

[10] Irenaeus, *Adversus Haereses*, 3, 3, 1, and *passim*; Eusebius, *Church History*,
books 4 and 5 especially, and *passim*.

[11] According to Isidore Loeb, the chain of tradition in Aboth is a fiction designed
to dispossess the Sadducees and their priests of their power, "Notes sur le chapître
premier des Pirke Abot," *Revue des études juives* 19 (1889): 188-201. Loeb also has
a good literary analysis of chapter one on pp. 197 f. Cf. also Louis Finkelstein,
New Light from the Prophets (London: Vallentine, Mitchell, 1969); W. D. Davies,
"Reflexions on tradition: the Aboth revisited," *Christian History and Interpretation*:
Studies Presented to John Knox, ed. W. R. Farmer, C. F. D. Moule and R. R.
Niebuhr (Cambridge: University Press, 1967), pp. 127-159, esp. pp. 138-143.

The Great Synagogue (*Kenesset ha-gedolah*) was, according to Jewish tradition, a legislative body of 120 members which was established in Jerusalem in the time of Ezra and Nehemiah (5th century B.C.). Its activities were held to have been largely concerned with the fixing of the canon and text of the Hebrew Scriptures. Whether such a body actually existed is uncertain. [12]

Turning to the actual content of the saying attributed to the men of the Great Synagogue, we note on the first part of the *tricolon* that judgment (*dîn*), that is to say, judicial activity, provided the context of much of the rabbis' thought. See 1:8 and 9.

Raise up many disciples (*talmidim*). This phrase turns our attention toward the learned, scholastic side of rabbinic activity. The word *talmid* as well as its English equivalent means *learner*, and learners were important to the rabbis both in order for the tradition to be transmitted orally, from memory, and yet accurately, but especially in order for the Torah to be lived out in detail. Jesus' followers are normally called disciples (*mathētai*) in the Gospels, committing them to lifelong learning from him. (See below and cp. Mk 1:17par.).

Make a fence around the Law. This famous saying has been interpreted in three main ways. The oldest and most common view, found for the first time in Aboth de Rabbi Nathan, ch. 2, is that the fence around the Torah means the need for the rabbis to formulate laws supplementary to those in Scripture, to act as a safeguard and protection for those chief laws, e.g., the minute rules about Sabbath observance spell out the implications of, and apparently go far beyond, the biblical commandment to keep holy the Sabbath day. They thereby insure a full and sure observance of the basic rule. Judah Goldin however proposes a second view, namely, that the original intent of the injunction to make a fence around the Torah is simply this: take great pains to ensure the exact reproduction of the consonantal text of the Hebrew Bible. This command was needed, he feels, because, with the rapid development of midrashic methods of exposition (after Hillel had formulated his seven *middoth* or exegetical principles) which made great play with alternative vocalizations, the consonantal text had to be exactly reproduced and preserved or Judaism would have disintegrated into a chaos of conflicting readings. [13] The third view,

---

[12] See Hugo [Haim Dov] Mantel, "The nature of the Great Synagogue," HTR 60 (1967): 69-91, and the sources and discussions there cited.

[13] "The end of Ecclesiastes," *Biblical Motifs*, ed. A. Altmann (Studies and Texts, 3; Cambridge, Mass.: Harvard U.P., 1966), pp. 135-158.

that of L. Finkelstein, [14] understands the hedge as a comment on the preceding "be deliberate in judgment." This was to be done by giving *supporting reasons* for one's judgment. This hedge of supporting argumentation would prevent the Torah being exposed to ridicule and rejection.

It seems to us that the older view of ARN should be upheld, because (a) it gives us the most penetrating understanding of the development of rabbinic law, (b) accurate reproduction of the biblical text belonged to the elementary levels of rabbinic education, (c) Finkelstein's view reduces the maxim to a banality, a banality which does not seem to have influenced the rabbis' legislative conduct very greatly.

1:2

ב   שִׁמְעוֹן הַצַּדִּיק הָיָה מִשְׁיָרֵי כְנֶסֶת הַגְּדוֹלָה. הוּא הָיָה אוֹמֵר: עַל שְׁלֹשָׁה דְבָרִים הָעוֹלָם
עוֹמֵד: עַל הַתּוֹרָה, וְעַל הָעֲבוֹדָה, וְעַל גְּמִילוּת חֲסָדִים.

2 Simeon the Just was of the remnants of the Great Synagogue. He used to say: By three things is the world sustained: by the Law, by the [Temple-]service, and by deeds of loving-kindness.

On three things does the world depend: (1) Torah (-study), (2) Temple-service, and (3) deeds of loving-kindness (*gemilut hasadim*). The relevant point for us is to determine precisely what is the relative weight given to each of these crucial values in Judaism (a) at any given time, (b) in any given place, (c) in any given branch of Judaism. (a) Obviously the balance shifted in all of Jewry after A.D. 70 when the Temple in Jerusalem was destroyed. At that time of crisis the Temple service was absorbed by the combination of Torah-study and synagogue worship. [15] (b) Before 70 a difference of stress would of necessity have existed between Diaspora Judaism and Jews of the mother country, and even possibly between Jews of Galilee and those of Judea. In the former, the synagogue would have enjoyed pre-eminence because of geographical convenience, in the latter the Temple. After 70, this difference was obliterated with the result that the balance as described in this saying was broken and the emphasis shifted to study and charity. (c) Even before 70, evaluation of the Temple varied from party to party within Judaism. The Temple was

---

14 "Introductory study to *Pirke Abot*," JBL 57 (1938): 13-50; *idem,* "The maxim of the Anshe keneset ha-gedolah," JBL 59 (1940): 455-469.
15 ARNA, ch. 4.

of central importance to the Sadducees who had a vested interest in it; the Pharisees were only slightly less interested if their extensive laws on Temple sacrifices are any indication. The Essenes of Qumran seem to have been hostile, at least to the Temple as it was then conducted. The attitude of Jesus is not perfectly clear. [16] The Samaritans are obviously a special case, since they had a Temple of their own.

Since both Judaism and Christianity emphasize the importance of deeds of loving-kindness, this common value is of no help in determining wherein the two great religious faiths diverge in their values. Thus, in terms of the triplet of Ab 1:2, what is characteristic of Pharisaic Judaism is Torah-study.

This saying finds a parallel in 1:18, with which it forms an *inclusio* (q.v.). [17]

1:3

ג   אַנְטִיגְנוֹס אִישׁ סוֹכוֹ קִבֵּל מִשִּׁמְעוֹן הַצַּדִּיק. הוּא הָיָה אוֹמֵר: אַל תִּהְיוּ כַּעֲבָדִים, הַמְשַׁמְּשִׁין אֶת הָרַב עַל מְנָת לְקַבֵּל פְּרָס; אֶלָּא הֱווּ כַּעֲבָדִים, הַמְשַׁמְּשִׁין אֶת הָרַב שֶׁלֹּא עַל מְנָת לְקַבֵּל פְּרָס; וִיהִי מוֹרָא שָׁמַיִם עֲלֵיכֶם.

3   Antigonus of Soko received [the Law] from Simeon the Just. He used to say: Be not like slaves that minister to the master for the sake of receiving a bounty, but be like slaves that minister to the master not for the sake of receiving a bounty; and let the fear of Heaven be upon you.

This saying is commonly understood to offer a rather Pauline motive of gratitude for ethical conduct and implicitly to reject reward-seeking as an adequate motive for ethical behavior. But E. Bickerman [18] takes it in the sense of the books of Job and Ecclesiastes: God may be capricious and hard to comprehend, indeed even from our point of view working evil, but in any case we must obey him and take what comes from him, like slaves who have no choice. It is best, on this view, to be fatalistically resigned to his will. New Testament parallels may be found in Lk 17:7-10, and, with respect to human masters, in 1 Peter 2:18.

---

[16] R. Hummel, *Die Auseinandersetzung zwischen Kirche und Judentum im Matthäusevangelium* (Beiträge zur evangelischen Theologie, Bd. 33; Munich: Kaiser, 1966), pp. 76-108.

[17] See further J. Goldin, "Three pillars of Simeon the Righteous," PAAJR 27 (1957): 43-57 (non vidi): on the identity of Simeon see G. F. Moore, "Simeon the Righteous," *Jewish Studies in Memory of Israel Abrahams* (New York: Jewish Institute of Religion, 1927), pp. 348-364.

[18] E. Bickerman, "The maxim of Antigonus of Socho," HTR 44 (1951): 153-165.

1:4

ד   יוֹסֵי בֶּן יוֹעֶזֶר אִישׁ צְרֵדָה וְיוֹסֵי בֶּן יוֹחָנָן אִישׁ יְרוּשָׁלַם קִבְּלוּ מֵהֶם. יוֹסֵי בֶּן יוֹעֶזֶר
אוֹמֵר: יְהִי בֵיתְךָ בֵּית וַעַד לַחֲכָמִים, וֶהֱוֵי מִתְאַבֵּק בַּעֲפַר רַגְלֵיהֶם, וֶהֱוֵי שׁוֹתֶה בְצָמָא
אֶת דִּבְרֵיהֶם.

4   Jose b. Joezer of Zeredah and Jose b. Johanan of Jerusalem received
[the Law] from them. Jose b. Joezer of Zeredah said: Let thy house
be a meeting-house for the Sages and sit amid the dust of their feet
and drink in their words with thirst.

This is a tripartite saying but each stich reinforces the previous one,
while making essentially the same point, namely, that learning should
be the chief goal not only of one's life as a whole but even of all one's
hospitality. The school room is thus brought directly into the living
room, the home becomes an academy, even the physical accoutrements
of the Sages (dust of their feet) become precious, the desire for Torah-
wisdom becomes a consuming thirst. Here is the whole ideology of the
rabbis *in nuce*. Ordinary life becomes academicized, that is, it is transformed into a life-long quest for wisdom. This saying stands in
dialectical tension with the following mishnah, which see.

The New Testament echoes this language at Lk 10:39 where Mary
sits at the feet of Jesus and in Acts 22:3 where Paul learns at the
feet of Gamaliel.

1:5

ה   יוֹסֵי בֶּן יוֹחָנָן אִישׁ יְרוּשָׁלַם אוֹמֵר: יְהִי בֵיתְךָ פָּתוּחַ לִרְוָחָה, וְיִהְיוּ עֲנִיִּים בְּנֵי בֵיתֶךָ,
וְאַל תַּרְבֶּה שִׂיחָה עִם הָאִשָּׁה. בְּאִשְׁתּוֹ אָמְרוּ, קַל וָחֹמֶר בְּאֵשֶׁת חֲבֵרוֹ. מִכָּאן אָמְרוּ
חֲכָמִים: כָּל זְמַן שֶׁאָדָם מַרְבֶּה שִׂיחָה עִם הָאִשָּׁה – גּוֹרֵם רָעָה לְעַצְמוֹ, וּבוֹטֵל מִדִּבְרֵי
תוֹרָה, וְסוֹפוֹ יוֹרֵשׁ גֵּיהִנָּם.

5   Jose b. Johanan of Jerusalem said: Let thy house be opened wide and
let the needy be members of thy household; and talk not much with
womankind. They said this of a man's own wife: how much more of
his fellow's wife! Hence the Sages have said: He that talks much with
womankind brings evil upon himself and neglects the study of the Law
and at the last will inherit Gehenna.

The dialectic commences. It is characteristic of the classical halachic
documents of Judaism that immediately after a weighty rabbinic decision has been delivered, another voice pipes up to give an alternative
viewpoint, a second opinion, e.g., M. Ber 1:1. This second opinion
is often introduced either by the formula *dabar aḥer* (another word)

or by the name of the dissenting rabbi, or by the words *we-ʾomrîm ha-ḥakamîm* (but the Sages say). This gives to the entire corpus of early rabbinic literature the character of an enormous, endless dialogue, stretching across the centuries, in which every male Jew is invited, even obliged (cf. Ab 2:16a) to participate. The only criterion was knowledge of the tradition, and also, in practice, rabbinic ordination. In spite of some excommunications on doctrinal grounds (see the case of R. Eliezer ben Hyrcanus, b. Baba Metzia 59b), and a large measure of uniformity in practice, one may speak of an intellectual democracy among the rabbis. The possibilities of both haggadic and halachic interpretation were rather open-ended. And though the method of self-government whether in civil or in religious matters varied some-what from place to place, and from period to period (consider especially the division of powers into that of the Patriarch (civil) and that of the Nasi and of the Ab Beth Din (religious) by which the Babylonian Jewish community was for a time governed), [19] both in effective power and in degree of centralization, Judaism throughout the whole Tan-naitic and Amoraic epochs lacked a centralized, all-powerful seat of authority in religious matters. Only at the time of the Renaissance did parts of Judaism (the Ashkenazim) receive codifications of halachic practice (e.g., J. Caro's *Shulḥan Aruch*) which tended to stifle the dialectic by their univocity and rigidity. We may be permitted to note a parallel development of the canon law of the Western Church. For a long time, its legislation was a piecemeal collection of letters from popes, synodical decisions, imperial decrees and the like (embodied in Friedberg's *Corpus iuris canonici*, 2 volumes, Leipzig 1879-81). Only in 1917 was a unified code achieved, the *Codex iuris canonici*, in which the confusion, and thereby most of the dialectic was removed.

Applying all this to the case in point we note that the first part of this verse, "let your house be opened wide and let the needy be members of your household," stands here as an alternative ideal of hospitality. In 1:4 only the Sages are invited. Here it is the needy who are wel-comed. This tension between Torah-study and deeds of loving-kindness, between the religion of a learned elite and the demands of a com-passionate humanity, between pure observance and openness to the world of ordinary men, characterizes other passages in Aboth and the rabbinic corpus as a whole; it pulled Hillel and the Essenes in different directions; and it provides the proximate location for the teaching

---

[19] J. Neusner, "The phenomenon of the Rabbi in late antiquity," *Numen* 16 (1969): 1-20; 17 (1970): 1-18.

of Jesus which specifically addresses the circle of problems which this tension raises. As with any worthwhile theological problem, both sides find abundant support in the canonical literature. Thus the Pentateuch stresses ritual purity and legal observance, not omitting a concern for the needy, while Jeremiah and some of the Psalms elevate the needy (*aniyyim* and *anawim*) to the level of a true religious elite, closer to God than other people. [20] Compare Lk 14:12-14, esp. v. 13: "When you make a feast, call the poor, the maimed, the lame, the blind."

The second part of this mishnah deals on the surface with women, but in fact with *betul Torah*, neglect of Torah-study. R. Jose b. Johanan warns against idle conversations, of which the vivid symbol for him is prolonged talk with women. He was not a misogynist on principle. He simply faced the (unfortunate) social reality of his day, that women were usually uneducated and confined and that therefore their conversation was often of a trivial kind, a distraction for serious students (cf. Ab 2:7: the more women the more witchcrafts; the more bondwomen the more lewdness). Had Jose been a social critic and a more rigorous thinker, he might have applied his first maxim to the situation assumed in the second, that is, he might have realized that women, by being kept in a state of cultural deprivation, were themselves spiritually "needy." But he was himself caught in the tension of conflicting demands. He opened the doors of hospitality wide enough to care for the materially (or male) needy, but not so far as to cover the needs of the spiritually deprived women.

The social position of women in Judaism at this time has been well treated by J. Jeremias. [21] Here we need only observe that, while Christianity was not long able to maintain the revolutionary position of Gal 3:28 ("there is neither male nor female; for you are all one in Christ Jesus") with respect to women, the incremental advance of 1 Tim 2:11 f. was not without considerable importance ("Let the woman learn in silence") when contrasted with the prevailing rabbinic view that women should not be taught Torah (M. Sotah 3:4; M. Ned 4:3). [22]

---

[20] Albert Gelin, *The Poor of Yahweh* (Collegeville, Minn: Liturgical Press, 1964) and the literature there cited.

[21] J. Jeremias, *Jerusalem at the Time of Jesus* (Philadelphia: Fortress, 1969), ch. 18, pp. 359-376. Cf. also his *New Testament Theology*, vol. 1, *The Teaching of Jesus* (New York: Scribners, 1971), pp. 223-227.

[22] On St. Paul and women see K. Stendahl, *The Bible and the Role of Women* (Philadelphia: Fortress, 1966), now carried further in a notable way by Wayne A.

1:6

ו   יְהוֹשֻׁעַ בֶּן פְּרַחְיָה וְנִתַּאי הָאַרְבֵּלִי קִבְּלוּ מֵהֶם. יְהוֹשֻׁעַ בֶּן פְּרַחְיָה אוֹמֵר: עֲשֵׂה לְךָ
רַב, וּקְנֵה לְךָ חָבֵר, וֶהֱוֵי דָן אֶת כָּל הָאָדָם לְכַף זְכוּת.

6   Joshua b. Perahyah and Nittai the Arbelite received [the Law] from
them. Joshua b. Perahyah said: Provide thyself with a teacher and get
thee a fellow[-disciple]; and when thou judgest any man incline the
balance in his favour.

In this mishnah two maxims are combined; the second, about judging
leniently, does not concern us. The first, a saying in two parts, sets out
clearly the primal necessity of studying Torah under an experienced
master, and, at the same time, in collaboration with an associate or
fellow-disciple. 23 The study of Torah is an essentially social enterprise.
Study with a teacher and a fellow-student is recommended in place of
solitary study for several reasons. (a) The danger presents itself that
the Scriptures would be wrongly vocalized if read apart from the
traditional vocalization, which, until the time of the Massoretes (sixth
to eighth centuries), was transmitted orally. (b) The halachic tradition
was formulated in such a compressed, short-hand fashion that without
the oral explanation it could easily become unintelligible or at least
wrongly understood; (c) Progress in understanding is made precisely
through the dialectical clash of opinion. (d) Every student needed
another student to test his mastery of the traditions by heart. 24

There is an exact verbal parallel to the first clause in 1:16, there
attributed to Rabban Gamaliel. It is hard to explain this state of
affairs. Probably Rabban Gamaliel took up that part of the earlier
saying which fitted his purpose and joined to it two other exhortations:
"Remove thyself from doubt, and tithe not overmuch by guesswork."
The effect of the three sayings together is to discourage those slipshod
methods of study which lead to a loss of exactitude in practice.

Two terms require some clarification: *rab* (teacher) and *ḥaber*
(fellow-disciple). It is disputed today when precisely the term *rabbi*

Meeks, "The image of the androgyne: some uses of a symbol in earliest Christianity,"
History of Religions 13 (1974): 165-208. On women in classical antiquity and
Christianity see the recent article by Thraede in RAC, s.v. Frau.

23 The need to study Torah in association with others is stressed in b. Ber 63a.
Further references may be found in Taylor's commentary on Aboth, pp. 44 f., 63 f.

24 See B. Gerhardsson, *Memory and Manuscript* (Lund: Gleerup, 1961), chapters
9 to 11, pp. 93-170, for a synthetic presentation of methods of study and memorization
in the Amoraic period, for which our information is fuller than for the Tannaitic
period.

came to designate a fixed office preceded by a certain course of studies and ordination (*semicha*) by a recognized master. B. Reicke, for example, thinks that the office existed already at the time of Jesus. [25] J. Neusner, on the other hand, thinks that the office became formalized only when R. Johanan ben Zakkai reorganized rabbinic Judaism after the fall of Jerusalem in A.D. 70. [26] R. Bultmann is undecided. [27] What is clear is that originally *rab* meant "great," and, as a title, "great one"; *rabbi*, "my great one." As such the word could be applied to leading figures in different fields, but was especially common in addressing religious teachers. No more than this need be implied when Jesus is addressed as rabbi. We have no certain evidence that Jesus studied at a rabbinical academy and received ordination, yet he was called rabbi because he taught in the synagogues and elsewhere. It is interesting that Pharisaic teachers earlier than Johanan ben Zakkai are not called rabbi either in Aboth or elsewhere. Probably Joshua ben Perahyah is using *rab* here in the same way that *rabbi* is used in the Gospels, viz., to designate a religious teacher, without implying any fixed system of qualification for the office or title. Neusner is probably right on this point. [28]

Ḥaber. This term commonly means friend, partner, member, associate. In Pharisaic circles it took on a special meaning: a member of an association who promised to be trustworthy in matters of second tithing, *terumah* and ritual cleanliness. Here the word has taken on a further, intellectual meaning: a member of a Pharisaic association, who is not only ritually observant, but who also agrees to join with another member to study together.

1:7

ז   נִתַּאי הָאַרְבֵּלִי אוֹמֵר: הַרְחֵק מִשָּׁכֵן רַע, וְאַל תִּתְחַבֵּר לָרָשָׁע, וְאַל תִּתְיָאֵשׁ מִן הַפֻּרְעָנוּת.

7   Nittai the Arbelite said: Keep thee far from an evil neighbour and consort not with the wicked and lose not belief in retribution.

25 B. Reicke, *The New Testament Era* (London: A & C Black, 1969), pp. 21 and 152.

26 J. Neusner, *A Life of Yohanan Ben Zakkai Ca. 1-80 C.E.* (Studia post-biblica, vol. 6; Leiden: Brill, 1970²).

27 *Jesus and the Word* (London: Collins, 1958), p. 48.

28 See H. Shanks, JQR 53 (1963): 337-45; S. Zeitlin, *ibid.*, pp. 346-9; *idem,* JQR 59 (1968): 152-160.

Taken as a whole this mishnah is a tristich containing an admonition to avoid evil companions and to preserve a moral sense (in biblical terms, fear of the Lord or retribution). The first thought is a commonplace of Old Testament wisdom literature: Prov 4:14; Ps 1:1; Sir 13:1, 15-19; cf. 1 Cor 15:33 citing Menander's play *Thaïs* (218).

If we are to give the rather generally expressed words of Nittai (or: Matthai) to avoid evil and wicked companions a specifically Pharisaic interpretation, we might think first of their quest for ritual purity. The Pharisees applied the biblical laws of purity, originally applicable to priests during their time of Temple service (two weeks a year, plus the three great pilgrim feasts), to all of their members, priestly and lay, at all times. [29] To maintain this level of purity they were obliged as much as possible to avoid contact with less scrupulous Jews, the *am ha-aretz*, as well as with Gentiles (cf. M. Ohol 18:7; Jn. 18:28). The evil neighbor referred to in the first stich would then be evil only in a special sense, not morally but ritually. But of course such a statement implies a moral viewpoint other than that of the Pharisees themselves. This is the dilemma we shall keep on meeting. Once the moral terms of reference differ, the evaluation of characteristically Pharisaic positions also changes radically. For the Pharisees, a violation of the laws of ritual purity was just as genuinely sinful and offensive to God as adultery or theft.

The words *we'al tithabber* (do not consort) of the second stich share the root *ḥbr* with the noun *ḥaber* (fellow, associate). As we have seen in the preceding mishnah, the noun *ḥaber*, while biblical, is especially associated in our period with the Pharisees as a technical term. Perhaps there is an overtone of this special usage in the choice of the verb here, in which case our specifically Pharisaic interpretation of the saying would be supported. On the other hand, the same verb is employed in Sir 13:1 in a similar context, and Sirach is thought to have been composed before the formation of the religious parties.

The third stich may be directed against the Sadducees, who did not

---

[29] The biblical basis of levitical purity is located in Lev 11:33 f.; 37 f. On its development see A. Büchler, *Der galiläische 'Am-ha'Areṣ des zweiten Jahrhunderts* (Vienna: Hölder, 1908); "The levitical purity of the Gentile in Palestine before the year 70," JQR n.s. 17 (1926/7): 1-81; W. Brandt, *Jüdische Reinheitslehre und ihre Beschreibung in der Evangelien*, BZAW, 19 (Giessen: Töpelmann, 1910), pp. 1-55; Wilfried Paschen, *Rein und Unrein*, SANT, 24 (Munich: Kösel, 1970); M. Hengel, *Judaism and Hellenism*, vol. 1 (London: SCM, 1974), p. 170 and cf. pp. 169-175; J. Neusner, "The idea of purity in ancient Judaism," JAAR 43 (1975): 15-26, where further references to his related works are given.

believe in the resurrection of the body (Mk 12:18 par; Acts 23:8), but clung to the old biblical view of life after death as a shadowy existence in Sheol. Thereby they undermined the whole theodicy and system of moral judgment and retribution which had been developed during the times of Israel's political eclipse and national travail by the writers of apocalyptic, and of which the Pharisees were the heirs and continuators, along with the Essenes. [30]

1:8, 9

ח   יְהוּדָה בֶּן טַבַּאי וְשִׁמְעוֹן בֶּן שָׁטָח קִבְּלוּ מֵהֶם. יְהוּדָה בֶּן טַבַּאי אוֹמֵר: אַל תַּעַשׂ
עַצְמְךָ כְּעוֹרְכֵי הַדַּיָּנִין; וּכְשֶׁיִּהְיוּ בַעֲלֵי הַדִּינִים עוֹמְדִים לְפָנֶיךָ, יִהְיוּ בְעֵינֶיךָ
כִּרְשָׁעִים; וּכְשֶׁנִּפְטָרִים מִלְּפָנֶיךָ, יִהְיוּ בְעֵינֶיךָ כְּזַכָּאִין, כְּשֶׁקִּבְּלוּ עֲלֵיהֶם אֶת הַדִּין.

ט   שִׁמְעוֹן בֶּן שָׁטָח אוֹמֵר: הֱוֵי מַרְבֶּה לַחְקוֹר אֶת הָעֵדִים; וֶהֱוֵי זָהִיר בִּדְבָרֶיךָ, שֶׁמָּא
מִתּוֹכָם יִלְמְדוּ לְשַׁקֵּר.

8   Judah b. Tabbai and Simeon b. Shetah received [the Law] from them. Judah b. Tabbai said: Make not thyself like them that would influence the judges; and when the suitors stand before thee let them be in thine eyes as wicked men, and when they have departed from before thee let them be in thine eyes as innocent, so soon as they have accepted the judgement.

9   Simeon b. Shetah said: Examine the witnesses diligently and be cautious in thy words lest from them they learn to swear falsely.

These sayings do not bear on our purpose except as pointing to an aspect of the rabbis' activity which must be kept in mind when assessing them, *viz.*, they were often engaged as judges or lawyers in what we would call civil suits (e.g., property rights and divorce proceedings). Of course the distinction between civil and religious or canon law did not exist for them, since both were included in the Pentateuch and therefore shared the character of sacred law (divine positive law, in the terminology of the Scholastics). Rather, they would have been concerned with the distinction between the law of Israel and the law imposed on them by Gentile conquerors. Some cases had to be tried first by Jewish courts and then remanded to Roman ones (e.g., the trial of Jesus).

---

[30] P. D. Hanson, "Jewish apocalyptic against its Near Eastern environment," **RB** 78 (1971): 31-58; W. D. Davies, "Apocalyptic and Pharisaism," *Christian Origins and Judaism* (Philadelphia: Westminster, 1962), pp. 19-30; and now W. Schmithals, *The Apocalyptic Movement* (New York: Abingdon, 1975), esp. pp. 127-150, and the literature cited in the book.

From probably the Persian period to the fall of Jerusalem in A.D.
70, the high court of the Jewish people was the great Sanhedrin which
held its sessions in the Temple, in the Chamber of the Hewn Stone
(*liškat ha-gazit*) on the south side of the great court (M. Mid 5:4).
Under the Roman proconsul Gabinus (57-55 B.C.), its authority was
fragmented for a time by its division into five courts judging five
districts (Jos. Ant. 14:91; B.J. 1:170). But its central constitution in
Jerusalem seems to have been re-established not very long thereafter,
for we find it active in the New Testament era. Though the rabbis
regarded their academy at Jamnia and at Usha as the continuation of
the Jerusalem Sanhedrin, they also realized that its authority was not
the same. "When the Sanhedrin ceased, singing ceased at the wedding
feasts," (M. Sot 9:11). In the tractates Sanhedrin and Makkoth, the
court is often spoken of as still in existence, yet at other times it is
mentioned in the past tense, e.g., Sanh 1:6 and Mak 1:10. According
to the tradition preserved in M. Hag 2:2, Judah ben Tabbai and
Simeon ben Shetah would have been one of the pairs (*zugoth*; cf. M.
Peah 2:6) which divided between them the offices of President (*Nasi*)
and Father of the Court (*Ab Beth Din*). Thus their words would come
as the result of a serious and prolonged judicial experience. [31]

This would be true, even if, as E. E. Urbach thinks, the pairs were
only sages who at some time rose to be influential members of the
Sanhedrin, their titles Nasi and Ab Beth Din being simply a retro-
jection of the situation at Jamnia and Usha back into an earlier time.

The competence of the Jewish courts tended to vary with the
political situation, and this variation was not without its effect on the
class status and social role of the rabbis. If Pharisaism had been in a
measure a lay and popular movement before 70, the attempt of the
Academy to fill the political vacuum left by the failure of the revolt
changed that. At the same time, the role of sage became more confined
to upper-class members, men of independent means, since there was
a ruling that judges could not take payment for their judicial work
(b. Bekh 29a). Simultaneously, study of Torah became recognized
as a full-time occupation, and, like other occupations, could be passed
on from father to son. By A.D. 150 the sages had become a separate

---

[31] For a survey of the history and competence of the Sanhedrin, and the numerous
problems connected with them, see T. A. Burkill, s.v. Sanhedrin, in the IDB 4:214-
218, with bibliography, to which add H. Mantel, *Studies in the History of the Sanhedrin* (Cambridge, Mass.: Harvard, 1965).

class, contemptuous of the unlearned *am ha-aretz* (though as we shall see in Ab 2:6 this class tension existed long before that date), distinctive even in their walk, dress and speech (*Sifre Deut.*, no. 343). [32]

The important point for us to note is the effect which this prolonged, responsible engagement in judicial work had on the mind and temper of the rabbis. A meticulous attention to verbal nuance and factual detail, subtlety in the analysis of concrete physical realities, rather than in the manipulation of abstract concepts, a sober ethical realism not untouched by deep piety, occasionally by mysticism, and even by apocalyptic political imprudence and heroism (one thinks of the martyrs under Hadrian), on the positive side; sometimes petty internal feuds (Beth Hillel and Beth Shammai), an often hair-splitting trivialization of the biblical precepts, with the notable exception of Josephus a flight from the often melancholy narration of historical facts into a legal never-never land, endlessly discussing powers they had long since lost, on the negative side—all this comprises the legal inheritance of the rabbis. Nevertheless, anyone raised on the kind of strenuous thinking which produced the Mishnah and the Talmuds could readily become an outstanding civil lawyer, if he so chose, and this is not a little tribute to the rabbis' achievement.

The New Testament attitude toward the judicial activity of Christians remains somewhat ambivalent. In Lk 12:14 Jesus is represented as refusing to adjudicate a case involving rights of inheritance (cf. M. Baba Bathra 8 and 9). Probably this is not to be taken as a rejection of all law suits, so much as an introduction to a parable warning against the excessive love of wealth. In Mt 5:22-26, the system of courts is presupposed, but men are advised to avoid litigation and to settle out of court. In Mt 18:15-18, part of a Matthean gemara, the stages of a Christian judicial proceeding are outlined, and judicial powers are given to church leaders, powers earlier mentioned in connection with Peter (16:19). Cf. Jn. 20:23. The most forthright argument for Christian courts and competent church lawyers occurs in 1 Cor 6:1-8. In vv. 1-6 Christians are advised to bring suits against fellow Christians only before church courts. In v. 5, Paul urges that there be Christians competent (*sophos*) to adjudicate such suits. Here is a basis from which to argue for learning as refined as that of the rabbis. One is frankly astonished to find Paul pleading for Christian jurists.

---

[32] See E. E. Urbach, "Class-Status ..." P.I.A.S.H., vol. 2, no. 4, pp. 11-37.

Then in vv. 7 and 8 follows a rebuke of Christian litigants, criminals, and perpetrators of fraud. [33]

1:10

שְׁמַעְיָה וְאַבְטַלְיוֹן קִבְּלוּ מֵהֶם. שְׁמַעְיָה אוֹמֵר: אֱהֹב אֶת הַמְּלָאכָה, וּשְׂנָא אֶת הָרַבָּנוּת,
וְאַל תִּתְוַדַּע לָרָשׁוּת.

10   Shemaiah and Abtalion received [the Law] from them. Shemaiah said: Love labour and hate mastery and seek not acquaintance with the ruling power.

Although these comments are not primarily concerned with bio-graphical information on the *zugot* except in so far as it would shed light on the interpretation of the sayings attributed to them, the case of Shemaiah and Abtalion is rather special. For they have been taken as transmitters of Alexandrian methods of interpretation to the rabbinic schools. First of all it may be taken as certain that Shemaiah and Abtalion are identical with the Sameias and Pollion mentioned in Jos. *Ant.* 15:3 f, and 370, as Pharisees especially honored by Herod the Great, and as living in Jerusalem. [34]

---

[33] In vv. 3 and 4 of 1 Cor 6, the word *biotika* has traditionally been translated "matters pertaining to this life" (AV, RV, RSV), supported by Phrynichus, who rejects the word. But the papyri employ the word in the sense of "business," a sense which has found its way into NEB, "business disputes."

See Matthias Delcor, "The courts of the Church of Corinth and the courts of Qumran," in *Paul and Qumran*, ed. J. Murphy-O'Connor (London: Chapman, 1968), pp. 69-84. This article is a useful collection of comparative material, and sets the question in a broad historical context, but its usefulness is diminished by several less than certain presuppositions and conclusions. First he dismisses the rabbinic materials as too distant in time to be really useful for the elucidation of the New Testament (pp. 70 f.), then later (p. 73) falls back upon those very same materials for the interpretation of Qumran texts. Second, and more seriously, he assumes that at the time Paul was writing, the Corinthian Christians had already set up a "system" of courts (pp. 70, 84, contradicted on p. 75), whereas in fact the text of 1 Cor 6:1-8 leads rather to the conclusion that the Corinthian Christians were taking their internal disputes to civil courts, and that Paul was urging them to set up courts of their own. To counterbalance this erroneous supposition, Delcor then concludes that in Corinth it was not a question of appointing judges but only a matter of calling for private arbitrators. This too seems unlikely to me, since Paul's language is too technical and precise to be weakened in this way. (See Delcor, p. 70, n. 2). As Delcor himself has pointed out, Diaspora Jews did have their own courts for civil cases (p. 71, based on Jos. *Ant.* 14:235). Lastly, a minor point, Delcor uses the word hierarchy to speak about church order in the first century, even though this word is never used in the New Testament, is not classical and came into currency only with the Pseudo-Dionysius in the sixth century.

[34] The arguments for this identification have been well set forth, and the objections refuted, by L. H. Feldman, "The identity of Pollio, the Pharisee, in Josephus," JQR n.s. 49 (1958-59): 53-62.

In the Talmud it is said that the *zugot* were proselytes, "descendants of the heathen" (b. Yoma 71b), indeed, that they were "scions of Sennacherib" (b. Git 57b). Though these statements may be un-historical, the result of a confusion, it has been argued that they were Alexandrians (either in the sense that they were born there, or in the sense that they passed a long time there) on the basis of their use of the measure *hin* when legislating. It is alleged that this measurement was no longer in use in Palestine at that time, but was used in Egypt. [35]

Hillel is recorded as having learned his rules of scriptural inter-pretation from them (b. Pes 66a). On the basis of this fact, and the rather fragile hypothesis that Shemaiah and Abtalion were Alexan-drians, David Daube has argued that Hillel's seven *middoth* derive from Hellenistic prototypes. [36]

Turning to Shemaiah's words, we note first of all an option for a "work-ethic." This orientation represents a permanent, important, and valuable stress in Judaism, and can be seen as standing in orthogonal relation to some interpretations of the teaching of Jesus against anxiety about material needs (Mt 6:25-33, especially v. 28: "consider the lilies of the field, how they grow; they neither *toil* nor spin"), though of course Jesus is not speaking against work, but against narrow pre-occupations with physical needs. (Cf. Ps 127:2; Lk 10:41; Phil 4:6; and contrast 2 Thess 3:10: "If any one will not work, neither let him eat.") The normal interpretation of the second and third parts of the saying (based on the translation given above) is that they contain "a clear warning against any position of (secular) authority or becoming intimate with the government." [37] Professor David Flusser however translates: Love a trade and hate the rank of rabbi. He then connects these words with the very similar words of Jesus in Mt 23:8: "But you are not to be called rabbi, for you have one teacher, and you are all brethren." [38] To be sure, Flusser's translation has provoked pro-test, [39] but no decisive philological arguments have been raised against

---

[35] H. Graetz, *Geschichte der Juden* (Leipzig: Leiner, 1888, 4th ed.), vol. 3, part 2, note 16, pp. 709-711.

[36] Daube, "Rabbinic methods of interpretation and hellenistic rhetoric," HUCA 22 (1949): 239-264; *idem*, "Alexandrian methods of interpretation and the rabbis," *Festschriebe Hans Lewald* (Basel: Helbing und Lichtenhahn, 1953), pp. 27-44 (non vidi). Of course, Daube's full demonstrations of the classical parallels to the *middoth* do not depend for their validity on these slender bases. They stand on their own intrinsic probability.

[37] E. E. Urbach, "Class-Status and Leadership...," p. 9.

[38] D. Flusser, *Jesus* (New York: Herder & Herder, 1969), p. 20.

[39] Cf. the review by S. Zeitlin, JQR n.s. 60 (1969/70): 187-196.

it, though perhaps it takes the word *rabbanut* too specifically, given
the Herodian date of the teacher involved. Cf. 2:3; 3:5; James 2:6;
Acts 18:3; Sir 38:24-34; Rom 12:16; Jn 13:1 ff; Sir 7:5 f; 13:9-13;
Prov 25:6 f.

1:11

יא   אַבְטַלְיוֹן אוֹמֵר: חֲכָמִים, הִזָּהֲרוּ בְדִבְרֵיכֶם, שֶׁמָּא תָחוּבוּ חוֹבַת גָּלוּת וְתִגְלוּ לִמְקוֹם
מַיִם הָרָעִים, וְיִשְׁתּוּ הַתַּלְמִידִים הַבָּאִים אַחֲרֵיכֶם וְיָמוּתוּ, וְנִמְצָא שֵׁם שָׁמַיִם מִתְחַלֵּל.

11   Abtalion said: Ye Sages, give heed to your words lest ye incur the
      penalty of exile and ye be exiled to a place of evil waters, and the
      disciples that come after you drink [of them] and die, and the name of
      Heaven be profaned.

An exhortation to teachers to be aware of their grave responsibility
seems to be the point of this somewhat elusively worded saying
(Herford). Herod sentenced those who acted subversively to banish-
ment abroad or to work in the mines. [40] The profanation of the name
is mentioned in 1:3; 4:4; 5:9. The words of the wise are compared to
water in 1:4 above. Cf. Jn 4:14; 7:37. Though it seems impossible
to find an exact parallel to the phrase "a place of evil waters" in the
Old Testament or in Qumran or the New Testament, the phrase "place
of waters" is found in CD 11:16, and "evil waters" in 2 Kg 2:19, in
reference to Jericho. Against carelessness in learning, see also 1:16;
2:5, 12, 14; 3:8, 9; 4:13.
    The saying can be interpreted in two different directions. If the
exile is meant literally, the saying warns against tactless criticism of,
or opposition to, the (Herodian) government. If all the terms are
purely metaphorical, then it could be a warning against the teaching of
error or heresy. If so, then perhaps it was directed at the widening
split among the *hasidim* or religious party, dividing them into Pharisees
and Essenes. This split was already an accomplished fact at the time of
Abtalion, but perhaps as teachers despaired of the impurity of the
Herodian government, they were tempted to look longingly at the
purity maintained at Qumran. The "place of evil waters" could then
be localized at the Dead Sea, truly a place of evil waters, and the site
of the Essene central community.

---

[40] Urbach, *art. cit.*, p. 9.

1:12

יב   הִלֵּל וְשַׁמַּאי קִבְּלוּ מֵהֶם. הִלֵּל אוֹמֵר: הֱוֵי מִתַּלְמִידָיו שֶׁלְאַהֲרֹן, אוֹהֵב שָׁלוֹם וְרוֹדֵף
שָׁלוֹם, אוֹהֵב אֶת הַבְּרִיּוֹת וּמְקָרְבָן לַתּוֹרָה.

12   Hillel and Shammai received [the Law] from them. Hillel said: Be
of the disciples of Aaron, loving peace and pursuing peace, loving
mankind and bringing them nigh to the Law.

BIBLIOGRAPHICAL NOTE ON HILLEL

(1) J. Goldin, "Hillel the Elder," JR 26 (1946): 263-277.

(2) A. Kaminka, "Hillel's Life and Work," JQR n.s. 30 (1939-
40): 107-122.

(3) N. N. Glatzer, *Hillel the Elder.* New York: Schocken, 1966.

(4) *Idem*, "Hillel in the Light of the Dead Sea Scrolls," in *The
Scrolls and the New Testament*, ed. K. Stendahl. New York: Harper,
1957, pp. 232-244.

On Paul as a Hillelite, see J. Jeremias, "Paulus als Hillelit," *Neotestamentica et Semitica* (M. Black Fs.). Edinburg: T & T Clark,
1969), pp. 88-94. On Jesus as a Hillelite, J. M. Ford, *Biblica* 48
(1967): 623-628.

Hillel in Aboth. In addition to mishnayoth 12-14 in chapter one,
mishnayoth 5-7 are ascribed to him in chapter two. Moreover 5:22-23
are ascribed to him, not in Aboth itself, but in Aboth de Rabbi
Nathan^A, ch. 12 (Goldin, p. 70).

Although we have no certain dates for the beginning and end of
Hillel's life (Glatzer conjectures c. 60 B.C. to A.D. c. 10), we are
doubtless moving with him into the lifetime of Jesus. Hillel and
Shammai form the fifth and final pair (*zugot*).

He, like Jesus (e.g., Mt 1:1), was said to have been a descendent
of David (j. Pes 33a), [41] though born in Babylonia. Most subsequent
presidents (*nasim*) of the Academy were lineal blood descendants of
his. This dynastic system of religious government, called a caliphate in
Islam, seems also to have been in operation in Jerusalem for a certain
time, as the deciding factor in the choice of Christian bishops, from
Jesus through his brother James, to Simeon. [42]

---

[41] Isidore Levi, "L'origine davidique de Hillel," REJ 31 (1895): 209 ff.

[42] Hegesippus, *apud* Eusebius, H. E. Vi 22, 4; 3, 11; Epiphanius, *Pan.* 29,4 4.
And cf. H. von Campenhausen, in H. Chadwick and von Campenhausen, *Jerusalem
and Rome* (Philadelphia: Fortress, 1966).

Hillel contributed a list of seven rules for the right interpretation of Scripture, rules he probably did not invent but derived at least in part from his teachers Shemaiah and Abtalion, who themselves, as we have seen, may have learned them from methods of interpreting the Greek classics in Alexandria current at that time. [43] These rules constituted a major breakthrough in rabbinic jurisprudence, allowing, as they do, each teaching of the oral (postbiblical) law to be deduced from Scripture, by deriving meaning even from slight pleonasms in the biblical text. It has been suggested (orally, by David Daube) that the earliest application by Hillel of his "new hermeneutic" was to the urgent case of conducting war on the Sabbath. The problem had arisen in an acute form during the initial rebellion of the Maccabees against their Seleucid overlords. At first they preferred to die in their innocence (1 Macc 2:37 f) rather than profane the Sabbath day. Realizing this was suicidal, Mattathias and his friends laid down a new halacha permitting defensive action on that day (1 Macc 2:39-41). But they provided no scriptural warrant for their decision. This omission proved such an embarrassment to strict Pharisees, that an author like 2 Macc (15:1 ff) does not cite the Sabbath decree. It was left for Hillel to supply the Scriptural warranty on the basis of the last three words of Dt 20:20: "until it falls." This interpretation of his is preserved in T. Erub 4:7, in T. Shab 15:17, and in Mek. Ex. 31:13. [44]

1. *Be of the disciples of Aaron.* (a) Somehow, in rabbinic circles (e.g., ARN^A, ch. 12), Aaron's character was defined in terms of Malachi's description (2:6b) of Levi: "He walked with me in peace and uprightness, and he turned many from iniquity." That is, he was a man of peace, and he made many converts. These two aspects of his (ideal) character are made more explicit in the other two parts of Hillel's saying. Perhaps Hillel's dictum has a finer point. "Be of the disciples of Aaron" could mean, not simply "love peace" but "even though you are lay scholars, learn the sacred tradition from them, the disciples of Aaron, that is, the priests, and confine your interests to ritual, cultic matters (in which they specialize), rather than to such dangerous matters as politics, rebellion, war." That is, do not be sons or disciples of *David*, but of Aaron.

---

[43] The rules are given in T. Sanh 7:8 (ed. Zuckermandel, p. 427); the introduction to Sifra, at the end (ed. Weiss, fol. 3a; ARNa, ch. 27). Cf. Strack, *Introduction*, pp. 93-98.

[44] For the background of this problem, and a description of pre-Hillelite unsuccessful attempts to solve it, see David Daube, "Zur frühtalmudischen Rechtspraxis," ZAW 50 (1932): 148-158.

(b) The idea that one could be a disciple of Aaron long after Aaron's death could be important for our purposes. It is commonly said that one of the differences between discipleship to a learned rabbi and discipleship to Jesus is that in the former case being a disciple is a preliminary stage to becoming a rabbi/*didaskalos* in one's own right, whereas in the latter case it implies a lasting relationship to Jesus as a disciple. [45] While in a narrowly titular sense this may be true for Matthew (23:8), it is not true for the early church as a whole. Paul (e.g., 1 Cor 12:28) and James (3:1) take it for granted that there are teachers (*didaskaloi*) in the early church, and even Matthew presupposes teaching activity by others than Jesus himself, including a body of Christian scribes (13:52; 23:34). On the other hand, the rabbis could consider themselves to have a lasting relationship to great figures of the past, as we see here. The difference then lies not in the duration of the attachment, but in its nature. For the early Christians, the master to whom they had this relationship was not simply a great figure of the past but a risen and present Lord.

2. *Loving peace and pursuing peace.* If this were to be given a concrete historical reference, we should probably take Hillel's admonition as directed to the rumblings of revolt on the part of zealous observant Jews against the secularisms of Herod's regime, and to the Roman domination which obtruded itself ever more conspicuously after Herod's death, rumblings which ended in the collapse of 66-73 A.D. Hillel belonged evidently to the politically quietist wing of the Pharisaic movement, which salvaged what it could from the disaster.

As a general statement, the admonition finds several biblical parallels, none closer than Ps 34:15: "Seek peace, and pursue it," quoted in 1 Peter 3:11. In the New Testament, the most significant parallel is doubtless the seventh beatitude "Blessed are the peacemakers, for they shall be called sons of God," (Mt 5:9). Cf. also Rm 14:19; Eph 2:17. But note also Mt 10:34.

3. *Loving mankind and bringing them nigh to the Law.* The Hebrew use of creation (*hab-briyoth*) to refer to mankind is found also in Sir 16:16; Mk 16:15; Rm 8:19 f; Col 1:23. The word is near in Dt 30:14, the Jews in Eph 2:17.

Hillel lived during the golden age of Jewish proselytism and the point of his saying is to encourage convert making, an endeavor which

---

45 So G. Bornkamm, "End-expectation and church in Matthew," in Bornkamm-Barth-Held, *Tradition and Interpretation in Matthew* (Philadelphia: Westminster, 1963), pp. 38-43.

withered away gradually after the political disasters of A.D. 70 and 132-5. Pharisaic energy in this direction is attested by Mt 23:15: "You traverse sea and land to make a single proselyte." [46] As we will see more distinctly later, Torah often functions in rabbinic Judaism in the same way as Christ does in the New Testament, as the visible, incarnate revelation of God. Here already there is a hint of that. "But now in Christ Jesus you who were far off have been brought near in the blood of Christ" (Eph 2:13).

1:13

יג   הוּא הָיָה אוֹמֵר: נְגֵד שְׁמָא אֲבַד שְׁמֵהּ, וּדְלָא מוֹסִיף יְסוּף, וּדְלָא יָלֵיף קְטָלָא חַיָּב, וְדִשְׁתַּמַּשׁ בְּתָגָא חֲלַף.

13   He used to say: A name made great is a name destroyed, and he that increases not decreases, and he that learns not is worthy of death, and he that makes worldly use of the crown shall perish.

This Aramaic mishnah is expressed in extremely condensed, almost poetic, staccato phrases. The four parts may hang together in that each is an escalation in gravity of offense of the preceding, but this is not clear in the last stich.

1. *A name made great is a name destroyed.* A simple exhortation to humility, such as we find in greater detail in Mt 23:5-12.

2. *He that increases not, decreases.* This clause expresses a very profound and important aspect of all learning and spiritual life both in Judaism and Christianity—growth. In the New Testament this theme is found both in parable form (e.g., Mt 13:32; Mk 4:8), as well as in direct instruction by Jesus (Mt 13:12 par = Mt 25:29), and by the early Christian letter-writers (2 Cor 10:15; Eph 2:21; especially 4:15 f; Col 1:10; 2:19; 1 Pet 2:2; 2 Pet 3:18). St. Paul's statement in 2 Cor 3:18 that Christians are being changed into the Lord's likeness "from one degree of glory to another" had a profound influence on the Greek Fathers, especially upon Gregory of Nyssa. [47] Perhaps most clear of all is Phil 3:12-14:

---

[46] Cf. D. Daube, *The New Testament and Rabbinic Judaism* (London: Athlone, 1956), pp. 109, 281, 339; B. J. Bamberger, *Proselytism in the Talmudic Period* (New York: Ktav, 1968).

[47] See his *Sixth Homily on the Song of Songs* (Migne, PG 44, 885A-888A) and the collection of his texts edited by J. Daniélou, *From Glory to Glory* (New York: Scribners, 1961). See further Louis Bouyer, *The Spirituality of the New Testament and the Fathers* (New York: Desclee, 1963), p. 364 f. On St. Paul, see G. T. Montague, *Growth in Christ: A Study in St. Paul's Theology of Progress* (Fribourg: Regina Mundi, 1961).

Not that I have already obtained this or am already perfect; but I press on to make it my own, because Christ Jesus has made me his own. Brethren, I do not consider that I have made it my own; but one thing I do, forgetting what lies behind and straining forward to what lies ahead, I press on toward the goal for the prize of the upward call of God in Christ Jesus.

The Western Fathers too shared this value. One reason for St. Augustine's break with Manichaeism was its static character, which contrasted strongly with the continuous progress expected of the Christian in his spiritual and intellectual life. [48] The same principle, to stand still in the way of God is to go backwards, is found in various Latin formulations throughout the Middle Ages, notably in Thomas Aquinas. [49] John Henry Newman learned the principle in his youth from reading the evangelical Thomas Scott, in the form Growth the only sign of life. It had a profound effect on him, leading finally to his elaborate *Essay on the Development of Christian Doctrine* (1845). [50]

3. *He that learns not is worthy of death.* From the point of view of our thesis, this is the most important stich. Its stress on religious learning as of life and death value is quite obvious. Hillel does not mean that the willfully unlearned should receive capital punishment, but rather that he deserves eternal death or gehenna in the world to come, for such a one has spurned the principal means of grace in Judaism.

The kind of clause which runs: "He who does x is worthy of (*lit.*, guilty of, *enochos*) x" occurs ten times in the New Testament, but only once is the punishment death: Mt 26:66 = Mk 14:64. Jesus is found by the Sanhedrin deserving of death.

There is no comparable general admonition to learn in the New Testament (except in the Pastorals), but rather a personal invitation: Learn of me, Mt 11:29.

4. *He that makes worldly use of the crown shall perish.* Cited also 4:5c. This means that it was forbidden that the scribes should be paid

---

48 Augustine, *Conf.* V, X, 18; cf. *De moribus Manichaeorum* (II), 22. See Peter Brown, *Augustine of Hippo* (London: Faber, 1967), chapter five, p. 59.

49 *Summa theologiae*, II-II, q. 24, a. 6 (Turin: Marietti, 1962), p. 122 and n. 1: "In via Dei stare retrocedere est." The sources of this saying are to be found in (1) Pelagius, *Epistula I, ad Demetriadem*, c. 27 (Migne, PL 30, 42B); (2) St. Augustine, *Sermo* 169, c. 15, n. 18 (PL 38, 926); (3) Gregory the Great, *Pastoral Rule*, III. c. 34 (PL 77, 118C); (4) Bernard of Clairvaux, Sermo II in festo Purificationis, n. 3 (PL 183, 369C).

50 John Henry Newman, *Apologia pro vita sua* (1864), ch. 2.

for exercising their profession (cf. M. Bek 4:6; b. Ned 37a, 62a). This principle is taken up in the Gospels: "You received without pay, give without pay. Take no gold, nor silver, nor copper in your belts, no bag for your journey, nor two tunics, nor sandals, nor a staff; for the laborer deserves his food" (Mt 10:8-10; cf. Mk 6:8; Lk 9:3). J. Jeremias argues that when Hillel paid an entrance fee to the school of Shemaiah and Abtalion (b. Yom 35b Bar.), the fee was not paid to the teacher, but to the caretaker of the school building. [51] Later this principle was abandoned, both in Judaism (b. Ket 105a), and in Christianity (1 Cor 9:4-11). [52] Some scribes practiced trades, some were supported out of the community charity fund, later some were maintained by the Patriarch. [53]

1:14

יד   הוּא הָיָה אוֹמֵר: אִם אֵין אֲנִי לִי, מִי לִי? וּכְשֶׁאֲנִי לְעַצְמִי, מָה אֲנִי? וְאִם לֹא עַכְשָׁיו,
אֵימָתַי?

14   He used to say: If I am not for myself who is for me? and being for mine own self what am I? and if not now, when?

Again we meet a saying of Sophoclean laconism, pregnant with meaning.

1. *If I am not for myself who is for me?* This question, to which the obvious unspoken answer is: no one, could be taken not only as encouraging self-reliance (cf. Hillel's "where there are no men strive to be a man," Ab 2:6 ad finem), but, theologically, as the definitive expression of that "works-righteousness" which, according to some theories, forever divides Judaism from Pauline-Christian salvation through God's grace and man's reliance on that grace by faith alone. Thus Eph 2:8 f: "For by grace you have been saved through faith; and this is not your own doing, it is the gift of God—not because of works, lest any man should boast" (but note also the important qualification in v. 10: "created ... unto good works"). More serious still, Hillel's remark could be construed as giving license to certain forms of selfishness and egotism which are by some thought to be characteristically Jewish. Such interpretations would have some color of truth were it not for the following clause:

---

[51] *Jerusalem in the Time of Jesus* (Philadelphia: Fortress, 1969), p. 112.
[52] On Paul, see D. Daube, *The New Testament and Rabbinic Judaism*, pp. 395 f.
[53] On these economic problems see E. E. Urbach, "Class-Status," pp. 24 f.

2. *Being for mine own self what am I?* I.e., if I am only for
myself, I am a wretchedly narrow, self-centered person. Earlier (on
1:4 and 5) we spoke of the dialectical arrangement of the sayings in
Aboth, which juxtaposes (partially) contradictory statements so that
they can qualify one another. Here we have an example of internal
dialectics, dialectics built into one mishnah by the author himself. Cf.
Rm 14:7: "None of us lives to himself, and none of us dies to himself."

3. *If not now, when?* Though its general applicability is not in
doubt, this stich finds its most appropriate point of reference in the
duty to learn and to study (cf. the preceding mishnah and especially
2:5 ad finem). New Testament parallels are: 2 Cor 6:2: Now is the
acceptable time; also Rm 13:11 f. Also Mt 6:34a: Therefore do not be
anxious about tomorrow, for tomorrow will be anxious for itself. [54]

1:15

טו   שַׁמַּאי אוֹמֵר: עֲשֵׂה תוֹרָתְךָ קֶבַע; אֱמֹר מְעַט וַעֲשֵׂה הַרְבֵּה, וֶהֱוֵי מְקַבֵּל אֶת כָּל הָאָדָם
בְּסֵבֶר פָּנִים יָפוֹת.

15   Shammai said: Make thy [study of the] Law a fixed habit; say little
and do much, and receive all men with a cheerful countenance.

1. So highly was study valued that a fixed amount of time was to
be set aside each day for its pursuit. Nothing was to be left to chance.
The amount of material to be mastered was in fact so vast (all the
written and oral Torah) that without method there was little hope of
accomplishing the task. The time allotted at Qumran is known from the
rule of the community (1 Q S 6:6-8) and will be considered in our
second chapter.

A comparable early Christian daily (or weekly) program may be
found in the summary in Acts 2:42, where attention to the apostolic
teaching is integrated into a wider range of activities: social action
(*koinonia*), the breaking of bread (= either communal meals or the
eucharist or both), and the prayers.

Note that in Shammai's dictum Torah means Torah-study. This
usage reminds us that though the principle object of our consideration,
the rabbinic ideal of study, is to be found throughout the sources we
are considering, there is in fact no single clear distinct word for study
in Hebrew, or at least none which is used very often. Thus *limmûd* or

---

[54] On this verse of Mt see the classical, Egyptian and rabbinical parallels collected
by J. G. Griffiths, "Wisdom about tomorrow," HTR 53 (1960): 219-221.

talmud correspond most closely to the idea but occur infrequently in the earlier material. *Torah, mishnah* and *midrash* are more common but have other meanings. All but *limmûd* become the names of specific books or bodies of literature. *Ḥeqer, meḥqar,* and *ᶜiyyun* are on the periphery of the circle of meaning.

A late Christian parallel to this part of Shammai's saying may be adduced from Cardinal Cajetan (Thomas de Vio, 1469-1534) to whom is attributed the remark: I can hardly excuse from grievous sin a brother Dominican who failed to devote at least four hours a day to study. [55] Contrast the opposing advice with regard to prayer in Ab 2:13; M. Ber 4:4a.

2. Here the stress is on action, deeds. Cf. Mt. 5:37: "Let what you say be simply 'Yes' or 'No'; anything more than this comes from evil."

3. Cf. 3:13. The same is said more pointedly in Mt 5:47. Contrast Lk 10:4: Salute no one on the road.

1:16

טז רַבָּן גַּמְלִיאֵל אוֹמֵר: עֲשֵׂה לְךָ רַב, וְהִסְתַּלֵּק מִן הַסָּפֵק, וְאַל תַּרְבֶּה לְעַשֵּׂר אוֹמָדוֹת.

16 Rabban Gamaliel said: Provide thyself with a teacher and remove thyself from doubt, and tithe not overmuch by guesswork.

From 1:16 to 2:7 we have a break in the chain of tradition, which amounts either to a digression on the descendants of Hillel (Taylor) or to a later insertion made for tendentious reasons (so, with differing nuances Marti-Beer *in loco,* and L. Finkelstein). [56] Rabban Gamaliel (I) is generally identified with the member of the Sanhedrin who figures in Acts 5:34-39 and is mentioned in Acts 22:3 as the teacher of Paul. He is further thought to have been the grandson (or son) of Hillel, who flourished in the mid-first century. K. Marti disagrees with this, and maintains that this mishnah belongs after 1:17, and that therefore the Gamaliel in question is Gamaliel II, who succeeded Johanan ben Zakkai as head of the Academy ca. A.D. 90-110. But O. Holtzmann, one of the final editors of the series in which Marti's commentary appears, in a note *in loco,* defends the tradition presented above, especially on the basis of M. Git 4:3; Orl 2:12; RH 2:5; Yeb 16:7.

---

[55] Quétif-Echard, *Scriptores Ordinis Praedicatorum* (Paris, 1722), II, p. 16a.
[56] L. Finkelstein, "Introductory Study to Pirke Aboth," JBL 57 (1938): 13-50.

The first stich is reproduced from 1:6, where it has been discussed.

The doubt referred to in the second stich is doubtless made more specific in the third: doubt in tithing, but also in observing the other details of the ceremonial and ritual precepts, is to be sedulously avoided. Positively one must study to make one's observance as accurate as possible. We have already seen that it was precision in tithing which distinguished the Pharisaic *ḥaber* (associate) from the unscrupulous *am ha-aretz*. Compare M. Ter 4:6b: To count the fruits is praiseworthy, to measure them is more praiseworthy, but to weigh them is the most praiseworthy of the three.

The Gospels make tithing a matter of secondary importance. "But woe to you Pharisees! for you tithe mint and rue and every herb, and neglect justice and the love of God; these you ought to have done, without neglecting the others" (Lk 11:42; cf. Mt 23:23 f, and by contrast Heb 7:1-10). In the Gospels Lev 27:30 is played off against Mic 6:8.

1:17

יז   שִׁמְעוֹן בְּנוֹ אוֹמֵר: כָּל יָמַי גָּדַלְתִּי בֵּין הַחֲכָמִים, וְלֹא מָצָאתִי לַגּוּף טוֹב אֶלָּא שְׁתִיקָה.
וְלֹא הַמִּדְרָשׁ הוּא הָעִקָּר, אֶלָּא הַמַּעֲשֶׂה. וְכָל הַמַּרְבֶּה דְבָרִים מֵבִיא חֵטְא.

17   Simeon his son said: All my days have I grown up among the Sages and I have found naught better for a man than silence; and not the expounding [of the Law] is the chief thing but the doing [of it]; and he that multiplies words occasions sin.

Simeon is mentioned by Josephus in *Vita* 190-198; 216; 309; Bell. Jud. 4:159 as a leader in Jerusalem.

1. *Nothing better than silence.* In Simeon's reference to his childhood we catch a glimpse of the exhausting schedule of studies imposed upon sons of the Hillelite and similarly illustrious families in Jerusalem. The whole saying could almost be read as an outburst of adolescent rebellion. It breathes a certain weariness with the interminable and excessive wrangling, with the overproduction of secondary refinements, which characterized one side of the Sages' learned activity. Precisely because the problem was so real, we find an amazing number of reservations concerning the tendency of the whole learned ideal of Aboth within Aboth itself. Deeds are valued more highly than words in 1:15, here, and in 3:9 (Danby 10); in 4:5a and in 6:5. In 3:17 (D 18) and in 5:14 a kind of even balance is maintained between them. The criticism of Jesus, which we will consider in detail in our

chapter three, does not spring from weariness so much as from concern
for those social classes excluded and thereby alienated from the ideal,
as well as from an opposition to the trivializing of the Law which
makes everything in it of equal importance, while stressing the physical
and material details (e.g., of tithing 1:16) rather than the inner
motivation.

Other texts (1) in praise of silence are Ab 3:13b (D 14); 2 Thess
3:12; cf. Mk 14:61 = Mt 26:63.

2. On the relative merits of talkers (hearers) and doers, Jas 1:22-26
is especially strong, but note too Rm 2:13 and 1 Cor 4:20.

3. Against many words are Prov 10:19; Qoh 5:2; Jas 3:5-8. Mt 6:7
is not relevant in this context.

1:18

יח רַבָּן שִׁמְעוֹן בֶּן גַּמְלִיאֵל אוֹמֵר: עַל שְׁלֹשָׁה דְבָרִים הָעוֹלָם עוֹמֵד: עַל הַדִּין, וְעַל
הָאֱמֶת וְעַל הַשָּׁלוֹם, שֶׁנֶּאֱמַר¹ : 'אֱמֶת וּמִשְׁפַּט שָׁלוֹם שִׁפְטוּ בְּשַׁעֲרֵיכֶם'.
₁ זכריה ח, טז.

18 Rabban Simeon b. Gamaliel said: By three things is the world sustained:
by truth, by judgement, and by peace, as it is written, *Execute the
judgement of truth and peace.*

Formally, this mishnah is a variant of 1:2. At first glance, the
contents are so general and vague as to put the reader off. There is
nothing especially Jewish here. But recently an interpretation has come
forward which finds significance precisely in its barely Jewish character:

> [No. 18] clearly presents a post-135 revision of no. 2: the Torah now
> is truth, a philosophizing tendency; the Temple service is now replaced
> by justice; and deeds of lovingkindness are replaced by peace. Morton
> Smith observes that the basis of "the world" is no longer the coherent
> "brotherhood of Israel," but the *pax Romana.* 57

This interpretation is interesting but uncertain. The displacement of
Torah by truth supposes that truth comes first in the list. This is true
for the Baer edition of the printed text and for Taylor's edition, but
not for the Römm edition of the printed text (Vilna), or for the
Kaufmann ms. or the Loewe (Palestinian) edition or for the Geniza
fragments in the Antonin collection or for the edition of Ch. Albeck.
Following this order, Torah is replaced by *dîn* (judgment), not a

---

57 J. Neusner, *The Rabbinic Traditions about the Pharisees before 70*, V. I: The
Masters (Leiden: Brill, 1971), p. 18.

very significant shift, whereas the Temple-service would be replaced
by truth, also quite understandable in view of the substitution of
Torah-study for the sacrificial system after the destruction of the
Temple. [58] It is further to be doubted whether the rabbis of the period
immediately following the Bar Kokhba debacle (ca. A.D. 140-165)
were yet ready to perceive the *pax Romana* as *shalom.*

2:1

פרק שני

א   רַבִּי אוֹמֵר: אֵיזוֹהִי דֶרֶךְ יְשָׁרָה שֶׁיָּבֹר לוֹ הָאָדָם? כָּל שֶׁהִיא תִפְאֶרֶת לְעוֹשָׂה וְתִפְאֶרֶת
לוֹ מִן הָאָדָם. וֶהֱוֵי זָהִיר בְּמִצְוָה קַלָּה כְּבַחֲמוּרָה, שֶׁאֵין אַתָּה יוֹדֵעַ מַתַּן שְׂכָרָן
שֶׁלַּמִּצְוֹת. וֶהֱוֵי מְחַשֵּׁב הֶפְסֵד מִצְוָה כְּנֶגֶד שְׂכָרָהּ, וּשְׂכַר עֲבֵרָה כְּנֶגֶד הֶפְסֵדָהּ.
וְהִסְתַּכֵּל בִּשְׁלֹשָׁה דְבָרִים, וְאִי אַתָּה בָא לִידֵי עֲבֵרָה; דַּע מַה לְמַעְלָה מִמְּךָ: עַיִן
רוֹאָה, וְאֹזֶן שׁוֹמַעַת, וְכָל מַעֲשֶׂיךָ בַּסֵּפֶר נִכְתָּבִין.

1   Rabbi said: Which is the straight way that a man should choose? That
    which is an honour to him and gets him honour from men. And be
    heedful of a light precept as of a weighty one, for thou knowest not the
    recompense of reward of each precept; and reckon the loss through
    [the fulfilling of] a precept against its reward, and the reward [that
    comes] from transgression against its loss. Consider three things and
    thou wilt not fall into the hands of transgression: know what is above
    thee—a seeing eye and a hearing ear and all thy deeds written in a book.

Rabbi [Judah ha-Nasi] is mentioned again in Aboth 4:20, as well
as in 2:2. As we leave the trichotomous sayings in chapter one, the
literary structure of the mishnayoth becomes more complex. Here,
for example, we could divide the teaching into three or four sayings,
the last of which itself ends in a three-fold division. We will consider
it in three steps.

The first part then is concerned with *derech eretz* or ethical right
conduct. With this metaphorical use of *derech* (way) may be compared
the hard and easy ways in Mt 7:13 f and the two ways of the Qumran
community rule (there expressed as two spirits, 1 Q S 3:13-4:26, but
as two ways in the Didache 1-6 and the Epistle of Barnabas 18-20).
The same usage is applied in a specific way to Christianity in Acts
18:25 f; 19:9, 23; 24:14. That the theme of honorable, praiseworthy
conduct enjoys a certain importance, or at least is taken for granted
in the New Testament, may be seen by a glance at the concordances

---

58 See A. I. Katsh, "Unpublished Geniza Fragments of Pirke Aboth in the Antonin
Geniza Collection in Leningrad," JQR 61 (1970): 4.

under *timē, doxa, epainos, semnos, axios*, and their respective cognates.
See especially Rom 2:6-10, Phil 4:8.

The second teaching, about light and heavy precepts, and about
loss and reward, is the most important for our purposes. It was one
of the major differences between early Christianity and rabbinic
Judaism that for the latter all 613 commandments of the Pentateuch,
both positive and negative, were of eternally valid divine force, whereas
for the former the Law had, with the advent of Christ, been effectively
reduced to the ten great commandments. The Jewish Christians based
their position on the words which immediately follow the giving of
the ten commandments in Deuteronomy: "These words the Lord spoke
to all your assembly at the mountain out of the midst of the fire, the
cloud, and the thick darkness, with a loud voice; *and he added no more*"
(Dt 5:22). [59]

The rabbis quickly realized the polemical and practical consequences
of such a radical reductionism, and countered with some drastic
measures of their own. Chief among these was the elimination of the
recitation of the ten commandments from the daily prayer service.
They also eliminated them from the phylacteries. Such a singling out
of the Ten for special esteem seemed to them to give a handle to the
heretics who had lately risen in their midst. By contrast, they were at
pains to teach that every one of God's commands revealed to Moses
at Sinai was of equal importance with the rest, and could not be
neglected with impunity. This message is pounded home three times
at least in Aboth alone: here, in 3:18 (D 19), and in 3:2. [60]

---

[59] The importance of the ten commandments in early Christianity may be seen
by a study of Mk 10:19 par; Rm 13:9; Did 2:1-3; Ep. Barn. 19:4-6; see R. M. Grant,
"The Decalogue in Early Christianity," HTR 40 (1947): 1-18.

[60] The fundamental text for evidence of the elimination of the Decalogue from the
prayer service is b. Ber 11b-12a. J. Neusner, *History of the Jews in Babylonia*, V
(Leiden: Brill, 1970) dates this passage to late Sassanian times, perhaps around
A.D. 400. For the phylacteries, see Sifre Deut, sections 34-35, as well as M. Men 3:7;
M. Kel. 18:18, M. Sanh 11:3; M. Tamid 5:1. Further K. G. Kuhn, *Phylakterien aus
Höhle 4 von Qumran* (Heidelberg: Winter, 1957); G. Vermeš, "Pre-mishnaic Jewish
worship and the phylacteries from the Dead Sea," VT 9 (1959): 65-72; H. Schneider,
"Der Dekalog in den Phylakterien von Qumran," BZ 3 (1959): 18-31; W. D.
Davies, *Setting of the Sermon on the Mount* (Cambridge: University Press, 1964),
p. 281 f; p. 401, n. 2. Unfortunately, Prof. Davies brings into the discussion M.
Horayoth 1:3, whose meaning he seems to misrepresent, turning it into the exact
opposite of what the text teaches. Recently Vermeš has returned to the question in
"The Decalogue and the Minim," *In Memoriam P. Kahle*, ed. M. Black and G.
Fohrer, BZAW, 103 (Berlin: Töpelmann, 1968), pp. 232-240. Here the attempts to
identify the *minim* in question exclusively as "Jewish Gnostics," that is, Jewish
Hellenists like Stephen. He thinks of them as liberal, enlightened Diaspora Jews,

Nevertheless, both the rabbinic literature and the Gospels recognize the distinction between light and heavy precepts. For the rabbis, it is not a real distinction, but only in the popular mind. For the Gospels, the distinction is a real one, but, curiously, where the distinction is mentioned, emphasis is also laid on keeping the whole law. Mt 5:19 reads: "Whoever then relaxes one of the least (*elachistōn, qallah*) of these commandments and teaches men so, shall be called least in the kingdom of heaven." Mt 23:23: "Woe to you, scribes and Pharisees, hypocrites! for you tithe mint and dill and cummin and have neglected the weightier matters of the law (*ta barytera tou nomou*), justice and mercy and faith; these you ought to have done, without neglecting the others." 61

A difference may however underlie the rabbinic and Gospel understandings of light and heavy commandments. It may be that the rabbis meant by the distinction easy as opposed to burdensome commands, whereas the Gospel text implied rather a distinction between trivial rules of little or no ethical significance, and rules of crucial moral import. These latter, as can be seen from the six antitheses of the Sermon on the Mount (Mt 5:21-48), the early Christians, or at least those among them of a somewhat nomistic turn of mind, were concerned to intensify, to bring out their real point.

The remainder of the second saying speaks of (heavenly) rewards as a motive for keeping even the minor laws. This motive is not foreign to the Christian scriptures, however much some would have it otherwise. See Mt 5:12; 6:1, 6, and the concordances generally under *misthos* and *apodidonai*. 62

With greater justice one could argue that the Gospel rejects too

---

located especially in Egypt. This view he asserts against the common opinion that the *minim* were Jewish Christians. Rabbinic descriptions of them as denying the divine origin of the rest of the Mosaic legislation Vermeš takes at face value as an accurate reflexion of the extreme views of radical antinomians who go far beyond Paul. But the signpost of their radicalism is the thesis that the Law was given through angels (Acts 7:53; cf. Acts 7:38; Gal 3:19; Heb 2:1 f). Here Vermeš draws the lines too finely. Gal 3:19 is an embarrassment to his thesis, since he has already admitted that Paul and his disciples did not deny the divine origin of the Torah but only taught that it was not universally obligatory (p. 238). Probably the Rabbis exaggerated the claims of the *minim*.

61 The Lucan parallel (11:42) to Mt 23:23 omits the phrase "the weightier matters of the law," and replaces mercy and faith with the love of God. On keeping the *whole* law see also James 2:10.

62 For resistance to the reward-motive, see, *inter alia*, J. Jeremias, *New Testament Theology, vol. I, The Teaching of Jesus* (New York: Scribner's, 1971), section 19, par. 3, pp. 214-218.

3

nice a calculation of rewards and penalties, the turning of the doing
of the will of God into a kind of niggardly bookkeeping. To this one
could apply Mt 6:33: "Seek first his kingdom and his righteousness,
and all these things shall be yours as well." See also Mt 20:1-16, the
parable of the laborers in the vineyard.

To the third saying we need only list the biblical parallels to the
imagery. For the all-seeing eye of God, see Ps 34:16 (E.V., 15),
cited in 1 Pet 3:12. The heavenly book of Ex 32:32 f; Mal 3:16;
Dan 7:10 is taken into the New Testament at Lk 10:20 (names written
in heaven), Phil 4:3; Rev 20:12. 63

On the rabbinic parallel to this third saying in Aboth 3:1 (Akabya
ben Mahalaleel) and possible Gnostic influence on its formulation,
see W. D. Davies, "Reflexions on tradition: the Aboth revisited,"
Christian History and Interpretation. Studies presented to John Knox.
Ed. W. R. Farmer *et al.* (Cambridge: University Press, 1967), pp.
149-151.

2:2

ב   רַבָּן גַּמְלִיאֵל בְּנוֹ שֶׁלְרַבִּי יְהוּדָה הַנָּשִׂיא אוֹמֵר: יָפֶה תַלְמוּד תּוֹרָה עִם דֶּרֶךְ אֶרֶץ,
שֶׁיְּגִיעַת שְׁנֵיהֶם מְשַׁכַּחַת עָוֹן. וְכָל תּוֹרָה שֶׁאֵין עִמָּהּ מְלָאכָה, סוֹפָהּ בְּטֵלָה וְגוֹרֶרֶת
עָוֹן. וְכָל הָעֲמֵלִים עִם הַצִּבּוּר, יִהְיוּ עֲמֵלִים עִמָּהֶם לְשֵׁם שָׁמַיִם, שֶׁזְּכוּת אֲבוֹתָם
מְסַיְּעָתַן וְצִדְקָתָם עוֹמֶדֶת לָעַד. וְאַתֶּם, מַעֲלֶה אֲנִי עֲלֵיכֶם שָׂכָר הַרְבֵּה כְּאִלּוּ עֲשִׂיתֶם.

2   Rabban Gamaliel the son of R. Judah the Patriarch said: Excellent is
    study of the Law together with worldly occupation, for toil in them
    both puts sin out of mind. But all study of the Law without [worldly]
    labour comes to naught at the last and brings sin in its train. And let all
    them that labour with the congregation labour with them for the sake
    of Heaven, for the merit of their fathers supports them and their
    righteousness endures for ever. And as for you, [will God say,] I count
    you worthy of great reward as though ye [yourselves] had wrought.

This mishnah again is formally curious and resists tidy classification.
It may be analysed into two, three, or four separate sayings. As
commonly punctuated it yields four sentences. But the first two stand
together as antithetically parallel. The third and fourth could possibly
be linked, but the fourth is so peculiar that it is hard to say for sure.
(Herford and Marti-Beer link them.) All four sentences mention
labor, but all employ a different vocabulary for it, so that while they

---

63 On *šakhar* and its range of meanings, see D. Daube, *The New Testament and
Rabbinic Judaism* (London: Athlone, 1956), pp. 355-361.

may have a thematic common denominator, the *Stichwort* principle of grouping orally transmitted sayings may not be invoked. [64]

1 and 2. The clear expression of what we take to be the dominant theme of Aboth should be noted first of all. *Talmud Torah* leaves no ambiguity. Yet in the antithetical statement, *talmud* is not mentioned, though clearly understood. Torah there stands, as elsewhere, for study of Torah. *Derech eretz*, here taken to mean worldly occupation, elsewhere means general ethics, or simply the way of the world.

The exhortation to balance one's study with a secular trade may have been motivated by a variety of social situations. In times of persecution and general poverty, the ability to earn a livelihood in other than the proscribed way of Torah study would be of self-evident value. Indeed Gamaliel may have been provoked to this utterance by a very concrete fact: as Patriarch in succession to this father, he was quite rich. Poor scholars were often maintained at the expense of the patriarchal treasury. Gamaliel may have found the burden more than he cared to bear. When the scholars migrated from Judea, they were often totally dependent on wealthy but ignorant landowners in Galilee. The landowners, at first impressed by the distinction and learning of their guests, soon began to contemn the scholars as a useless nuisance. So "R. Eleazar [b. Pedath in Sepphoris] said: How is the scholar regarded by the ignorant?—At first, like a golden ladle; if he converses with him, like a silver ladle; if he [the scholar] derives benefit from him, like an earthen ladle, which once broken cannot be mended" (b. Sanh 52a. b. Par. ARN[B], ch. 31, Schechter ed., p. 68). [65]

It may be that the primary intention of the saying is a concern for mental health and a balanced life, on the principle of Acts 26:24: "Your great learning is turning you mad," but this seems unlikely in

---

[64] This saying, and the next two sayings, all three attributed to Rabban Gamaliel III (ca. A.D. 200-220), son of R. Judah the Patriarch, may indicate the relative lateness of the final redaction of Aboth vis-a-vis the rest of the Mishnah. On the other hand, his brother Simeon is cited in four scattered tractates of the Mishnah (M. Shab 3:6; Makk 3:6; Shebu 1:5; Neg 10:8), for which no special lateness is usually claimed. Recently their tombs have very likely been uncovered in the necropolis of Beth Shearim in Lower Galilee. See Nahman Avigad, *Beth She^carim*, vol. 3, *The Archaeological Excavations during 1953-1958*, the catacombs 12-23 (Jerusalem: Israel Exploration Society with the assistance of Mosad Bialik, 1971), pp. 33-48 on catacomb 14 (in Hebrew). In English, see N. Avigad, "The Necropolis of Beth Shearim," in *Archaeological Discoveries in the Holy Land*, compiled by the Archaeological Institute of America (New York: Crowell, 1967), pp. 175-185.

[65] See further Adolf Büchler, *The Political and the Social Leaders of the Jewish Community of Sepphoris in the Second and Third Centuries*. Jews' College Publications, no. 1 (London: Jews' College, n.d.), esp. chapters four and five, pp. 50-92.

view of the general absence of this kind of psychological consideration from the rabbinic literature. Alternatively, Gamaliel's intent may have been to stave off a growing estrangement between the ordinary Jewish people, highly assimilated to the surrounding Gentile culture, and a small elite of observant scholars, closeted away in the yeshivot. This split was already a social fact by Gamaliel's time, Torah-study having become a full-time profession at least by the second century. Practice in this matter has always varied, as might have been expected. Many scholars also worked at trades, but some belonged to the landed gentry, with many slaves. That Karl Marx derived his peculiar doctrine of the right relation between theory and praxis from this kind of rabbinic view must remain a distinct possibility. See his *Theses on Feuerbach.*

The concluding thought of the first saying, that study and work put sin out of mind, reveals the normal rabbinic optimism about the capacity of human nature to resist temptation and sin. [66]

The antithetical statement betrays either polemical sharpness or exaggeration for the sake of literary effect.

Several parallels within Aboth may be noted. 1:10: love labor. 2:12: learning is (should not be) the hereditary privilege of an elite. 3:18: study and *derech eretz.* In 4:10 we find the dialectical antithesis which overturns the balance of 2:2 by giving the primacy unequivocally to study. Business is only a *pis aller.*

The third saying finds parallels to its motives in Rm 15:17 (for the glory of God) and Rm 11:28 (for the sake of their forefathers). The merits of the fathers may be derived from passages like Ex 32:13 and Lev 26:45. [67]

The fourth saying, with which may be compared Rm 4:4, presents a textual problem (singular or plural main verb). Whichever reading be adopted, God is undoubtedly the unnamed subject, the plural being simply a reverential form, like the theological passive. Who are the "you"? Albeck: those who labor with the congregation.

2:5

ה הִלֵּל אוֹמֵר: אַל תִּפְרשׁ מִן הַצִּבּוּר, וְאַל תַּאֲמֵן בְּעַצְמָךְ עַד יוֹם מוֹתָךְ, וְאַל תָּדִין אֶת חֲבֵרָךְ עַד שֶׁתַּגִּיעַ לִמְקוֹמוֹ. וְאַל תֹּאמַר דָּבָר שֶׁאִי אֶפְשָׁר לִשְׁמוֹעַ, שֶׁסּוֹפוֹ לְהִשָּׁמַע. וְאַל תֹּאמַר: לִכְשֶׁאֶפָּנֶה אֶשְׁנֶה, שֶׁמָּא לֹא תִפָּנֶה.

---

[66] W. D. Davies, *Paul and Rabbinic Judaism* (London: SPCK, 1948), pp. 22 f and literature there cited. Contrast Rm 1, 2, 5:12 f, and especially 7.

[67] See G. F. Moore, *Judaism*, I, pp. 535-545; III, detached note 249.

5   Hillel said: Keep not aloof from the congregation and trust not in
thyself until the day of thy death, and judge not thy fellow until thou
art come to his place, and say not of a thing which cannot be understood
that it will be understood in the end; and say not, When I have leisure
I will study: perchance thou wilt never have leisure.

We return to sayings attributed to Hillel, picking up from 1:14 where
we had left him. This mishnah contains five thoughts which might be
taken as discrete entities or as ethical maxims arranged in an ascending
order with maxims relating to study as the crown of the whole. All
are formulated in the imperative mood.

1. This saying has been located against the background of early first
century Jewish sectarianism, and specifically against the alternative
to Pharisaic Judaism which the Essene community at Qumran offered.
Palestinian Jewry, so far as we can tell from Josephus, was restless and
fissiparous, earnest young men, zealous for their national religious
heritage, trying now one school, now another (cf. Jos, *Vita*, 9-12).
Then as now the more eager, disgusted at how far the majority of
Jews were from the religious ideal of purity set before them in their
scriptures (especially, as had by then become the case, when that ideal
had widened to apply not only to the priests but to plain Israelites as
well), banded together in "holy clubs" (*ḥaburoth*) to make the living
of the Law easier and more sure. Still, even so, as long as one remained
in the city, one was never free from defilement for long. And so arose
the further temptation to leave behind the imperfect Jewry of the
cities, and to join a holy community in the desert, leaving the larger
community bereft of its natural leaders and divided in spirit. It was to
meet such a temptation that Hillel framed this reply, or so runs a
plausible hypothesis. 68

In Aboth 4:5 the saying is repeated, in the name of R. Zadok,
though this repetition is omitted in the Taylor and Albeck editions.
The meaning of this variant attribution and wavering in the textual
tradition is difficult to assess with certainty. It has recently been argued
that since R. Zadok not only in Ab 4:5 but elsewhere states maxims in
his own name which are otherwise attributed to Hillel, he had not
heard of their Hillelite origin. Probably therefore he was the first

---

68 See N. N. Glatzer's works cited in the note to 1:12. It has been further
suggested that the Menahem mentioned in j. Hag 77d as Hillel's colleague, is the
same person as the Menahem mentioned by Josephus (*Ant.* 15:373-379) as an
Essene. Were such a connection verifiable, which unfortunately it is not, it would
give a personal point to Hillel's saying. On Menahem, see further J. Neusner,
Rabbinic Traditions, I, pp. 184 f and the literature there cited.

to enunciate them. Later, during the final redaction of the Mishnah, as many as possible such maxims were attributed to Hillel. [69] In this case the omission of sayings in Ab 4:5 would have been a late, deliberate attempt to eliminate any rivals to the Hillelite authorship of these *bons mots*. Such elaborate, even if tentative, deductions seem to rest on rather fragile bases, since we do not find any very thorough-going attempt to attribute all early sayings to Hillel. On the contrary, attributions seem to be rather widely distributed in the tannaitic literature. The Mishnah has no hero, no central dominant figure. Certainly Judah ben Ilai, the most frequently mentioned teacher in the Mishnah (some 650 times), is not. We must also realize that we are not yet dealing with a critically edited text. On the other hand, there can be no doubt that in the course of oral transmission some attributions must have floated from one teacher to another, especially in the case of earlier material. (R. Zadok was a second generation tanna, fl. A.D. ca. 80-120.) On balance, we are inclined to a verdict of *non liquet*.

Cf. Heb 10:25 and the example of Jesus, who, though he withdrew into the desert from time to time for prayer, had compassion on the crowds (Mt 9:36) and rejected no one, not even the *am ha-aretz*.

2. This warning against exaggerated self-confidence should be balanced by the saying attributed to Hillel in 1:14 which encourages a reasonable self-trust. Similar thoughts are common in the New Testament; e.g., 1 Cor 10:12; Gal 6:3 (paralleled in Plato, *Apol.* 41E); Jas 4:6; 1 Pet 5:5 and their Old Testament source Prov 3:34LXX. Cf. also the conversation between Solon and Croesus in Herodotus (I, 32-34) where we are advised not to call a man happy until we know the outcome of his life.

3. The obvious parallel to this invitation to put ourselves in the other fellow's shoes is Mt 7:1-5, par Lk 6:37 f. Perhaps one should further see here a variant of the Golden Rule (Mt 7:12, par Lk 6:31) or of the so-called Silver Rule attributed to Hillel (b. Shab 31a).

4. This statement is important for our theme, because it stresses the personal responsibility each disciple should feel for the resolution of difficulties found in the Torah. There is to be no pious appeal to a higher, more distant authority, with its concomitant shirking the task of tackling the problem oneself. This spirit of the personal responsibility of each individual Jew for the maintenance of the learned tradition, as reflected in the later remarks "where there are no men

---

[69] J. Neusner, *Rabbinic Traditions*, III, pp. 185-199.

strive to be a man" (2:6), and "it is not thy part to finish the task, yet thou art not free to desist from it" (2:16), goes far to explain the impressive vitality of Jewish culture in later ages. To be sure, from time to time, this vitality has been overshadowed by the feeling that the men of earlier ages were giants, that we of a later time are pygmies by comparison, or at least that we are much farther away from the sources of the tradition, and that therefore we should not dare to change or criticize anything. This is the spirit of M. Sotah 9:15: "When R. Meir died there were no more makers of parables, etc." Of course in times of persecution or grave social dislocation, when men lacked the circumstances conducive to a mastery, let alone a development, of the tradition, such a feeling of inadequacy may have some basis in fact. Still, such an attitude could only lead in the long run to uncreative stagnation. The spirit of the present maxim represents the healthier tradition. [70]

5. For the ancient Greeks leisure (*scholē*) was the basis of culture (cf. Aristotle, *Metaphysics* I, 1, 18; Sir 38:24). The rabbis feared that an illusory quest for full leisure might become the basis of sloth. The point is that one must not wait for time to be given one, one must make time available through one's own efforts. The rabbis have really anticipated Parkinson's Law: work expands in proportion to the time allotted for its accomplishment. The maxim contains the same message as 1:14c: "if not now, when" applied more specifically, and may be connected with the recommendation to combine study with worldly occupation (2:2). Since the word for study used here is *shanah* (to repeat), the maxim may have in mind something more modest than what we mean by the word, viz., the simple repetition of mishnayoth and bible texts which one had in fact first learned in the leisure of one's youth. Understood in this way, the principle may be compared with the "pray without ceasing" of 1 Thess 5:17, an ideal taken up into monastic *meditatio*, which has been well explained as the muttered repetition and savoring of Scriptural (especially Psalm) verses. In Greek monasticism this practice received a narrowing but intense development in hesychasm. [71]

---

[70] For a thorough discussion of a problem in the textual transmission and translation of this maxim, see Herford, p. 46.

[71] On *meditatio*, see J. Leclercq, *The Love of Learning and the Desire for God* (New York: Fordham U.P., 1961), Mentor Omega edition, pp. 23-26; 77-80.

J. Neusner, *Rabbinic Traditions*, I, pp. 224-226, brings forward (inconclusive) arguments for denying the attribution of Aboth 2:5-7 to Hillel, and for dating them to the Amoraic period. On pp. 297-302 of the same volume, he argues that most

2:6

ה   הוּא הָיָה אוֹמֵר: אֵין בּוּר יְרֵא חֵטְא, וְלֹא עַם הָאָרֶץ חָסִיד, וְלֹא הַבַּיְשָׁן לָמֵד, וְלֹא הַקַּפְּדָן מְלַמֵּד, וְלֹא כָל הַמַּרְבֶּה בִסְחוֹרָה מַחְכִּים, וּבִמְקוֹם שֶׁאֵין אֲנָשִׁים הִשְׁתַּדֵּל לִהְיוֹת אִישׁ.

6 He used to say: A brutish man dreads not sin, and an ignorant man cannot be saintly, and the shamefast man cannot learn, and the impatient man cannot teach, and he that engages overmuch in trade cannot become wise; and where there are no men strive to be a man.

In the Judaism of the first century we find "an emphasis on study for its own sake, on nonpractical, pure study, on study that approaches the character of worship," [72] and this emphasis is true both of the more sectarian, as of the more "normative" strains. Though this stress has already been noticed in many of the sayings of Aboth which we have considered, it is to a marked degree pregnant in this saying attributed to Hillel.

Formally the saying contains five rather too terse value judgments in the indicative, judgments having to do with five types of men related negatively to this ideal of study; then follows an exhortation in the imperative. Since this exhortation has no self-evident formal or material connection with the rest of the mishnah it may have had a separate origin, but this cannot be certain. It has been suggested that the three Hillel pericopes Aboth 2:5-7 form a kind of catechism, but this seems highly unlikely, on formal grounds alone. Thus, there is no clear division into two ways, no basic ethical or halachic instruction, nor other characteristics of catechetical literature.

1. Since the definitions of the *bor* (brutish man) in later rabbinic literature are somewhat fanciful, we will not delay over them. What

---

of the material traditionally ascribed to Hillel must probably not be judged historically reliable, with the exception of his teachings on the festivals, purity-laws, and legal theory. The Hillel stories are first referred to chiefly at Usha, rather than at Jamnia, that is, in the mid-second century. For our purposes all of this is not of decisive importance, though it does seem rather extravagant to say, as Neusner does on p. 299, that "Hillel had neither masters nor disciples."

In this sequence of Hillel sayings (2:5-7) there is a slight discrepancy in the numbering and division of the texts between the Albeck text and the Danby translation. Albeck makes Danby's 2:5 (on which we have just commented) part of Rabban Gamaliel's last mishnah (2:4). Danby's 2:6 then becomes 2:5; his 2:7 is divided into the apophthegm about the floating skull, numbered 2:6, and the chain of brief antitheses, numbered 2:7. Both editions then agree on numbering the next mishnah (containing Johanan b. Zakkai material) 2:8. We will follow the Danby division here as being more logical.

[72] Glatzer, "Hillel the Elder in the light of the Dead Sea Scrolls," p. 236.

is clear is that he was regarded as one step worse than the *am ha-aretz*. Paul's "sin is not counted where there is no law" (Rm 5:13b) may be adduced as a somewhat remote parallel. [73]

2. Our central thesis is that Jesus differed from his Pharisaic contemporaries primarily in respect of the relation between this ideal of Torah study as a means of salvation and the various classes of the Jewish people of that day. This saying constitutes the star witness of the case, if our understanding of it is correct. We must proceed therefore with care, beginning with the matter of the translation. For, though commonly rendered, by both Jewish and Christian translators, "an ignorant man *cannot* be saintly," the very brief Hebrew literally runs: "not *am ha-aretz* a *hasid*." Thus, holding *au pied de la lettre*, one could understand the phrase as the neutral recognition of an unfortunate social state of affairs, with no trace of either contempt or *parti pris*. That the statement means more than this may be gathered both from the context, for as we have seen we have here a list of five value judgments, and from a critique of its content. On the face of it, there is no reason whatever why a man ignorant of the details of the Law could not nevertheless be morally upright, God-fearing, and pious. But here everything depends on the definition of piety. According to the presuppositions of Hillel (as we may conveniently name the author of the statement, whoever he may have been), piety meant precisely the observance not only of the ten commandments, or of the biblical precepts taken as a whole, but the extension and application of those rules of purity which in the Bible were intended only for the priests now to all devout Israelites, as well as all the other developments of the Law which had been made through the Oral Tradition, notably the extreme regulations concerning Sabbath rest, which far exceeded the scriptural rule. [74] Now the keeping of all these regulations was not possible without a serious study of them in all their subtlety. Thus piety depended upon study. Study was in a measure salvific. To be sure, in the list of those Israelites who will have no share in the world to come, the ignorant as such are not mentioned (Sanh 10:1-4), unless they be included under the "Epicureans" and

---

[73] Cf. *Seder R. Amram Gaon*, Part I, ed. D. Hedegard (Lund: Lindstedts, 1951), p. 18 f. Paragraph V contains a discussion of the morning prayer which thanks God "who has not made me an uncultivated person (*bor*)." The tendency of the discussion is to remove the prayer as tending toward self-praise, or, as we would say, arrogance.

[74] Cf. the well known admission of M. Hag 1:8, "The rules about the Sabbath ... are as mountains hanging by a hair, for teaching of Scripture thereon is scanty and the rules many."

those who say that the Law is not from Heaven. At the very least they were felt not to be fully justified, not to be standing quite right with the Heavenly Father.

The obvious question here is what exactly were the *amme ha-aretz?* Was theirs a voluntary status resulting from their positive refusal to study, or from a deliberately heterodox choice, or was it at least at times a fate to which they were condemned by social circumstances? Were the Pharisees trying to impose a life-style possible in an urban setting on rural inhabitants? How deep did the class antagonism go? These questions are rather difficult to answer since the term *am ha-aretz* changed meanings several times in the course of its history. At first it seems to have meant the native inhabitants of what was to become the land of Israel whom Abraham found when he arrived in Canaan (cf. the use of the term in this sense in Gen 23:7, 12, 13). At the time of the kings it seems to have meant the Israelite rural gentry, the squirarchy, conservative in religion and politics. [75] When the Jews returned from the exile in Babylon, the term seems to have meant the Samaritans (cf. Ezra 4:4; 10:2, 11). There is more abundant material for the rabbinic usage but the interpretation of it remains a matter of delicate judgment. Clearly for the rabbis the *am ha-aretz* were the common people, the masses, as opposed however not to an aristocracy of birth or wealth (both priests and rich men could be classed as *am ha-aretz*), but rather to the disciples of the Sages. They were held to be ignorant at least of the refinements of Torah and their observance. The rabbis held them in great contempt, and discouraged marriage with their daughters. The locus classicus for stories about the rabbis' dislike of them is b. Pesahim 49b. A less well known statement, the most extreme I have come across, may stand for the others (though its authenticity must remain doubtful):

> R. Simeon b. Yohai said: An Am ha-aretz, even if he is pious, even if he is a saint, even if he is honest, cursed be he to the Lord, the God if Israel. [76]

With this frightful statement may be compared a remark attributed to Pharisees in Jn 7:49: "But this crowd, who do not know the law, are accursed." More moderately, they were thought to be trustworthy

---

[75] See R. de Vaux, *Ancient Israel* (New York: McGraw-Hill, 1961), pp. 70-72; M. H. Pope, s.v. ᶜAm ha'arez, IDB, vol. I, p. 106 f.

[76] *Pirke de Rabbenu ha-Kadosh*, ed. Schoenblum, 21b, ed. Grunhut, p. 76. Cited by S. Lieberman, "The discipline in the so-called Dead Sea Manual of Discipline," JBL 71 (1952): 199-206.

on the matter of tithes, but not with regard to second tithes and priests' dues (*Terumah*). Still, they were regarded as ritually unclean. [77] Many other too precise definitions are given; for example, they are Jews who recite the eighteen benedictions but not the Shema^c, or who do not use phylacteries, or who do not wear the tassels, or who eat their secular food (*ḥullin*) in a state of uncleanness. (The matter of hand-washing in Mk 7:2 refers to this regulation.) Such almost capriciously varied definitions give one the uneasy feeling that the exact boundary line between the *am ha-aretz* and the *ḥaber* was not precisely fixed, but that there was a peculiar religious affinity between them. In some cases at least the *am ha-aretz* seem to have been sincerely religious Jews, but Jews who simply did not live up to the full, high standards of the Pharisees, a kind of outer fringe or penumbra of the Pharisaic movement. Since the difference between them was one of culture and piety, the transition from one status to the other may have been relatively easy. On the other hand, the *am ha-aretz* seem to have been sufficiently cohesive as to have their own synagogues (Ab 3:10). The extreme hatred expressed against them may then be explained as due to their being so near and yet so far, as is the bitterness which has often existed between Latin and Greek Christians. This too could explain such a statement as: "If an *am ha-aretz* is pious (*ḥasid*), do not dwell in his neighborhood" (b. Shab 63a).

It is sometimes assumed that from a Pharisaic point of view both Jesus and his disciples would have been considered *am ha-aretz*. [78] It is better however to observe the precision of the Gospels in this case. The disciples of Jesus are there reproached for, e.g., not washing their hands, but not Jesus himself (Mk 7:2, 5). If such a detail were reliable, then we might suspect that Jesus was a Jew who personally maintained a Pharisaic level of observance and the religious knowledge which such observance presupposed, but that he could not bring himself to reject all religious association with his fellow Jews of a lower standard of observance. In so doing he would only have been giving a wider application to rules which existed apart from him, rules permitting association with not fully observant Jews on the occasion of the great festivals, for the sake of the brotherhood of all Israel (b. Betz 11b; b. Hag 26a). Such a comparatively small difference in

---

[77] L. Finkelstein, *Pharisees*, v. 2.

[78] So G. F. Moore, in Appendix E of *Beginnings of Christianity*, vol. I, ed. by K. Lake and Foakes-Jackson (New York: Macmillan, 1920), p. 445; S. S. Cohon, "The Place of Jesus in the religious life of his day," JBL 48 (1929): 82-108.

practice seems eventually to have led to a more radical break with Pharisaism on his part.

To return to the Hillelite statement. Fiebig's remark that "in these words the difference between Hillel's way of thinking and Jesus' way of thinking can be seen most clearly" must be taken with full serious-ness. [79] But what is the difference? Most likely this, that while Jesus shared to the full Hillel's zeal for sacred learning, for the Word of God, while he too venerated many of the religious traditions of his people, he nevertheless displaced them in his understanding of God's plan of salvation for men. To him this knowledge, this sacred study, sanctifying though it may be, could not be made a condition for salvation. Salvation could not be reserved for a learned elite. What must have decisive weight was a right intention, i.e., the desire to do the will of God, the faith in his promises, and deeds of loving kindness, even though these not be strictly according to the halacha. Perhaps no other statement in Aboth more clearly reveals that inner flaw in the otherwise noble and praiseworthy ideal of study as a form of worship, a flaw which compelled Jesus, and the early church with him, to take their distance from it in that form, while presupposing its values and retaining them in a new synthesis.

3. The other parts of the mishnah may be dealt with more quickly. The reference to the shamefaced man may refer either to an incipient schizophrenic's shyness, or to the need for nerve to make headway in life, learning included.

4. The same emphasis on the need to teach, and to teach with patience, may be noticed in Ezra 7:25b; 1 Tim 3:2 f; 2 Tim 2:24 f; Tit 1:7 f.

5. This statement may be regarded as an emphatic riposte to Ab 2:2. It too echoes the thought of Sirach 38:24, that leisure is the basis of culture, itself an Aristotelian theme.

6. Though couched in general terms, the context might incline us to understand the "manliness" in this case as pertinacity in study, rather in the same way as Ab 2:16a is to be taken. Although precise dating is impossible, if the saying arose at a time of persecutions, it might mean the manliness to recreate singlehandedly a Jewish community which had been destroyed. The general effect is to encourage that sense of individual responsibility which alone has enabled Judaism to survive and to revive itself down through the centuries of counter-pressure.

---

[79] Cited in Marti-Beer, p. 44.

2:7

ו אַף הוּא רָאָה גֻלְגֹּלֶת אַחַת שֶׁצָּפָה עַל פְּנֵי הַמַּיִם. אָמַר לָהּ: עַל דַּאֲטֵפְתְּ אַטִיפוּךְ,
וְסוֹף מְטִיפַיִךְ יְטוּפוּן.

ז הוּא הָיָה אוֹמֵר: מַרְבֶּה בָשָׂר – מַרְבֶּה רִמָּה; מַרְבֶּה נְכָסִים – מַרְבֶּה דְאָגָה; מַרְבֶּה
נָשִׁים – מַרְבֶּה כְשָׁפִים; מַרְבֶּה שְׁפָחוֹת – מַרְבֶּה זִמָּה; מַרְבֶּה עֲבָדִים – מַרְבֶּה גֶזֵל;
מַרְבֶּה תוֹרָה – מַרְבֶּה חַיִּים; מַרְבֶּה יְשִׁיבָה – מַרְבֶּה חָכְמָה; מַרְבֶּה עֵצָה – מַרְבֶּה
תְבוּנָה; מַרְבֶּה צְדָקָה – מַרְבֶּה שָׁלוֹם. קָנָה שֵׁם טוֹב – קָנָה לְעַצְמוֹ; קָנָה לוֹ דִּבְרֵי
תוֹרָה – קָנָה לוֹ חַיֵּי הָעוֹלָם הַבָּא.

7 Moreover he saw a skull floating on the face of the water and he said
unto it, Because thou drownedst they drowned thee and at the last they
that drowned thee shall be drowned. He used to say: The more flesh
the more worms; the more possessions the more care; the more women
the more witchcrafts; the more bondwomen the more lewdness; the
more bondmen the more thieving; the more study of the Law the more
life; the more schooling the more wisdom; the more counsel the more
understanding; the more righteousness the more peace. If a man has
gained a good name he has gained [somewhat] for himself; if he has
gained for himself words of the Law he has gained for himself life in
the world to come.

Three distinct units are herein contained, and the second of them
must be further subdivided into five negative and four positive observations on life expressed in a *marbeh* form: the more this, the more
that. This form, once established, is so simple to duplicate that we must
reckon with additions to an originally brief set.

1. The saying over the skull has the form of an apophthegm, with
just enough of a preamble to make the aphorism intelligible. The
lesson of retribution it imparts is common elsewhere, e.g., Obad 15;
M. Sotah 1:7, 8; M. Peah 8:9 ad finem; Mt 7:2; 26:52. It is seen to be
inadequate by Job, Jn 9:3, and Lk 13:1-5.

2. a. What is the point? Birth-control? A slim figure? Neither.
Rather this. A retiring scholar, living a life of almost monastic dedi-
cation, apart from his marriage, the author warns against setting too
great store by the pleasures of the flesh, the pursuit of women (in his
terms probably this means building up a large harem), and so on.
The precise use of "flesh" to mean "pleasures of the flesh" is not
common in the two Testaments. But it is found in documents reflecting
the philosophy of Epicurus, though usually in the fuller phrase *hē kata
sarka hēdonē*. Whence it is taken up as an anti-Epicurean slogan, [80]

---

[80] Philodemus Philosophus, *De Epicuro*, II, Fr. 6, col. II (ed. A. Vogliano, 1928)
in *Epicuri et epicureorum scripta*.

which becomes especially popular in Hellenistic Jewish religious polemic (see 4 Macc 7:18 "weakness of the flesh" in the context of following one's passions, and Philo). The rabbis then assimilated this development in meaning, closely connecting the flesh with the origin of evil. It is well known that the label "Epicurean" was used by the rabbis to denote the very type of an unbeliever (cf. Ab 2:14; M. Sanh 10:1). [81] "Flesh" just might be taken here in the older biblical meaning of the total human person, man simply, but the saying would not yield as good sense, turning its author into a misanthrope. As it stands, the statement is true but sour.

On worms as the fate of man, a biblical commonplace, see, for example, Is 66:24; Sir 7:17 (alluded to in Ab 4:4a); Judith 16:17; Mk 9:48parr.

b. This is an altogether evangelical assertion, but see Lk 16:14: "The Pharisees, who were lovers of money..."

c. Women, witchcraft and superstition are connected in 1 Sam 28:7 (Endor); Jer 44:15 (astral religion); Ezek 13:18; 2 Kg 23:7. Had more pains been taken with their education, this state of affairs would have been less likely to exist.

d. If lewdness was associated with women slaves, this was so partly because they had to submit themselves to their master's pleasure. This is taken for granted, e.g., in M. Yeb 6:5 and in M. Ket 1:4. In this last we are given to expect that female slaves would have been violated after their third year and a day of age! Partly however their condition was rendered difficult because they were not guaranteed a normal married life of their own, so that their relations with male slaves were legally out of wedlock. Hillel's judgment seems to us too cynical. Christians would want to stress the saintly exceptions to the rule. Both miss the mark. The only cure for such a state of affairs is a change in the social structure, foreshadowed in Gal 3:28, though it took two millenia and the invention of the cotton gin to effect that change.

e. Thieving is a lesser crime than either slave rebellion (such as occurred in the Italian provinces of the Republic, e.g., under Spartacus [d. 71 B.C.]), or the murder of the master by the household servants (as not uncommonly happened in nineteenth century Russia). This criminal restraint may be put down to the relatively better conditions which slaves enjoyed among the Jews, probably in part due to the humanitarian legislation of Deuteronomy (15:12-18) as well as to

---

[81] See further E. Schweizer and R. Meyer, s.v. *sarx*, TDNT, VII, pp. 98-151, esp. pp. 103-5, 110-124. Also the phrase *hēdonōn tou biou*, Lk 8:14.

the generally high ethical standards of the Jews. [82] Several of the early second century rabbis, e.g., Eleazar b. Harsum, are said to have had large numbers of slaves to work their estates. [83] Thieving in the sense of embezzlement of funds is mentioned in the Gospel parable of the dishonest steward (Lk 16:1-13). [84]

a'. The Hebrew merely says "the more Torah, the more life," which links up with several Old Testament passages: Dt 30:15-20; Prov 3:1 f, 18. This last, "it is a tree of life to them that lay hold of it" points back to the tree of life and the tree of the knowledge of good and evil in Genesis 2 and 3, but was applied to the Torah in rabbinic tradition, e.g., in the prayer said when bringing the Torah-scroll back to the ark after it has been read at the service. This connection between Torah and life is alluded to in Jn 5:39, but there the further point is made that for the life contained in the Torah to be appropriated by the individual he must search (study) the Scriptures, thus justifying Danby's expanded translation of our passage. Since in any religion that is called life which is at the center of that religion's set of values, since all religion is intended somehow to resolve or illuminate the mystery of life and thereby to improve our individual lives, it is evident in this short affirmation that the highest religious evaluation in Judaism is accorded to Torah. With this compare the Johannine affirmation of Jesus the Logos, the Torah incarnate, as the life of men (Jn 1:4; 8:12; 14:6).

b'. The practical concomitant of such a high evaluation of study is the need for schools (*yeshivah*), education, assiduity in study (*yeshivah* literally means sitting). Though wisdom may be hypostatized in the Old Testament (Prov 8:21 ff, etc.), for the rabbis it is acquired through painstaking labor over the sacred text.

c'. Couched in such general terms as not to require comment.

d'. The intellectual emphasis is now once again balanced by practical "deeds of loving-kindness" (Ab 1:2). For righteousness (*ṣedaqah*) acquired in rabbinic literature the specific meaning "almsgiving" as did charity in English. This concern for the welfare of the Jewish

---

[82] Jeremias, *Jerusalem*, p. 348.

[83] b. Yoma 35b Bar; cf. Lam R. 2:4 on 2:2 (Sonc. ed., p. 162).

[84] On slavery see especially the minor tractate of the Talmud, "Abadim," and Jeremias, *Jerusalem*, pp. 312-316, and ch. 16, pp. 345-351, with the literature there cited, to which add E. E. Urbach, "The laws regarding slavery," *Annual of Jewish Studies* (London: University Press, 1963). This article appeared originally in Hebrew in *Zion* 25 (1960).

community has always been an important part of Jewish piety. [85]
Shalom here could refer either to social peace or to welfare, well-
being itself.

3. Here the study of Torah is presented as a foretaste of heaven,
eternal life already begun, implying a kind of eschatology realized
by anticipation. On the value of a good name, see Qoh 7:1; Sir 41:12;
on gaining treasure in heaven, cf. Mt. 6:19 f. [86]

2:8

ח   רַבָּן יוֹחָנָן בֶּן זַכַּאי קִבֵּל מֵהִלֵּל וּמִשַּׁמַּאי. הוּא הָיָה אוֹמֵר: אִם לָמַדְתָּ תוֹרָה הַרְבֵּה,
אַל תַּחֲזִיק טוֹבָה לְעַצְמָךְ, כִּי לְכָךְ נוֹצָרְתָ. חֲמִשָּׁה תַלְמִידִים הָיוּ לְרַבָּן יוֹחָנָן בֶּן זַכַּאי,
וְאֵלּוּ הֵן: רַבִּי אֱלִיעֶזֶר בֶּן הָרְקָנוֹס, וְרַבִּי יְהוֹשֻׁעַ בֶּן חֲנַנְיָה, וְרַבִּי יוֹסֵי הַכֹּהֵן, וְרַבִּי
שִׁמְעוֹן בֶּן נְתַנְאֵל, וְרַבִּי אֶלְעָזָר בֶּן עֲרָךְ. הוּא הָיָה מוֹנֶה שְׁבָחָן: רַבִּי אֱלִיעֶזֶר בֶּן
הָרְקָנוֹס – בּוֹר סִיד, שֶׁאֵינוֹ מְאַבֵּד טִפָּה; רַבִּי יְהוֹשֻׁעַ – אַשְׁרֵי יוֹלַדְתּוֹ; רַבִּי יוֹסֵי –
חָסִיד; רַבִּי שִׁמְעוֹן בֶּן נְתַנְאֵל – יְרֵא חֵטְא; וְרַבִּי אֶלְעָזָר בֶּן עֲרָךְ – מַעְיָן הַמִּתְגַּבֵּר.
הוּא הָיָה אוֹמֵר: אִם יִהְיוּ כָל חַכְמֵי יִשְׂרָאֵל בְּכַף מֹאזְנַיִם, וֶאֱלִיעֶזֶר בֶּן הָרְקָנוֹס בְּכַף
שְׁנִיָּה – מַכְרִיעַ אֶת כֻּלָּם. אַבָּא שָׁאוּל אוֹמֵר מִשְּׁמוֹ: אִם יִהְיוּ כָל חַכְמֵי יִשְׂרָאֵל בְּכַף
מֹאזְנַיִם וְרַבִּי אֱלִיעֶזֶר בֶּן הָרְקָנוֹס אַף עִמָּהֶם, וְרַבִּי אֶלְעָזָר בְּכַף שְׁנִיָּה – מַכְרִיעַ
אֶת כֻּלָּם.

8   Rabban Johanan b. Zakkai received [the Law] from Hillel and from
    Shammai. He used to say: If thou hast wrought much in the Law claim
    not merit for thyself, for to this end wast thou created. Five disciples
    had Rabban Johanan b. Zakkai, and these are they: R. Eliezer b. Hyr-
    canus, and R. Joshua b. Hananiah, and R. Jose the Priest, and R.
    Simeon b. Nathaniel, and R. Eleazar b. Arak. Thus used he to recount
    their praise: Eliezer b. Hyrcanus is a plastered cistern which loses not a
    drop; Joshua b. Hananiah—happy is she that bare him; Jose the Priest
    is a saintly man; Simeon b. Nathaniel is fearful of sin; Eleazar b. Arak
    is an ever-flowing spring. He used to say: If all the Sages of Israel were
    in the one scale of the balance and Eliezer b. Hyrcanus in the other,
    he would outweigh them all. Abba Saul said in his name: If all the
    Sages of Israel were in the one scale of the balance and with them
    Eliezer b. Hyrcanus, and Eleazar b. Arak was in the other, he would
    outweigh them all.

With the material attributed to Rabban Johanan ben Zakkai and his
disciples we may feel ourselves on historically firmer ground than with

---

[85] See Is 32:17 and Jeremias, *Jerusalem*, pp. 126-134; Moore, *Judaism*, II, pp.
162-179.

[86] On the sense of *qana* as winning or acquiring spiritual goods see Ab 1:6; Sir 6:7
and Daube, *New Testament and Rabbinic Judaism*, p. 355.

the sayings attributed to Hillel. [87] At least starting with him we have chains of oral tradition likely preserved unbroken until written down, though at times interpolated. [88]

Formally we are again confronted with a composite and complex pericope which we may divide into five parts. The *qibbel* formula is used for the last time in Aboth here. With this passage therefore the oldest stratum of Aboth, which seems to have consisted of a genealogy of teachers and pupils, comes to an end. With Johanan occurs the transition from Pharisaism properly so-called to rabbinic Judaism.

1. For our purposes, this is the most important, as well as the best authenticated, part. What it says in effect is that Jewish man's *raison d'être*, the purpose of his entire life on earth, is to occupy himself with Torah. Thus Johanan states in the strongest possible way the centrality of Torah for rabbinic Judaism, its preeminence in value.

Unfortunately, when we try to pin him down more precisely, we run into a textual problem: is it "if you have *done* much Torah" or "If you have *learned* much Torah"? *ᶜasita* (done) is better attested than *lamadtta* (the Kaufmann Ms, for example), and that is doubtless the reading we must follow, although probably with a harmonizing translation such as Danby offers: "if thou has wrought much in the Law...," that is, *do* in the sense of *work at*, though there is no preposition in the text. Still, the variant may not be without theological significance. It could of course have arisen accidentally, in which case the scribe may have felt that there was little difference between learning and doing Torah. Or the change may have been deliberate, to bring the words of Johanan into line with the decision of the sages in favor of

---

[87] On the life of Johanan, the savior of rabbinic Judaism after the debacle of 66-73 A.D., the sage of the academy at Jamnia, see esp. J. Neusner, *A Life of Yohanan ben Zakkai ca. 1-80 C.E.* (Studia post-biblica, vol. 6; Leiden: Brill, 1970[2]); also the same author's form-critical study *Development of a Legend* (Studia post-biblica, vol. 16; Leiden: Brill, 1970). The same author has recently published two articles on the rabban of Jamnia: "Priestly views of Yohanan ben Zakkai," *Kairos,* N.F. 11 (1969): 303-312; "Some early traditions concerning Yohanan ben Zakkai," in *Studies in Jewish Bibliography, History and Literature in Honor of I. E. Kirv* (New York: Ktav, 1971), pp. 333-345.

[88] See the methodological presupposition (better, working hypothesis) of Neusner, *Rabbinic Traditons,* vol. 3, p. 3: "I take seriously the attributions of sayings to post-70 masters, and moreover, regard post-140 attributions as absolutely reliable." And see his note in *A Life,* 2nd ed., p. 107: "The antiquity of these sayings ... is proven by the high praise recorded for Eleazar ben Arakh. Since Eleazar was isolated from the rabbis at Yavneh, one must assume that this collection of logica was edited before his reputation for learning was lost, and, therefore, during Eleazar's lifetime, if not during Yohanan's."

Akiba's position in the famous disputation at Lydda (b. Kid 40b) which we shall examine at the end of this chapter.

"Doing Torah" is good biblical language: Jos 22:5; Neh 9:34; Sir 19:20. Internal parallels, more or less close, are to be had at 1:3 (claim no reward); 1:17; 2:15 and 16; 6:1 (abundant rewards). New Testament parallels can be found in the unprofitable servants of Lk 17:10 and in the necessity to preach the gospel of 1 Cor 9:16.

2. Johanan's list of five disciples may be compared with Jesus' Twelve (Mk 3:13-19; Mt 10:1-4; Lk 6:12-16). In Aboth de Rabbi Nathan, Recension A, ch. 14, the same five act as his comforters on the death of his son. On that occasion too Eleazar ben Arak succeeded where the others had failed. Note the use of the title Rabbi for the first time in Aboth (though some manuscripts omit them). [89]

3. a. The plastered cistern is a metaphor for the meticulous, faithful preservation of the oral traditions. He was what the later Tannaim would call a basket of books, though at this time the tradition was probably not so rigidly fixed as later when it positively required such prodigies of memory. In the end, according to the tradition, such fidelity was his undoing (on which see, among other texts, b. Suk 28a and b. Yoma 66b). Cf. Ab 6:6 *ad finem*.

b. With this phrasing we may compare Lk 11:27 and 1:42. Cf. j. Yeb 1:6.

c. As a *ḥasid*, he was certainly not an *am ha-aretz*. See Ab 2:6.

d. It is hard to see how, on rabbinic grounds, R. Simeon b. Nathaniel could be regarded as fearful of sin, if, as is reported in Tos. AZ 3:10, he ate his secular food (*ḥullin*) in a state of uncleanness. One or the other tradition must be awry, unless he later mended his ways, or something else is meant by fearing sin than observing the minutiae of the halacha.

e. The metaphor speaks of creative originality and copiousness. He was only remembered for his incursions into mysticism, having isolated himself from the rabbinic movement by retiring to Lydda.

---

[89] On two of the disciples there are modern monographs. R. Eliezer ben Hyrcanus, called in M. Sotah 9:15 "the Great," has been so honored by B. Z. Bokser's *Pharisaic Judaism in Transition* (New York: Bloch, 1935, repr. Arno Press, 1973); R. Joshua b. Hananiah by Joshua Podro's *The Last Pharisee* (London: Vallentine, Mitchell, 1959). Eliezer is mentioned four hundred times in the Mishnah, though excommunicated for his conservatism; Joshua some eighty times. Of the others, Jose is mentioned outside this chapter only in M. Eduy 8:2, the remaining two only in this chapter. On R. Simeon b. Nathaniel see J. Jeremias, *Jerusalem*, p. 256, as an example of a non-Pharisaic scribe and teacher, an interpretation he bases on the slender evidence of Tos. AZ 3:10, ed. Zuckermandel, p. 464.

On the ever-flowing spring, see especially Jn 4:14, which has many
biblical roots, e.g., Ps 36:10. It should be noted that these praises of
the disciples are expanded and varied in ARN^A, ch 14. There, to take
the more noteworthy variants, Simeon ben Nathaniel is called "oasis in
the desert, which holds on to its water." To Joshua ben Hananiah are
applied the words of Qoh 4:12, "a three-fold cord not quickly broken."

4. The high praise accorded to R. Eliezer ben Hyrcanus, an excom-
municate at the end of his days, may indicate the antiquity of the
saying and the authenticity of its attribution. [90] On the image of the
scale of the balance see Daniel 5:27.

5. Abba Saul has added a gloss which may be a secondary correction
of the high praise accorded to Eliezer ben Hyrcanus. (In that case it
is hard to see why he transferred the praise to the equivalently delin-
quent Eleazar.) Or he may simply be recording the earlier opinion
of Rabban Johanan.

2:9

ט אָמַר לָהֶם: צְאוּ וּרְאוּ אֵיזוֹהִי דֶרֶךְ יְשָׁרָה שֶׁיִּדְבַּק בָּהּ הָאָדָם. רַבִּי אֱלִיעֶזֶר אוֹמֵר:
עַיִן טוֹבָה. רַבִּי יְהוֹשֻׁעַ אוֹמֵר: חָבֵר טוֹב. רַבִּי יוֹסֵי אוֹמֵר: שָׁכֵן טוֹב. רַבִּי שִׁמְעוֹן
אוֹמֵר: הָרוֹאֶה אֶת הַנּוֹלָד. רַבִּי אֶלְעָזָר אוֹמֵר: לֵב טוֹב. אָמַר לָהֶם: רוֹאֶה אֲנִי אֶת
דִּבְרֵי אֶלְעָזָר בֶּן עֲרָךְ, שֶׁבִּכְלָל דְּבָרָיו דִּבְרֵיכֶם. אָמַר לָהֶם: צְאוּ וּרְאוּ אֵיזוֹהִי דֶרֶךְ
רָעָה שֶׁיִּתְרַחֵק מִמֶּנָּה הָאָדָם. רַבִּי אֱלִיעֶזֶר אוֹמֵר: עַיִן רָעָה. רַבִּי יְהוֹשֻׁעַ אוֹמֵר: חָבֵר
רַע. רַבִּי יוֹסֵי אוֹמֵר: שָׁכֵן רַע. רַבִּי שִׁמְעוֹן אוֹמֵר: הַלֹּוֶה וְאֵינוֹ מְשַׁלֵּם. אֶחָד הַלֹּוֶה
מִן הָאָדָם כְּלֹוֶה מִן הַמָּקוֹם בָּרוּךְ הוּא, שֶׁנֶּאֱמַר[1]: 'לֹוֶה רָשָׁע וְלֹא יְשַׁלֵּם, וְצַדִּיק חוֹנֵן
וְנוֹתֵן'. רַבִּי אֶלְעָזָר אוֹמֵר: לֵב רַע. אָמַר לָהֶם: רוֹאֶה אֲנִי אֶת דִּבְרֵי אֶלְעָזָר בֶּן עֲרָךְ,
שֶׁבִּכְלָל דְּבָרָיו דִּבְרֵיכֶם.

[1] תהלים לז כא.

9 He said to them: Go forth and see which is the good way to which a
man should cleave. R. Eliezer said, A good eye. R. Joshua said, A good
companion. R. Jose said, A good neighbour. R. Simeon said, One that
sees what will be. R. Eleazar said, A good heart. He said to them: I
approve the words of Eleazar b. Arak more than your words, for in his
words are your words included. He said to them: Go forth and see which
is the evil way which a man should shun. R. Eliezer said, An evil eye.
R. Joshua said, An evil companion. R. Jose said, An evil neighbour.
R. Simeon said, He that borrows and does not repay. He that borrows
from man is as one that borrows from God, for it is written, *The wicked
borroweth and payeth not again but the righteous dealeth graciously and*

---

[90] Neusner applies the same argument to the praise of R. Eleazar ben Arak,
A Life of Yohanan b. Zakkai, 2nd ed., p. 107, n. 1.

giveth. R. Eleazar said, An evil heart. He said to them: I approve the
words of Eleazar b. Arak more than your words for in his words are
your words included.

At first glance this double inquiry seems banal in the extreme: a conventional question, uninteresting answers, limp conclusions (a good/
evil heart). It can be shown that this is not the case at all. It helps to
locate the dialogue in the context of a philosophical debate of the kind
held in late Hellenistic schools. Such schools were no longer primarily
centers of scientific research, as had been the early Aristotelian Lyceum.
For philosophy had begun to take on a traditional character. Loyalty
to the teaching of the founder became a paramount virtue. A. D. Nock
has even described it as a "dogmatic philosophy seeking to save
souls." [91] The questions discussed were not merely academic, but were
concerned with the meaning of life itself. The discussion here has been
reduced to the bare bones, accounting for the stylized form.

1. The question Johanan poses is not strictly halachic, but generally
ethical, and so are the answers given, though the idiom remains fundamentally Semitic-rabbinic. With this kind of inquiry compare the
famous contest of the three pages in 3 Ezra 4:13-41, concluding with
the well known proverb: Magna est veritas et praevalet! Detailed
parallels: 1. for "go and see," Mt 9:13 and Jn 1:46; 2. for the good
way, Ab 2:1; 1 Pet 3:16; Jas 3:13 (*anastrophē* = conduct, way of
life). [92] The verb "cleave" (*dabaq*) has been plausibly interpreted as
indicating a certain urgency or fervor, appropriate to a life-question. [93]

a. On the good eye see Prov 20:27 [21]; 22:9; Mt 6:22 f (par
Lk 11:34 ff). If taken as a symbol of the inner light of intelligence,
quickness, acuteness of observation, it would not differ greatly from the
prize-winning answer, but that is presumed in the conclusion in any case.

b. For the good *ḥaber*, see Qoh 4:9-12, Sir 6:14-17; 37:1-6, and
Ab 1:6.

c. Cf. the allusion in 1 Cor 15:33 to Menander, *Thais* (218).

d. Cf. Ps 22:32.

e. If the "correct" answer is to be rescued from banality, it is crucial
that we not understand it in the English sense of good-heartedness,
meaning kindliness, nor even in the sense defended by Melamed, viz.,

---

91 Nock, *Conversion* (Oxford: University Press, 1933), p. 181.
92 On *derech* see the remarks of Daube, *New Testament and Rabbinic Judaism*,
p. 99.
93 Thus J. Goldin, "A philosophical session in a Tannaite academy," *Traditio* 21
(1965): 1-19. Goldin proposed the Hellenistic analogue.

cheerfulness, inner joy, but rather in the good biblical and rabbinic sense of *mind*. *Leb* in the Old Testament is the seat of mental or spiritual powers and capacities, the seat of rational functions, of planning and volition and all purposiveness. Even among the Greeks this sense is not unknown. While for Aristotle the heart is the center of the emotions, the Stoics made of it the seat of reason. Philo and Josephus only speak of the heart as a physical organ, but in rabbinic literature the Old Testament range of meaning persists, as it does in the New Testament. [94]

So then Eleazar asserts and Johanan agrees, that, naturally speaking, man's best guide to life in his reason or mind, comprising of course both intellectual and affective functions. All else flows from this. Eleazar is simply teaching the Greek commonplace that man is the reasonable animal. Following one's reason need not imply a detachment from Torah, since if Torah were held to be really God's gift and instructions to man, it would be reasonable to accept and follow it. [95]

Johanan's approval is given not only to the content but also to the inclusive compactness of Eleazar's answer, a model of *kelal* summary. [96]

2. a. On the evil eye see Prov 23:6 f; 28:22; Sir 14:8-10; 29:4 ff; Ab 2:11; 4:21; 5:13; Mt 20:15; Mk 7:22.

b. Cf. Ps 37:21.

c. Cf. Prov 19:17; Haggai 2:8; Ab 1:17; Mt 25:40; Lk 16:10.

d. This answer is followed by a homiletic interpolation or gloss supported by a citation from Ps 37:21. Goldin (*art. cit.*) here finds an explicit reference to Plato, *Res pub.* 1:331d, the definition of justice as "truth-telling and paying back what one has received."

e. Perhaps we should see in this answer, verbally parallel to part 1.e., a shift in content. It seems unlikely that "an evil heart" should mean simply "poor intelligence." Doubtless the heart as the seat of moral impulses and decision is meant. There need be no tension between the two meanings, since intelligence was essentially moral intelligence

---

[94] For many examples see the article by Baumgärtel and Behm, s.v. *Kardia* in TDNT, III, pp. 605-613. E. Melamed's view is defended in *Leshonenu* 20 (1957): 108-9.

[95] Reason seems to have been the content of the Greek doctrine of the law of nature, assimilated to Judaism through a process of radical transformation by Philo. See the important article by H. Koester, "Nomos physeōs: the concept of natural law in Greek thought," in *Religions in Antiquity* (Goodenough Festschrift), ed. J. Neusner (SHR, 14: Leiden: Brill, 1968), pp. 521-542.

[96] See thereon B. Gerhardsson, *Memory and Manuscript*, pp. 136-148, esp. p. 140.

for the Bible and rabbinic thought. Cf. Parallels in Mk 7:21 f; Eph 1:18; Clem. Rom. 36 and 59.

In his article already mentioned J. Goldin has located the entire dialogue in a Stoic school context on the basis of a summary of Stoic teaching on the virtues drawn up in Diogenes Laertius 7:92 ff, presenting the matter first positively, then negatively. [97]

There is a parallel version of the dialogue in ARN[A], ch. 14 (Goldin ed., pp. 75 f) with a few interpretative glosses, of which the most important explains the "good heart" as being "toward heaven, toward the commandments, and toward mankind."

2:10

הֵם אָמְרוּ שְׁלֹשָׁה (שְׁלֹשָׁה) דְּבָרִים. רַבִּי אֱלִיעֶזֶר אוֹמֵר: יְהִי כְבוֹד חֲבֵרְךָ חָבִיב עָלֶיךָ
כְּשֶׁלָּךְ; וְאַל תְּהִי נוֹחַ לִכְעוֹס; וְשׁוּב יוֹם אֶחָד לִפְנֵי מִיתָתָךְ. וֶהֱוֵי מִתְחַמֵּם כְּנֶגֶד אוּרָן
שֶׁלַּחֲכָמִים; וֶהֱוֵי זָהִיר בְּגַחַלְתָּן שֶׁלֹּא תִכָּוֶה, שֶׁנְּשִׁיכָתָן נְשִׁיכַת שׁוּעָל, וַעֲקִיצָתָן עֲקִיצַת
עַקְרָב, וּלְחִישָׁתָ   לְחִישַׁת שָׂרָף, וְכָל דִּבְרֵיהֶם כְּגַחֲלֵי אֵשׁ.

10 They [each] said three things. R. Eliezer said: Let the honour of thy
    fellow be dear to thee as thine own, and be not easily provoked, and
    repent one day before thy death; and warm thyself before the fire of
    the Sages, but be heedful of their glowing coals lest thou be burned,
    for their bite is the bite of a jackal and their sting the sting of a
    scorpion and their hiss the hiss of a serpent, and all their words are
    like coals of fire.

---

[97] W. D. Davies, in his article "Reflexions on tradition: the Aboth revisited," in
Christian History and Interpretation (John Knox Festschrift), ed. W. R. Farmer *et al.*
(Cambridge: University Press, 1967), p. 148, has expressed reserve at the parallel
from Diogenes Laertius on the grounds that its structure is "too elaborate." One
could argue in a counter sense to the same conclusion, that is, the Diogenes text is
not a true parallel because its structure is not elaborate enough, in that no "right
answer" concludes each part; there is no dialogue between master and disciples,
no living situation but only a listing of various opinions apparently by the author
himself. But the prominence in the lists of *phronesis* (prudence, wisdom) and
aphrosynē (imprudence) provides a striking counterpart to the good/evil heart of our
text, especially since *phronesis* can mean intention, understanding, insight as well
(see Bauer, s.v.). See further M. Smith's comment on our passage, contributed to
J. Neusner, *Development of a Legend*, p. 55, wherein he expresses doubts as to the
authenticity of this material, because of its highly stylized form. This too may bear
on the relevance of the Stoic parallel, since Aboth and Diogenes Laertius' *Lives of the
Philosophers* were probably finally redacted around the same time, the first part of the
third century. If Ab 2:9 is authentic, i.e., if it indeed dates from the time of Johanan
and his immediate disciples, it probably could not have been related to this Stoic
text. If however it is late, redactional material, the possibility of contact becomes
more plausible.

As regards form, this mishnah, containing the teaching of R. Eliezer ben Hyrcanus, presents a problem of division. At first glance, there seem to be four members to the paragraph. But, since the introductory clause leads us to expect only three members, and the fourth is of a markedly different form and character from the others, we are led to the conclusion that the fourth member is a secondary component, a gloss added when the heat of passion had cooled and such a saucy saying could be admitted to the collection without wounding.

1. The first stich treats of honor, and in this resembles 2:1. In content however it can be seen as a variant form of the Golden Rule, with its roots in the deutero-canonical (Tob 4:15; Sir 31:15) and apocryphal (Letter of Aristeas, 207) books, emerging clearly in the New Testament (Mt 7:12 par Lk 6:31) and the Apostolic Fathers (e.g., Didache 1:2), and attributed in one form to Hillel (b. Shab. 31a). [98]

2. The warning against anger is paralleled in Jas 1:19 f and 1 Cor 13:5.

3. Of the centrality of repentance both in Judaism and in the New Testament there can be no doubt. [99] The fifth of the Eighteen Benedictions is a prayer for repentance. Here what is said is, on the fact of it, of a rather low order, conjuring up the man who postpones repentance till his revels are over, rather than making the will of God his way of life. But it would be unwise to press the text too far, in the absence of a clarifying context. Such contexts were provided by later Jewish tradition: since no one can know the day of his death, we should repent every day, it was reasoned. Besides, there is always room for minimalist religious instruction to support the weak, so that no one be lost.

4. The first part of this ironic saying may be an intentional parody of the dust-saying in Ab 1:4 above. There are loose verbal parallels to some of the imagery in Sir 8:3, 10 and Prov 25:22 (taken up in Rm 12:20). The sharp language was elicited by the painful personal experience of excommunication due to R. Eliezer's refusal to accept the ruling of the majority, and he died under the ban. The harshness

---

[98] See Daube, *New Testament and Rabbinic Judaism*, pp. 343 ff, and Albrecht Dihle, *Die goldene Regel* (Göttingen: Vandenhoeck & Ruprecht, 1962), Studienhefte zur Altertumswissenschaft, **no. 7.**

[99] On repentance in Judaism, see Moore, *Judaism*, I, pp. 507-519; S. Schechter, *Aspects of Rabbinic Theology* (New York: Schocken, 1969, 1st ed. 1909), ch. 18, pp. 313-343; for the New Testament, see the bibliography to *metanoeō* in Bauer's **Lexicon (E.T., p. 513).**

of the sentiments is perhaps only exceeded by the fierce denunciation
of the scribes and Pharisees found in the twenty-third chapter of
Matthew. There the stakes are higher. [100]

2:12

יב רַבִּי יוֹסֵי אוֹמֵר: יְהִי מָמוֹן חֲבֵרְךָ חָבִיב עָלֶיךָ כְּשֶׁלָּךְ; וְהַתְקֵן עַצְמְךָ לִלְמוֹד תּוֹרָה,
שֶׁאֵינָהּ יְרֻשָּׁה לָךְ; וְכָל מַעֲשֶׂיךָ יִהְיוּ לְשֵׁם שָׁמַיִם.

12 R. Jose said: Let the property of thy fellow be dear to thee as thine
own; and fit thyself for the study of the Law, for [the knowledge of]
it is not thine by inheritance; and let all thy deeds be done for the
sake of Heaven.

In this mishnah we return to the regular three-clause pattern, the
second clause being fitted out with an explanatory or causal rider
which is doubtless original.

1. This injunction is perfectly parallel with that in 2:10a, thus
another variant of the Golden Rule, only substituting *mammon*
(wealth, property) for *chabod* (honor). Mammon is a word that does
not occur in the Hebrew Bible, being first attested in Sir 34:8, and
later immortalized in Lk 16:9, 11, 13, and Mt 6:24. Herford suggests
that this formulation represents a decline from the elevated principle
of 2:10a, but it may rather amount simply to a concretization of that
principle. The commentary in ARN[A], ch. 17, wisely extends the
meaning of this principle to the sharing of learning as well as of
material property and does not attain a wider social view.

2. This is the clause of greatest concern to us. R. Jose warns that
there can be no learning by proxy. The Torah is Israel's inheritance
(Dt 33:4), but must be personally appropriated by each Israelite
through serious and prolonged study. As Goethe said: Was du ererbt
von deinen Vätern hast, erwirb es, um es zu besitzen: In the first
century, "to the aristocracy of money and lineage was added that of
Torah-learning, and the conception of Torah-study as an occupation
opened the way for its transmission as an inheritance from father to
son, like other occupations." R. Jose attacks the "tendency to bequeath
Torah-learning and its status, including the prerequisites attaching
thereto, which manifested itself among the families of the Sages, who,

---

[100] On R. Eliezer's life, see B. Z. Bokser, *Pharisaic Judaism in Transition* (New
York: Bloch, 1935; repr. Arno Press, 1973).

as 'Sons of the Sages,' were candidates for the inheritance of their
fathers' positions." [101]

Since the tendency to pass on to one's children what they have not
themselves earned, whether it be a heritage of learning, or money,
or aristocratic blood, is so persistent, protests of this type are always
needed. The New Testament provides examples of protest against
thinking that salvation can be inherited merely by being born into a
certain race, or by the performance of physical rites: "Do not presume
to say to yourselves, 'We have Abraham as our father'; for I tell you,
God is able from these stones to raise up children to Abraham"
(Mt 3:9 par Lk 3:8); "For he is not a real Jew who is one outwardly,
nor is true circumcision something external and physical. He is a Jew
who is one inwardly, and real circumcision is a matter of the heart,
spiritual and not literal" (Rm 2:28 f).

But more to R. Jose's point is the danger that religious learning
will be used to create or at least to reinforce class divisions rather than
to nourish the spiritual life of the whole people by being put freely
at the service of all as a humble service. It is at this point that Jesus
anticipates Jose's reservations at the learning of the rabbis, as we shall
see, though Jose is only exhorting to real as opposed to sham learning,
whereas Jesus is concerned for the moral attitudes with which it is
undertaken, and for the social consequences to which it leads.

(In the New Testament the inheritance is thought of as salvation,
eternal life. Cf. e.g., Gal 3:18 on inheritance and the law.)

3. With this admonition to have a right intention for all the deeds of
one's life (kawwanah), compare 1 Cor 10:31; Col 3:17, and the motto
of the Jesuits. [102]

2:13

יג רַבִּי שִׁמְעוֹן אוֹמֵר: הֱוֵי זָהִיר בִּקְרִיַת שְׁמַע וּבִתְפִלָּה; וּכְשֶׁאַתָּה מִתְפַּלֵּל, אַל תַּעַשׂ
תְּפִלָּתְךָ קֶבַע, אֶלָּא רַחֲמִים וְתַחֲנוּנִים לִפְנֵי הַמָּקוֹם בָּרוּךְ הוּא, שֶׁנֶּאֱמַר [1]: 'כִּי־(אֵל)
חַנּוּן וְרַחוּם הוּא אֶרֶךְ אַפַּיִם וְרַב־חֶסֶד וְנִחָם עַל־הָרָעָה'; וְאַל תְּהִי רָשָׁע בִּפְנֵי
עַצְמְךָ.

[1] יוֹאֵל יג.

---

101 See E. E. Urbach, "Class-Status and Leadership in the world of the Palestinian
sages," *Proceedings of the Israel Academy of Sciences and Humanities*, vol. II, no. 4
(Jerusalem: Central Press, 1968), p. 25. And, in Hebrew, Gedaliah Allon, "The
sons of scholars," *Tarbiz* 20 (1950): 84 f. A classic early rabbinic account of
academic arrogance and the conflict between talent and the rights of blood is the
case of the fight between Gamaliel, Eleazar ben Azariah and Akiba, told in j. Ber 4:2
and b. Ber 27b-28a.
102 See Moore, *Judaism*, II, pp. 223 ff.

13   R. Simeon said: Be heedful in the reciting of the *Shema*ᶜ and in the
     Tefillah; and when thou prayest make not thy prayer a fixed form,
     but [a plea for] mercies and supplications before God, for it is written,
     *For he is gracious and full of compassion, slow to anger, and plenteous
     in mercy, and repenteth him of the evil*; and be not wicked in thine
     own sight.

Rabbi Simeon's mishnah retains the three-part structure. The first
two sayings are related to one another in content, and indeed mutually
interpret each other. The second saying is outfitted with a scriptural
quotation. Marti-Beer regard this as a late gloss, though the community
of vocabulary is so great that the rabbinic saying might well have been
originally formulated on the basis of the Scripture words, which after
all are very great, often repeated in the Old Testament, and lead
naturally to meditation upon themselves.

   1. The first clause is concerned with set prayers: the *Shema*ᶜ, a
selection of Scripture passages, the *Tefillah* meaning prayer simply, but
the prayer par excellence in Judaism was, and is, the Eighteen (later
Nineteen) Benedictions, and these seem particularly to be in view
here. [103] R. Simeon is here either directly encouraging the recitation
of fixed prayers, or at least presupposing that fixed prayers will be
and should be said, while he exhorts to a special attentiveness in their
recitation.

   2. In either case, at first blush his first two sayings seem to stand in
contradiction to one another, since in the second he cautions against
fixed prayers. This contradiction can be resolved in several ways.
J. Jeremias implicitly assumes that the first clause is not authentic, and,
stressing that this R. Simeon was not a Pharisee, interprets the second
saying as an attack on the whole Pharisaic practice of prayer. [104] The
more usual resolution is to understand the second saying not as a
criticism of fixed prayer as such, but rather as a warning against the
permanent temptation to make such prayer merely perfunctory. In
this sense we may understand the parallel from R. Eliezer in M. Ber
4:4a: "He that makes his prayer a fixed task, his prayer is no supplica-
tion." Contrast Aboth 1:15 above, where one is encouraged to make

---

[103] On the *Shema*ᶜ see M. Berakoth 1-3 and the Talmuds thereon, as well as
Bousset-Gressmann, *Die Religion des Judentums*, p. 176, and J. Elbogen, *Der jüdische
Gottesdienst in seiner Geschichtlichen Entwicklung*, 1913. The laws relating to the
Tefillah are given in M. Berakoth 4 and 5, and the Talmuds thereon. See further
Moore, *Judaism*, II, pp. 212-238. Mk 12:29 gives the opening line of the *Shema*ᶜ.
[104] Jeremias, *Jerusalem*, p. 256.

study a fixed habit. Prayer and study are the two poles of the rabbis' world, with many points of contact yet with different rules and different problems.

Jesus' instructions on prayer (Mt 6:5-8; Mk 12:40par Lk 20:47 and the textually doubtful Mt 23:14) hover in the vicinity of R. Simeon's concern, although they are explicitly only about undue ostentation and excessive length (see Qoh 5:1). The real Gospel parallel to this mishnah is Mt 23:23 where one is sharply brought back from the externals of observance to the "weightier matters of the law." Here Jesus (or Matthew) and Simeon can be seen as men who share a common concern that the inner depths of religious life not be lost to view as the result of hurried preoccupation with a multiplicity of superficial details.

At first glance, these sayings chiefly on prayer have nothing to do with our theme of study. But our further thesis is that Jesus shared the main, positive, elements of the rabbinic religious evaluation of study, though he did so with discrimination, protesting against certain social and religious abuses to which it led. Our task is made difficult by the fact that he did not express himself directly on the role of Torah-study in the process of sanctification. Therefore his attitude must be apprehended indirectly. If, as here, it can be shown that he directly shared certain other viewpoints with the rabbis which are, in rabbinic literature, intimately connected with Torah-study, the probability increases that he also shared at least in part their views on Torah-study. The visible connections attest to a common *Denkwelt*, and lend support to the likelihood of invisible connections where our texts are unfortunately silent.

3. The third saying is too terse for commentators to be very sure of its original meaning. The most likely views are those of Maimonides who takes it as a warning against a self-hatred which leads to discouragement and moral disintegration, and of those who take it as an exhortation to maintain a clean conscience however great the corruption of your neighbors might be.

W. D. Davies raises the possibility of anti-Pauline polemic here (contrast for example Rm 7:18), but dismisses the suggestion as too explicit to be supported by the text. [105]

---

105 W. D. Davies, "Reflexions on tradition: the Aboth revisited," *John Knox Fs.* (Cambridge: University Press, 1967), p. 154.

2:14

יד   רַבִּי אֶלְעָזָר אוֹמֵר: הֱוֵי שָׁקוּד לִלְמוֹד תּוֹרָה; וְדַע מַה שֶׁתָּשִׁיב לָאֶפִּיקוֹרוֹס; וְדַע לִפְנֵי
מִי אַתָּה עָמֵל; וְנֶאֱמָן הוּא בַּעַל מְלַאכְתָּךְ, שֶׁיְשַׁלֶּם לָךְ שְׂכַר פְּעֻלָתָךְ.

14   R. Eleazar said: Be alert to study the Law and know how to make
answer to an unbeliever; and know before whom thou toilest and who
is thy taskmaster who shall pay thee the reward of thy labour.

The conclusion of this mishnah comes down to us in an unstable
condition. Danby translates the text preserved in ARN and the Prayerbook. Albeck's text reads: "... and faithful is thy task-master who
shall pay thee the reward of thy labor," which is verbatim identical
with part of the saying of R. Tarfon in 2:16 below, and has perhaps
been contaminated thereby.

Commentators waver on the division of the text, but it seems clear
that the three-fold division normal in Aboth immediately emerges
when one divides the text on the principle that the three main verbs
each begin a separate thought. The problem of division no doubt arose
out of a desire to join the first two clauses more closely than the obvious
division would allow. Thus one might read: study Torah *in order to*
be able to answer an Epicurean, or even, study Torah rather than anything else, including philosophy, for Torah knowledge alone suffices to
answer an Epicurean. These readings however do not flow naturally
from the text, since the *waw* of the apodosis is not common in Mishnaic
Hebrew, and the Mishnah is rich enough in subordinating conjunctions
to be able to express purpose clauses when it wishes to (e.g.,
lemaᶜan). [106] Therefore it seems best to take the text in three stages.

1. This simple injunction is only apparently banal. The verb *šaqad*
(Danby's "be alert") normally means to be watchful, to keep watch,
and is often used as a parallel to *šamar*. It is first applied in a cognitive
sense in Prov 8:34, where the man who keeps daily watch at Wisdom's
gates is pronounced happy. It occurs in connection with Torah-study
in an almost verbal parallel to our mishnah in the important passage
1 Q S 6:6-8, "... and the Many shall watch (*yišqodu*) together a
third of all the nights of the year, to read in the books, to investigate
judgment, and to bless together...," to which we shall return in our
second chapter. B. Gerhardsson understands it to have taken on the

---

[106] M. H. Segal, *A Grammar of Mishnaic Hebrew* (Oxford: University Press,
1927), p. 54 (sect. 104), pp. 227-231 (sects. 483-492), p. 242 (sects. 514, 515).
Compare P. Joüon, *Grammaire de l'Hébreu biblique* (Rome: PBI, 1923), pp. 529-532
(sect. 176), for biblical usage.

sense of "to persist obstinately," "be assiduous." He then finds a
parallel between this daily (or day and night, Qumran) assiduity in
study and the apostles' steadfast devotion to the service of the Word
(Acts 6:4). [107] So it appears that R. Eleazar is urging a peculiarly
intense study, day and night (Ps 1:2), which reflects a general rise
in temperature of the religious party atmosphere, as each group girded
its loins to meet the challenge of the other Jewish sects, as well as the
ever-present threat of pagan hedonism. To this may be added the consideration that for Johanan b. Zakkai and his disciples Torah-study
substituted for the temple-sacrifices as atonement for sin (ARN^A, 4).

2. That one goal of study should be to know how to answer the
objections of opponents is self-evident because utilitarian. As such
R. Eleazar's demand finds its close parallel in 1 Pet 3:14-16, particularly
in the well-known words: "always ready with a defense (*apologia*) to
everyone who asks of you a reason (*logos*) for the hope which is within
you." What is important to note is that this motive for study ranks
as rather secondary among the rabbis; indeed it is often suppressed
altogether in the desire to avoid religious controversy with outsiders,
which Jewish experience after the disasters of 66-73 and 132-5 generally
found to be futile and even counterproductive. Further, some feared
that an over-concern with apologetics in turn would lead to the sin of
beṭul Torah (neglect of Torah).

The "unbeliever" of Danby's version is of course literally an
Epicurean. We meet him elsewhere by name in M. Sanh 10:1, Acts
17:18, Jos. *Ant.* 10:277-280. Though scholars for long thought it
unlikely that the rabbis could have been in close enough contact with
Greek philosophy to be able to use the term Epicurean in anything but
the very loose sense of unbeliever, a consensus is emerging which takes
the term (in these early rabbinic texts) as referring to a particular
school of philosophy. To be sure, generally in antiquity the Epicurean
was popularly taken as a lay figure of a hedonist. [108]

3. With reference to the third of R. Eleazar's sayings, Davies
continues:

> On this view, the verse in Aboth 2:14 is a direct warning against
> Epicurean philosophy. Eleazar ben Arak has in mind the refutation
> of Jews who had succumbed to the philosophy of Epicurus. Among

---

107 B. Gerhardsson, *Memory and Manuscript* (Lund: Gleerup, 1961), pp. 240 ff.
108 Cf. A. Marmorstein, "Les 'Épicuriens' dans la littérature talmudique," *Revue
des études juives* 54 (1907: 181-193, and W. D. Davies, "Reflexions on tradition,"
p. 146 f.

other things, that philosophy argued against the conception of God
as either creator or providence—at least as popularly held. Against this
R. Eleazar ben Arak roundly asserts "... know before whom thou
toilest and who is thy task-master who shall pay thee the reward of
thy labour ..." There *is* a God who watches and rewards. Here R.
Eleazar ben Arak joins hands with the traditional opponents of the
Epicureans, the Stoics. 109

2:15, 16

טו   רַבִּי טַרְפוֹן אוֹמֵר: הַיּוֹם קָצָר, וְהַמְּלָאכָה מְרֻבָּה, וְהַפּוֹעֲלִים עֲצֵלִים, וְהַשָּׂכָר הַרְבֵּה,
וּבַעַל הַבַּיִת דּוֹחֵק.

טז   הוּא הָיָה אוֹמֵר: לֹא עָלֶיךָ הַמְּלָאכָה לִגְמוֹר, וְלֹא אַתָּה בֶן חֹרִין לִבָּטֵל מִמֶּנָּה; אִם
לָמַדְתָּ תוֹרָה הַרְבֵּה, נוֹתְנִים לְךָ שָׂכָר הַרְבֵּה; וְנֶאֱמָן הוּא בַּעַל מְלַאכְתָּךְ, שֶׁיְּשַׁלֶּם
לְךָ שְׂכַר פְּעֻלָּתָךְ; וְדַע: מַתַּן שְׂכָרָן שֶׁלַּצַּדִּיקִים לֶעָתִיד לָבֹא.

15   R. Tarfon said: The day is short and the task is great and the labourers
     are idle and the wage is abundant and the master of the house is urgent.
16   He used to say: It is not thy part to finish the task, yet thou art not
     free to desist from it. If thou hast studied much in the Law much
     reward will be given thee, and faithful is thy taskmaster who shall pay
     thee the reward of thy labour. And know that the recompense of the
     reward of the righteous is for the time to come.

These two sayings are attributed to Rabbi Tarfon, an older associate
of Rabbi Akiba. Described as a priest, well-to-do country squire, and
down-to-earth jurist and exegete, he has also been identified with the
Jew Trypho of St. Justin Martyr's *Dialogue*. Though this is question-
able, it will always remain a tantalizing possibility. If all the biographical details preserved in the Talmuds are accepted as historical
(particularly his having served as a priest in the Temple around A.D.
66), he would have been too old to meet Justin around 150. But
the historical reliability of this information is not very great. Normally
his dates are given as A.D. 50-130, and it has been supposed that he
perished in the Hadrianic persecution, though again there is no direct
evidence of this. 110

The two sayings ascribed to Tarfon here are closely related to each
other in content. Both affirm the urgency of sacred study and the

---

109 W. D. Davies, *loc. cit.*, p. 146 f.
110 On R. Tarfon, see the brief biography of him given by Jacob Neusner in his
essay, "Learning and Deeds," reprinted in his *History and Torah* (New York:
Schocken, 1965), pp. 76-102. On Tarfon's, for our purposes crucial, debate with
Akiba at Lydda on the relative merits of study and action, recorded in b. Kiddushin
40b and elsewhere, see below.

greatness of its reward. The first is expressed in five terse, even staccato, metaphorical assertions, so that the second saying might be understood as a partial commentary on it, pinning down the metaphors, especially the identification of "the task" with study in the Law.

Formally the saying in 2:15 diverges, as we have noted, from the tripartite form common to most of Aboth. In form, as well as in content, it bears a strong resemblance to Akiba's saying in 3:16 (Danby 3:17), where the metaphorical assertions are increased to eleven, a cause is introduced, the metaphors begin to wear thin, and the whole mishnah becomes stylistically overloaded. Tarfon's saying in 2:16 possesses tripartition, though the second part contains two distinct clauses, and the third part has been deemed a later gloss by A. Geiger and Marti-Beer (q.v.). If their view is correct, perhaps the gloss was added by the final editors of the tractate in order to regularize form, though this must remain uncertain, since the present second part could conceivably have been considered as distinct, or, what is more likely still, 2:15 and the first two parts of 2:16 could have been taken as one tripartite mishnah. The judgment of Geiger and Marti-Beer is however not based on formal grounds but rather on the unlikelihood of a belief in the after-life in the Mishnah. This doctrinaire assumption seems to us singularly ill-founded (see M. Ber 9:5; Sanh 10:1; Sotah 9:15) but to pursue the matter further would distract from our purpose.

The point of both sayings is plain: the task of Jewish man during his belief lifetime is the study of Torah. His salvation depends upon it. The measure of his reward is in proportion to the amount of the tradition which he has mastered. (We should here sound a cautionary note. If the first saying (2:15) is taken in isolation, its parabolic language leaves it open to other interpretations. Thus Herford can give the saying a vaguely ethical meaning, with no reference to Torah study. Even if he has fairly represented the original sense of the saying, which seems unlikely, the saying will have taken on the special coloration of its context once it had been inserted into the tractate *Aboth*, and there fairly plainly the task in question is Torah-study.) Thus study is intrinsically salvific, and the reward of each individual is geared to the level of mastery he has attained therein (see M. Kiddushin 1:10 and below), though this agressively intellectualist viewpoint is qualified (a) by the reminder that no one is expected to master the whole tradition, so long as he keeps working at it (2:16), (b) by the here implicit, elsewhere explicit (b. Kid 40b), assumption that study leads to doing.

2:15 has frequently been brought into comparison with the parable of the laborers in the vineyard (Mt 20:1-16, Matthean special material). There are certain resemblances: in both the day is a life-time (cf. Jn. 9:4), the idle laborers are men (cf. Mt. 9:37, laborers = ministers of the Gospel), the master-householder is God. But the differences are significant too. While in the Matthean parable the work is un-defined, and undoubtedly refers to the service of God in general, the task of which R. Tarfon speaks amounts, if what we have argued above be correct, to labor in the Torah. The parable moreover seems to be sharply pointed; it is concerned to emphasize the incalculable generosity of God as rewarder and the impossibility of man's knowing in advance how God will award his blessings. (Note the inclusion created by the twice-repeated statement: "the last shall be first, and the first last" Mt 19:30 and 20:16.) Contrariwise the paratactic style of the rabbinic logion inhibits it from marking any special emphasis. Marti-Beer's lyrical explanation of the labor in the Matthean parable as the demonstration of our divine sonship in true love of God and the spontaneous fulfilling of his will seems ill-founded in the text and derived from theological prejudice.

2:16 offers consolation in place of the laconic gruffness of 2:15. The Hippocratic lament "ars longa, vita brevis" does not count as an excuse. Neither the wisdom of the Torah nor the Christian life operates as a Gnostic key to the universe in ten easy steps, but is rather a continual growth in understanding, worthy of a whole lifetime. Every man is invited to it, to the limits of his time and ability. Great stress is here laid on God's fidelity as rewarder of those who study. This close connection of study and heavenly reward is not found in the New Testament (cf. 1 Cor 9:16), nor does the accent normally fall on the human achievement (see the Matthean parable above, and Lk 17:7-10), but the early Christians had no doubt of God's fidelity as a rewarder (see, e.g., 1 John 1:9), and in this their attitude does not differ from the rabbis'. [111]

---

[111] On the matter of divine reward in the New Testament, see G. Bornkamm, "Der Lohngedanke im Neuen Testament," *Studien zu Antike und Urchristentum, Gesammelte Aufsätze* II, B. Ev. Th. 28 (Munich: Kaiser, 1959 = 2nd ed., 1963), pp. 69-92; W. Pesch, *Der Lohngedanke in der Lehre Jesu,* Münchener Theologische Studien, Historische Abteilung 7 (Munich: K. Zink, 1955), and the bibliography in Bauer's *Lexicon,* s.v. *misthos.* See also Benjamin W. Helfgott, *The Doctrine of Election in Tannaitic Literature* (New York: King's Crown, 1954), p. 73, who suggests that Tarfon's statement (2:16a) sounds like a direct response to the implica-tions of Paul's antimomian charges in Rm 3 and 7 and Gal 3 and 5 that the burden

Prenote to Comments on Aboth, Chapter Three

The medieval commentator Simeon ben Zemah Duran (1361-1444) notes: "Up to this chapter the Mishnah cited authorities according to some sequence. From here on no particular sequence is followed. The Sages are quoted neither according to chronological order not according to their excellence, and not even according to some sequence of subject matter." [112] So with chapter three we begin a new section. The literary structure of the sayings undergoes a corresponding change. The triadic pattern does not occur so regularly as before.

3:2a

רַבִּי חֲנַנְיָה סְגַן הַכֹּהֲנִים אוֹמֵר: הֱוֵי מִתְפַּלֵּל בִּשְׁלוֹמָהּ שֶׁלַּמַּלְכוּת, שֶׁאִלְמָלֵא מוֹרָאָהּ ב
אִישׁ אֶת רֵעֵהוּ חַיִּים בָּלָעוּ.

2 R. Hanina the Prefect of the Priests said: Pray for the peace of the ruling power, since but for fear of it men would have swallowed up each other alive.

The text of this mishnah (3:2) is rather unstable, but the divergences between the Kaufmann manuscript and the common text given by Albeck do not notably affect the sense. Marti-Beer believe the third section, on the solitary student (see below), to be a later addition, because it is wanting in the best manuscripts K R. [113]

a. The saying of R. Hanina the *sagan* [114] of the priests is not strictly to our purpose, but its expression of a pacifist or quietist attitude with respect to the Roman government is an interesting example of that wise and sober pragmatism which enabled at least one branch of Pharisaic Judaism to survive the ensuing political upheavals. If uttered on the eve of the A.D. 66 revolt, as is commonly supposed

---

of the Law is unbearable and that the Law must be observed in its entirety or not at all. But, since Paul is not a complete antinomian (see Rm 2:6 and 13 and 13:8-10 among other passages), and, since the doctrine of God's fidelity in rewarding good deeds is a rabbinic commonplace (Aboth 3:15, 16; 4:10; 5:23 among other passages), it seems unlikely that Tarfon's dictum should be given such a narrowly specific polemical point (Neusner, *History and Torah*, p. 99, n. 2, has garbled Helfgott's references to Paul). See further literature on the doctrine of reward in note 150 on Ab 4:10.

112 Cited in Goldin, *The Living Talmud*, p. 118.

113 See also Taylor, II, p. 147.

114 On the office of *sagan*, see Jeremias, *Jerusalem*, pp. 160-163, and compare Acts 4:1, 5:24; Ez 23:6, 12, 23; Is 41:25, etc.

by modern, historically minded commentators, it would represent a
highly controversial *pris de position*, a position the zealots would
quickly have branded as pusillanimous, not to say mistrustful of God's
power to save his people. Hanina's mastery of the arts of survival
was shared by Paul (Rm 13:1-7) and his followers (1 Tim 2:1 and 2;
Tit 3:1; 1 Pet 2:17; cf. also Mk 12:17parr and Mt 17:25-27). It finds
good prophetic precedent in Jer 29:7. Similarly circumspect attitudes
toward the ruling powers that be, less vividly expressed, can be found
in Ab 1:10, 2:3. Weiss's view that Hanina later changed his mind
and became a zealot is not well founded. [115]

3:2b, 3, 6

רַבִּי חֲנַנְיָה בֶּן תְּרַדְיוֹן אוֹמֵר: שְׁנַיִם שֶׁיּוֹשְׁבִין וְאֵין בֵּינֵיהֶן דִּבְרֵי תוֹרָה, הֲרֵי זֶה מוֹשַׁב
לֵצִים, שֶׁנֶּאֱמַר[1]: 'וּבְמוֹשַׁב לֵצִים לֹא יָשָׁב'; אֲבָל שְׁנַיִם שֶׁיּוֹשְׁבִין וְיֵשׁ בֵּינֵיהֶם דִּבְרֵי
תוֹרָה, שְׁכִינָה בֵינֵיהֶם, שֶׁנֶּאֱמַר[2]: 'אָז נִדְבְּרוּ יִרְאֵי ה' אִישׁ אֶל־רֵעֵהוּ' וַיַּקְשֵׁב ה'
וַיִּשְׁמָע וַיִּכָּתֵב סֵפֶר זִכָּרוֹן לְפָנָיו לְיִרְאֵי ה' וּלְחֹשְׁבֵי שְׁמוֹ'. אֵין לִי אֶלָּא שְׁנַיִם; מִנַּיִן
שֶׁאֲפִלּוּ אֶחָד שֶׁיּוֹשֵׁב וְעוֹסֵק בַּתּוֹרָה, שֶׁהַקָּדוֹשׁ בָּרוּךְ הוּא קוֹבֵעַ לוֹ שָׂכָר? שֶׁנֶּאֱמַר[3]:
'יֵשֵׁב בָּדָד וְיִדֹּם כִּי נָטַל עָלָיו'.

1 תהלים א, א.
2 מלאכי ג, טז.
3 איכה ג, כח.

ג רַבִּי שִׁמְעוֹן אוֹמֵר: שְׁלשָׁה שֶׁאָכְלוּ עַל שֻׁלְחָן אֶחָד וְלֹא אָמְרוּ עָלָיו דִּבְרֵי תוֹרָה, כְּאִלּוּ
אָכְלוּ מִזִּבְחֵי מֵתִים, שֶׁנֶּאֱמַר[1]: 'כִּי כָּל־שֻׁלְחָנוֹת מָלְאוּ קִיא צֹאָה בְּלִי מָקוֹם'; אֲבָל
שְׁלשָׁה שֶׁאָכְלוּ עַל שֻׁלְחָן אֶחָד וְאָמְרוּ עָלָיו דִּבְרֵי תוֹרָה, כְּאִלּוּ אָכְלוּ מִשֻּׁלְחָנוֹ
שֶׁלַּמָּקוֹם בָּרוּךְ הוּא, שֶׁנֶּאֱמַר[2]: 'וַיְדַבֵּר אֵלַי זֶה הַשֻּׁלְחָן אֲשֶׁר לִפְנֵי ה''.

1 ישעיה כח, ה.
2 יחזקאל מא, כב.

ו רַבִּי חֲלַפְתָּא אִישׁ כְּפַר חֲנַנְיָה אוֹמֵר: עֲשָׂרָה שֶׁיּוֹשְׁבִין וְעוֹסְקִין בַּתּוֹרָה, שְׁכִינָה שְׁרוּיָה
בֵּינֵיהֶם, שֶׁנֶּאֱמַר[1]: 'אֱלֹהִים נִצָּב בַּעֲדַת־אֵל'. וּמִנַּיִן אֲפִלּוּ חֲמִשָּׁה? שֶׁנֶּאֱמַר[2]: 'וַאֲגֻדָּתוֹ
עַל־אֶרֶץ יְסָדָהּ'. וּמִנַּיִן אֲפִלּוּ שְׁלשָׁה? שֶׁנֶּאֱמַר[3]: 'בְּקֶרֶב אֱלֹהִים יִשְׁפֹּט'. וּמִנַּיִן אֲפִלּוּ
שְׁנַיִם? שֶׁנֶּאֱמַר[4]: 'אָז נִדְבְּרוּ יִרְאֵי ה' אִישׁ אֶל־רֵעֵהוּ וַיַּקְשֵׁב ה' וַיִּשְׁמָע' וגו'. וּמִנַּיִן אֲפִלּוּ
אֶחָד? שֶׁנֶּאֱמַר[5]: 'בְּכָל־ הַמָּקוֹם אֲשֶׁר אַזְכִּיר אֶת־שְׁמִי אָבוֹא אֵלֶיךָ וּבֵרַכְתִּיךָ'.

1 תהלים פב, א.
2 עמוס ט, ו.
3 תהלים פב, א.
4 מלאכי ג, טז.
5 שמות כ, כד.

---

[115] *Dor dor ve-dorshav* I, p. 191. He bases his suspicion on ARN, ch. 20, but
there is nothing therein to support such a reconstruction.

R. Hananiah b. Teradion said: If two sit together and no words of the Law [are spoken] between them, there is the seat of the scornful, as it is written, *Nor sitteth in the seat of the scornful*. But if two sit together and words of the Law [are spoken] between them, the Divine Presence rests between them, as it is written, *Then they that feared the Lord spake one with another: and the Lord hearkened, and heard, and a book of remembrance was written before him, for them that feared the Lord, and that thought upon his name*. Scripture speaks here of 'two'; whence [do we learn] that if even one sits and occupies himself in the Law, the Holy One, blessed is he, appoints him a reward? Because it is written, *Let him sit alone and keep silence, because he hath laid it upon him*.

3   R. Simeon said: If three have eaten at one table and have not spoken over it words of the Law, it is as though they had eaten of the sacrifices of the dead, for it is written, *For all tables are full of vomit and filthiness without God*. But if three have eaten at one table and have spoken over it words of the Law, it is as if they had eaten from the table of God, for it is written, *And he said unto me, This is the table that is before the Lord*.

6   R. Halafta b. Dosa of Kefar Hanania said: If ten men sit together and occupy themselves in the Law, the Divine Presence rests among them, for it is written, *God standeth in the congregation of God*. And whence [do we learn this] even of five? Because it is written, *And hath founded his group upon the earth*. And whence even of three? Because it is written, *He judgeth among the judges*. And whence even of two? Because it is written, *Then they that feared the Lord spake one with another: and the Lord hearkened, and heard*. And whence even of one? Because it is written, *In every place where I record my name I will come unto thee and I will bless thee*.

3:2b. R. Hananiah ben Teradion was the father of the famed Beruria (Valeria), distinguished for her learning among all the women of the rabbis, and wife to R. Meir. He flourished ca. A.D. 100-135, and was thus contemporary with Akiba. Hananiah's words are important to us because of their amazing parallel in Mt 18:19 and 20. He asserts that when two Jewish men converse together they fail in their duty if they do not discuss Torah. But when they discuss Torah, the act they thereby perform is so pleasing to God that his shimmering presence (Shekinah) hovers over them as it did over the Ark of the Covenant in the Holy of Holies in the (by then destroyed) Temple. In this sense then Hananiah's teaching develops that of Johanan ben Zakkai, viz., that Torah-study replaces the sacrificial system of the Temple as atonement for sin. [116]

---

[116] On the *Shekinah*, see Bousset, *op. cit.*, p. 315 and esp. p. 346, bolder than G. F. Moore, *Judaism*, I, pp. 434-8, on the possibility of the hypostatization of this and

Internal and other rabbinic parallels to this saying abound. Aboth 3:3; 3:6 and 4:11 (to which there is a further parallel in 5:17) may be adduced. One almost has the impression that R. Hananiah's saying created a literary subgenre, the recurring elements of which are 1. a concern that assemblies of Jewish men should always somehow involve Torah, 2. an assurance of the Divine Presence at such assemblies, and 3. (usually) a concern with the number of men necessary in order for the Divine Presence to be engaged.

Underlying these sayings may be a concern that the common events of Jewish life (e.g., eating, sitting) not be secularized or desacralized. But the means of hallowing these events is not exclusively or even primarily prayer, as might be found in other sacral societies, but precisely in the joint (or solitary, if need be) study of the religious tradition.

Old Testament roots of this teaching may be found in Ps 1, as well as in Ex 20:21 and Mal 3:16, cited by the Talmud (see below). Indeed, the phrase "seat of the scornful" (*moshav letzim*) in the original teaching of R. Hananiah is a direct borrowing from Ps 1:1, where that curious phrase is first found. This fact leads us to suspect that this teaching of R. Hananiah arose in the first place as a midrash on Ps 1. And the structure of Ab 3:2b is the same as that of Ps 1, viz., antithetical parallelism. The use of the psalm phrase by R. Hananiah would naturally have led, at a later period, to the direct quotation of the appropriate verse.

Besides the close parallel in Mt. 18:19-20 (on which see below), there are New Testament resonances of the Shekinah concept in the weighty passages Jn 1:14; Rev 21:3.

The Talmud (b. Ber 6a, Sonc. ed., pp. 24 f) contains a remarkably similar passage which sheds some light on this group of sayings in Aboth, though the authorities involved are all Babylonian, and the Scriptural supports differ except for the use of Mal 3:16. To the occasions when the Divine Presence rests over devout Israelites it adds the case of synagogue prayer where a full quorum (*minyan*) of ten is present, and the case of three sitting as a court of judges.

---

other manifestations of the divine in the Jewish literature of that time. Also A. M. Goldberg, *Untersuchungen über die Vorstellung von der Schekinah in der frühen rabbinischen Literatur* (Berlin: de Gruyter, 1969; Studia judaica, no. 5), pp. 385-388. On substitutes for the sacrificial system, see ARN[A], ch. 4 (Goldin, pp. 32-38) and the unpublished dissertation of Michael Marsch, Paris: le Saulchoir, 1969.

Rabin b. R. Adda says in the name of R. Isaac: ... And how do you
know that if ten people pray together the Divine Presence is with
them? For it is said: "God standeth in the congregation of God"
(Ps 82:1). And how do you know that if three are sitting as a court
of judges the Divine Presence is with them? For it is said: In the midst
of the judges He judgeth (Ibid.). And how do you know that if two
are sitting and studying the Torah together the Divine Presence is with
them? For it is said: They that feared the Lord spoke one with another,
and the Lord hearkened and heard, and a book of remembrance was
written before Him, for them that feared the Lord and that thought
upon His name (Mal 3:16).... And how do you know that even if one
man sits and studies the Torah the Divine Presence is with him? For
it is said: In every place where I cause My name to be mentioned
I will come unto thee and bless thee (Ex 20:21).

Further rabbinic parallels may be noted at: Mekilta de Rabbi Ishmael,
tract. Baḥodesh, ch. 11 (Lauterbach ed., II, p. 287); Mekilta de Rabbi
Simeon ben Yohai on Ex 20:21 (ed. J. N. Epstein, p. 156); ARN[B],
chs. 18 and 34 (Schechter ed., pp. 40 and 74). [117]

These parallels add little to our inquiry save the nuance that the
rabbinic norm would be that it is necessary for ten men to be present
at prayer in order for the Shekinah to hover over them. That he would
be present even when only three or two or one pray is something over
and above the call of duty, so to speak. A subsidiary question raised by
Goldberg is: does the Shekinah remain present in the synagogue at all
times, so that the ten (etc.) go there to be in its presence, or does the
Shekinah wait till they are gathered and *then* come?

c. This section is most likely a later addition, whose text remained
somewhat unstable. [118] The quotation, cited with the regular academic
formula for introducing a proof text, is from Lam 3:27 f.

Aboth 3:2b, 3 and 6 and Mt 18:18-20

These four passages have a common pattern: if (where) x number
of men do x together and it (the doing) is accompanied by a devout
practice/awareness, the divine presence will be among them. A major
variation in the pattern occurs when the proposition is first stated in
positive terms and then repeated in a negative form. This variation
occurs in Ab 3:2b and 3. The positive form alone occurs in Ab 3:6
and Mt 18:20. Other variables are as follows: A. the number of men

---

[117] These parallels have been collected and analyzed by A. M. Goldberg, *op. cit.*,
in his sections 379, 380.

[118] See Taylor, II, p. 147.

involved: 2 (Ab 3:2b); 3 (Ab 3:3); 10, 5, 3, 2, 1 (Ab 3:6, according to a descending scale reminiscent of Gen 18:22-33); 2 or 3 (Mt 18:20); B. the common activity: sitting (Ab 3:2b, 6); eating (Ab 3:3; cf. Ab 3:18); gathering (Mt 18:20); C. the devout practice/awareness: words of Torah (Ab 3:2b, 3); occupying themselves in the Torah (Ab 3:6); "in my name" (Mt 18:20).

It will be seen that the passage in Mt has affinities with all three of the Aboth passages. What strikes the reader especially is how for Matthew Jesus functions as both words of Torah and as divine presence, or, to put it the other way round, how for the rabbis the Torah and the Shekinah function as Jesus.

This raises the question of relative chronology and of dependence. These questions can probably not be settled with certainty, but a hypothesis may be advanced. Let us suppose with Hummel that Matthew dates from A.D. 80, no later. The approximate dates of the three rabbis in question are variously given. Danby and Strack place Hananiah ben Teradion between 80/90 and 135, Montefiore and Loewe toward the end of that period. Simeon ben Yohai is assigned to 100-170 (Danby), 130-160 (Strack), 140-165 (Montefiore and Loewe); Halafta ben Dosa is put in 140-165 by Danby, 80-120 by Montefiore and Loewe, and is not treated by Strack.

My assumption is therefore that Matthew, or his special source, created (or received) the saying as referring to Jesus from the beginning. The rabbis created a counter-saying of the same type, in opposition to but in imitation of Matthew 18:20.

A possible argument for this may be that it is not clear where the rabbis acquire their numbers, except that Ab 3:6 may derive its first number (10) from the *minyan* for prayer, though prayer is not at issue here. But Matthew likely got his "two or three" from his v. 16b, a quotation from Dt. 19:15. As the saying stands in Matthew now, it is closely built in to the unit 18:15-20, serving as a brief commentary or gloss (*gar*) on v. 19. Verse 19 is a rather commonplace instruction about efficacious prayer (here probably a prayer for light to settle the criminal cases alluded to in Mt 18:15-18, so Boismard), with many New Testament congeners (Mt 7:7; 21:22; Mk 11:24; Jn 15:7; 16:23; Jas 1:5; 1 Jn 3:22; 5:14 f). It was not originally Christological, as some of these congeners indicate. ("By my father in heaven" is not original, is indeed rendered superfluous by the presence of a divine passive (*genēsetai*), but a Matthean addition in his most characteristic language.) The commentary in v. 20 helps to make v. 19 explicitly Christological. More broadly, it links up the Emmanuel prophecy of Mt 1:23 with the close and climax of the whole Gospel (28:20). [119]

3:7 (D 8)

ז   רַבִּי אֶלְעָזָר אִישׁ בַּרְתּוֹתָא אוֹמֵר: תֶּן לוֹ מִשֶּׁלּוֹ, שֶׁאַתָּה וְשֶׁלְּךָ שֶׁלּוֹ; וְכֵן בְּדָוִד הוּא
אוֹמֵר[1]: 'כִּי־מִמְּךָ הַכֹּל וּמִיָּדְךָ נָתַנּוּ לָךְ'. רַבִּי שִׁמְעוֹן אוֹמֵר: הַמְהַלֵּךְ בַּדֶּרֶךְ וְשׁוֹנֶה
וּמַפְסִיק מִמִּשְׁנָתוֹ, וְאוֹמֵר: מַה נָּאֶה אִילָן זֶה! וּמַה נָּאֶה נִיר זֶה! – מַעֲלֶה עָלָיו הַכָּתוּב[2]
כְּאִלּוּ מִתְחַיֵּב בְּנַפְשׁוֹ.

[1] דהי־א כט, יד.
[2] דברים ט, ד.

7   R. Eleazar b. Judah of Bartotha said: Give unto him what is his for thou and what thou hast are his; and it is written in [the Scripture concerning] David, *For all things come of thee, and of thine own have we given thee.*

8   R. Jacob said: If a man was walking by the way and studying and he ceased his study and said, 'How fine is this tree!' or 'How fine is this ploughed field!' the Scripture reckons it to him as though he was guilty against his own soul.

As noted earlier, from this point on in chapter three of Aboth there is a difference in numbering between the text (Albeck) and the translation (Danby) which we are following. Albeck joins the sayings attributed to R. Eleazar (b. Judah) of Bartotha and to R. Simeon (Danby, R. Jacob) into one mishnah numbered seven. We will follow Albeck, putting the Danby number afterward in parentheses.

The saying of R. Eleazar is not to our purpose.

The saying of R. Jacob (ben Korshai?) presents us with a textual difficulty, in that some text witnesses offer Simeon b. Yohai, others, Akiba, as the author. These variants merit little trust, as Taylor and Marti-Beer have shown. A second variant occurs at the end. Some texts, preferred by Taylor and Marti-Beer, read: "*They* reckon (pl.) it to him...," others read, "the *Scripture reckons* it to him." No Scripture is in fact quoted in any text. This may have led to an embarrassment, resolved by a change in wording in the direction of vagueness. Albeck keeps the "Scripture reckons" and in a note suggests Dt 4:9 as the text

---

[119] For the opposite view on dependence, see C. H. Dodd, *New Testament Studies* (Manchester: U.P., 1953), pp. 58-62: "any dependence of the Jewish saying upon the Christian is unlikely." Acute observations on the structure of the Gospel passage may be found in P. Benoit and M.-E. Boismard, *Synopse des quatre évangiles en français, vol. II, Commentaire* (Paris: Cerf, 1972), p. 268 (sect. 180).

alluded to. We may here safely follow him. (Dt 4:9 is cited in the next mishnah.)

Other Old Testament roots of the saying may be found at Dt 6:7; Prov 6:22; 23:5.

An obvious first clarification concerns the vocabulary for study, *shôneh* and *mishnathô*. Marti-Beer translate literally: "Who walking along the way *repeats* and breaks off his repetition...." What are involved then are not loose theological or devotional thoughts, but precise and accurate reproduction of the Scripture and customary law which have been memorized.

We must also avoid the misunderstanding which would in facile fashion conclude that the rabbis were heartless and indifferent to the beauties of nature. Their prayers prove the contrary (b. Ber 58b, j. Ber 13b.c.).

What does emerge sharply is the zeal, the ferocity of the rabbis for the tradition. This is radical discipleship to the Torah worthy of comparison with Jesus' "No one who puts his hand to the plow and looks back is fit for the kingdom of God" (Lk 9:62, Lucan special material; cf. Mt 8:21 f and par.). But it is not simply a matter of religious fanaticism. Pragmatical considerations also come in. How else could the Torah be grasped and lived, if not by study? If indeed it is true that the Mishnah was, in some sense, preserved orally at this period, how else could it be sustained in existence, much less applied, if it were not memorized and retained accurately, through frequent review and repetition? In this context, R. Jacob's exaggeration is pardonable.

We may compare with this saying two elements of the Christian religious tradition. The Rule of St. Benedict (ch. 43) says: "Let nothing be preferred to the work of God." This refers in context to the liturgical prayer of the monks. It differs from the saying of R. Jacob both in its aim, and in its inclusion of beauty. Of Saint Dominic early accounts [120] relate that he did not speak except to God or of God (nil nisi ad Deum vel de Deo), and this was also to be the rule for his friars. This ideal includes prayer, but also preaching and theological dispute and thus comes closer to R. Jacob. What is peculiar to the Mishnah is its singleminded and exclusive insistence on study.

---

[120] Process of Canonization, Testimony of Bonaventure of Verona, and the Primitive Constitutions (1228), Dist. II, c. 31, both translated in F. C. Lehner, ed., *St. Dominic: biographical documents* (Washington, D. C.: Thomist 1964), pp. 101, 247. Cf. the modern study by J. A. Weisheipl, *The Place of Study in the Ideal of St. Dominic* (River Forest, Ill.: Aquinas Institute, 1960).

3:9 (D 10)

ח　רַבִּי דּוֹסְתַּאי בַּר יַנַּאי מִשּׁוּם רַבִּי מֵאִיר אוֹמֵר: כָּל הַשּׁוֹכֵחַ דָּבָר אֶחָד מִמִּשְׁנָתוֹ, מַעֲלֶה
עָלָיו הַכָּתוּב כְּאִלּוּ מִתְחַיֵּב בְּנַפְשׁוֹ, שֶׁנֶּאֱמַר[1]: 'רַק הִשָּׁמֶר לְךָ וּשְׁמֹר נַפְשְׁךָ מְאֹד
פֶּן־תִּשְׁכַּח אֶת־הַדְּבָרִים אֲשֶׁר־רָאוּ עֵינֶיךָ'. יָכוֹל אֲפִלּוּ תָּקְפָה עָלָיו מִשְׁנָתוֹ? תַּלְמוּד
לוֹמַר[2]: 'וּפֶן־יָסוּרוּ מִלְּבָבְךָ כֹּל יְמֵי חַיֶּיךָ'; הָא אֵינוֹ מִתְחַיֵּב בְּנַפְשׁוֹ עַד שֶׁיֵּשֵׁב וִיסִירֵם
מִלִּבּוֹ.

[1] שָׁם שָׁם, שָׁם.
[2] שָׁם שָׁם, שָׁם.

9　R. Dosethai b. Yannai said in the name of R. Meir: He that forgets
one word of his study, the Scripture reckons it to him as though he was
guilty against his own soul, for it is written, *Only take heed to thyself,
and keep thy soul diligently, lest thou forget the words which thine
eyes saw.* Could this be even if his study was too hard for him?
Scripture says: *And lest they depart from thy heart all the days of thy
life*; thus he is not guilty against his own soul unless he sits and puts
them away from his heart.

Taylor's text offers a variant which proves rather helpful. Instead
of beginning with "he that forgets," it runs: "When a scholar of the
wise sits and studies [i.e., repeats] and has forgotten...." This introductory clause clarifies the saying by giving a more delimited subject
(*talmid ḥakam*) and a more specific setting in life, the traditioning
of Mishnah.

This saying follows upon that attributed to R. Jacob both because
of the similarity of subject matter and because of the common link-
word: "guilty against his own soul;" perhaps also because of the common Scriptural basis, Dt 4:9. Structurally the passage readily falls into
two parts: the original saying, having to do with forgetting one's
Mishnah, together with a Scriptural proof text. This is the only part
likely due to R. Meir and his tradent, R. Dosithai. Then follows the
later raising of an objection, followed by its answer, based on another
section of the same Scripture verse: only deliberate forgetting is sinful.

That the second part is secondary in time may also be suggested by
the introductory formula to the objection: *talmud lomar*, literally,
"instruction is to say." The instruction in question is only biblical, hence
the translation "Scripture says." This formula is common and technical
in the Tannaitic rabbinical discussions. Marti-Beer cite Rm 9:17 and
Gal 4:30 as early parallels, but *hē graphē* is not quite equivalent to
talmud.

The phrase "guilty against his own soul" requires some preliminary
comment. Soul (*nephesh*) often means life in Hebrew. Thus the sense

would be: guilty against his own life, or, guilty of his own death, i.e., guilty of suicide, or perhaps more simply (so Goldin), *mortally* guilty. In a word then, a grievous offense.

The secondary addition almost certainly does the original saying a disservice. It finds its point too rigorous and tries to soften it. It would have done better to try to understand its precise intent. In the period before A.D. 200, when the Mishnah was in large measure preserved orally, and the Roman authorities did persecute the rabbis, and part of that persecution, be it remembered, was the destruction of the sacred books (this was true for persecuted Christians as well), insistence upon the exact memorization and preservation of the customary laws is only what we must expect. It was not the luxurious exaggeration of a school-masterly crank. Such care was indispensable if a man were to live the Pharisaic way of life, if Jewish communities were to survive, if cases were to be adjudicated properly. The saying reflects precisely that difference of perspective which separated the early rabbis both from the early church and from the later Judaism of the Talmuds. Its legitimacy and reasonableness within its own terms must be respected and understood, not watered down. [121]

Parallel insistence on preserving the true teaching exactly may be

---

[121] B. Gerhardsson comments on this saying in his *Memory and Manuscript*, pp. 168-170, with parallels on p. 134 f. M. Smith (JBL 82 (1963): 169-176) and J. Neusner (*Rabbinic Traditions...*, III, pp. 146-149) have severely criticized him for assuming that the oral transmission of the Pharisaic customary law which prevailed after 80, and especially during the time of Aqiba, also occurred in the period before that. Neusner makes the point that Palestine was a literate society (III, p. 153) and that the sectarians at Qumran did not hesitate to set their *halachoth* down in writing. These statements are undoubtedly true, but what do they prove? That because Palestine was literate, there was no careful oral transmission before 80? Did Palestine cease to be literate in 80? Should we assume that if the Qumranites did something, the Pharisees did likewise? Sayings such as those of R. Dositbai (R. Meir), while deriving from the period after 80, do not give the impression of referring to an entirely novel situation. Neusner himself (III, p. 154) is not so careful as Gerhardsson in handling the matter of tradition in Paul (*Memory*, pp. 288-323). See further Davies, *Setting*, appendix 9, pp. 453-455, on Gal. 1:18, and the recent work by D. L. Dungan, *The Sayings of Jesus in the Churches of Paul* (Philadelphia: Fortress, 1971) on 1 Cor 9:4-18 and 7:1-16, showing their dependence on, and application of, the teaching of Jesus.

Moreover, Neusner's remark (III, p. 154) that "early Christian tradition is quite fluid and variable, even when the content is of crucial importance" is limited, with respect to the Synoptic Gospels, by the principle he cites with respect to Buddhist traditions (III, p. 151): "the narrative framework is apt to be less reliable than the logia." See for example Mk 12:13-17 and parallels (on paying tribute to Caesar), where the narrative varies somewhat, but the logion is word for word the same, except for the addition of a linking particle in Mt and Lk and a slight inversion of word order which does not affect the sense.

found in the New Testament at Mt 5:19; Rev 22:7; 18 f; 1 Thess 4:1 f,
8; 2 Thess 3:6; Gal 1:8; 1 Tim 6:20; 2 Tim 1:12, 14. Rabbinic parallels
abound, e.g., Aboth 4:13: "He who learns Torah and does not "repeat"
is as one who sows and does not reap. He who learns and forgets is
like a mother who bears and buries" (b. Sanh 99a, Sonc. ed., p. 673;
cf. ARN^A, ch. 23, Goldin, p. 102). Most useful of all is a teaching
attributed to R. Elisha b. Abuya, a contemporary of Akiba and possibly
of the author of our saying:

> He used to say: One may learn Torah for ten years and forget it (all)
> after two years. How so? For example, if for six months one neglects
> to review, he then says of the unclean "It is clean" and of the clean
> "It is unclean." If for twelve months he does not review, he then
> confuses the Sages with one another. If for eighteen months he does
> not review, he forgets the chapter headings. If for twenty-four months
> he does not review, he forgets the treatise headings. And after saying
> of the unclean, "It is clean," and of the clean, "It is unclean," after
> confusing the Sages with one another, after forgetting the chapter
> headings and treatise headings, he sits and keeps quiet in the end. And
> of him said Solomon, I went by the field of the slothful, and by the
> vineyard of the man void of understanding; and lo, it was all grown
> over with thistles; the face thereof was covered with nettles, and the
> stone wall thereof was broken down (Prov. 24:30 f): for once the
> wall of the vineyard falls, the whole vineyard is destroyed.
>
> (ARN^A, ch. 24, Goldin, p. 104)

3:9 (10)

ט   רַבִּי חֲנִינָא בֶּן דּוֹסָא אוֹמֵר: כָּל שֶׁיִּרְאַת חֶטְאוֹ קוֹדֶמֶת לְחָכְמָתוֹ, חָכְמָתוֹ מִתְקַיֶּמֶת;
וְכָל שֶׁחָכְמָתוֹ קוֹדֶמֶת לְיִרְאַת חֶטְאוֹ, אֵין חָכְמָתוֹ מִתְקַיֶּמֶת. הוּא הָיָה אוֹמֵר: כָּל
שֶׁמַּעֲשָׂיו מְרֻבִּין מֵחָכְמָתוֹ, חָכְמָתוֹ מִתְקַיֶּמֶת; וְכָל שֶׁחָכְמָתוֹ מְרֻבָּה מִמַּעֲשָׂיו, אֵין
חָכְמָתוֹ מִתְקַיֶּמֶת.

10   R. Hanina b. Dosa said:He whose fear of sin comes before his wisdom,
his wisdom endures; but he whose wisdom comes before his fear of
sin, his wisdom does not endure. He used to say: He whose works
exceed his wisdom, his wisdom endures; but he whose wisdom exceeds
his works, his wisdom does not endure.

Hanina ben Dosa and Onias (Honi) the Circle-Drawer are important
in any comparison of the New Testament with the world of rabbinic
thought and piety, because both are *Galilean* figures, both work miracles, a power which apparently rests on their humility and childlike
simplicity. These enable them to approach God with great confidence
and boldness. Both remained somewhat atypical and ill-at-ease in the

rather tight-knit world of Pharisaic-rabbinic sectarianism. It is even
possible that their peculiar "style" may reflect a persistence in the
Galilean folk-memory of the thaumaturgical, itinerant prophetic activity
of an Elijah and an Elisha. This divergent point of view comes to
expression in the three sayings attributed to R. Hanina in Aboth. [122]

All three of Hanina's Aboth sayings follow the same formal pattern:
each point is stated first positively, then negatively—a kind of antithetical parallelism (cf. Mk 8:35 par). Our two sayings contrast two
virtues and give the first of them preference. Both offer almost the
same content (good morals are more important than wisdom) but
the formulation of the second saying is of greater interest to us because
it is more readily inserted into the debates at Lydda (Tarfon versus
Aqiba, on which see below) and in the New Testament.

The style is so formal that we can speak of constants (*hokmatô*
(wisdom) and *mitqayyemet* (endure) and *col* (all)) and variables:
(verbal) *qodemet* (comes before) versus *merubbin* (is greater), (nominal) *yirat ḥeṭʾô* (his fear of sin) versus *maʿasaw* (his works).

In ARNᴬ, ch. 22, the sayings are provided with Scriptural support
from Ps 111:10 and Ex 24:7 respectively. The parallels within Aboth
(1:17b; 3:18b; 5:14) all belong to that minority strand we might call
anti-intellectual (comparatively), which maintains the dialectic and
nourishes the creative tension which give the tractate its life and
fascination.

The second saying finds an obvious parallel in Jas 2:24: "a man is
justified by works and not by faith alone," (cf. v. 26), itself a part
of a debate within the New Testament. Paul asserts that Torah does

---

[122] Onias is mentioned in the Mishnah once only, Taan 3:8; Hanina twice outside
of Aboth: Ber 5:5 where it is a matter of the efficacy of his prayer; Sot 9:15, the
rabbinic apocalypse, where he is listed with "the men of good deeds" or miracle-
workers. Stories about Hanina are found in b. Ber 17b, 34b, 61b, ARNᴬ, ch. 8
(Goldin, p. 53); this same story is told in a more developed form of R. Phinehas
b. Jair in j. Dem 1:3; see Montefiore and Loewe, *Rabbinic Anthology*, p. 46, pericope
121.

The most careful critical study of the traditions relating to Hanina is provided by
Geza Vermes, *Journal of Jewish Studies* 23 (1972): 28-50; 24 (1973): 51-64; see
also his *Jesus the Jew* (New York: Macmillan, 1974), pp. 58-82. But Hanina must
be dated a good deal later than Jesus, ca. A.D. 80-120, a second generation *tanna*.
Herford has him live *to* 70, thus opening the possibility of his contemporaneity with
Jesus. But hard evidence is lacking. He is said to have come from Arab near
Sepphoris in Galilee, thus also not far from Nazareth. The name Hanina is attested
archeologically in the Beth Alfa synagogue mosaic inscription which dates from the
sixth century. See E. R. Goodenough, *Jewish Symbols in the Greco-Roman World*
(New York: Princeton U.P., 1953), vol. I, p. 243.

not bind those in Christ because they have died with him in baptism
and Torah does not bind a man after his death (Rm 7:1-6). Thus
Christ is the end of the Law (Rm 10:4; cf. Gal 3). This mystical
doctrine was both useful and dangerous. It was useful because it enabled
Paul to replace physical circumcision with the circumcision of the heart
in baptism and thus to remove the one great stumbling block to mass
conversion of Gentiles to the religion of Israel. This no doubt was the
secret of Paul's missionary strategy and success. It was dangerous
because it could be taken in an ethically antinomian sense. (Paul himself inconsistently but reasonably rejected such an understanding, e.g.,
Rm 13:8-10.) Thus Paul's initial, somewhat unguarded statement of
his doctrine in Galatians 2:15-3:28 laid him open to the broadside
attack made in James, chapter 2. The letter to the Romans could
conceivably be among other things a cautious restatement of Galatians
so as to meet this attack. In any case, it seems plausible that the letter
of James is aimed directly at the teaching of Paul, even though its
precise date is impossible to determine beyond cavil.

As James insists that no doctrine of salvation should set aside plain
moral standards, even theoretically, so Hanina protests against the
danger of the rabbinic life degenerating into endless legal wrangling
and scholarly arrogance.

Though we will not treat the saying of R. Dosa b. Harkinas (Ab
3:10b) separately: "Morning sleep and midday wine and children's
talk and sitting in the meeting houses of ignorant people (*battē-
knesiyôt shel-amme-haaretz*) put a man out of the world," it deserves
a brief notice as indicating precisely some of the dangers just mentioned.
Meeting house (or synagogue) of the *amme-haaretz*, followed by R.
Eleazar's list of heresies in Ab 3:11, puts us in mind of the (Jewish)
Christian synagogues of Jas 2:2. Not all Jewish-Christians were *amme-
haaretz*, but many of them were, and in any case their *halacha* diverged
from that of the rabbis. Avoiding them meant avoiding the contraction
of ritual uncleanness, but also avoiding contamination by erroneous
interpretations of Scripture.

3:11 (D 12)

א. רַבִּי אֶלְעָזָר הַמּוֹדָעִי אוֹמֵר: הַמְחַלֵּל אֶת הַקֳּדָשִׁים, וְהַמְבַזֶּה אֶת הַמּוֹעֲדוֹת, וְהַמַּלְבִּין
פְּנֵי חֲבֵרוֹ בָּרַבִּים, וְהַמֵּפֵר בְּרִיתוֹ שֶׁלְּאַבְרָהָם אָבִינוּ עָלָיו הַשָּׁלוֹם, וְהַמְגַלֶּה פָנִים
בַּתּוֹרָה שֶׁלֹּא כַהֲלָכָה, אַף עַל פִּי שֶׁיֵּשׁ בְּיָדוֹ תּוֹרָה וּמַעֲשִׂים טוֹבִים – אֵין לוֹ חֵלֶק
לָעוֹלָם הַבָּא.

12   R. Eleazar of Modiim said: If a man profanes the Hallowed Things and despises the set feasts and puts his fellow to shame publicly and makes void the covenant of Abraham our father, and discloses meanings in the Law which are not according to the *Halakah*, even though a knowledge of the Law and good works are his, he has no share in the world to come.

For Jewish relations with Christians in the first century, this mishnah's importance has long been recognized. Unfortunately its exposition is hindered by several difficulties, especially textual ones. We will follow this course: translate the text again, shorn of what appear to be later glosses, then interpret this text and finally the glosses.

"R. Eleazar of Modiim said: If a man profanes the Hallowed Things, and despises the set feasts, and makes void the covenant of Abraham our father, and uncovers his own face in the Law [i.e., acts impudently in his treatment of the Law], even though he has good works, he has no share in the world to come." 123

R. Eleazar according to tradition was present at Jamnia, where the *Birkat ha-Minim* (the Blessing [euphemism for cursing] of Heretics) was legislated by R. Samuel the Little (Ab 4:19). His teaching in this mishnah serves as a list of heretical traits, such as would distinguish Jewish-Christians, as well as others within the Jewish community at that time. Similar lists are found in M. Meg 4:9; M. Ber 5:3; M. Sanh 10:1-3. Legend has it that he was executed by his nephew Bar Cochba on a false suspicion of treason in A.D. 135, at Beth Tor. 124

1. Hallowed Things or *Qodashim*. The kind of religious observances intended by this rubric are listed in the Seder of the Mishnah bearing this name. Most of the tractates deal with various kinds of sacrifices and would therefore have become rather irrelevant after 70, but one tractate, Hullin, deals with animals killed for food, ritual slaughtering, and thus with rules of *kashrut*. This was indeed a lively issue among the Jewish Christians all through the first century.

Mark 7:1-23 portrays Jesus as abolishing *kosher* laws, especially with its famous gloss in v. 19b. Matthew (15:1-20) portrays a more conservative attitude of Jesus, who sets aside Pharisaic religious law,

---

123 Albeck adds one gloss to the already overloaded text represented by Danby's translation: after the words "Abraham our father" he adds "may peace be upon him." This is obviously a pious phrase with no serious claim to authenticity.

124 The legends on the fall of Beth-Tor are found mainly in j. Taan 4:5 (6) (Fr. trans., pp. 189 f.) and in Midrash Echa rabbati, ch. 2.

but not the teachings of the Pentateuch, where distinctions of food into clean and unclean are found. [125]

Paul opposes Peter on this point, Gal. 2:11-16. Peter receives a revelation about it in Acts 10. (We may note here the suggestion of G. Vermeš, made orally, that if the Marcan version of the Synoptic pericope just referred to were the authentic one, the vision of Acts 10 would have been superfluous.) In Acts 15, a church council is held to adjudicate the matter. Christians must be warned against submitting to these rules, Col 2:21. As Herford notes, what is involved is not deliberate sacrilege, but the treating of holy things as if they were not holy, as if they were profane. Here rabbinism and at least Pauline Christianity did indeed differ.

2. Set feasts or *Moadoth*. For these too an entire seder of the Mishnah is set aside: Moed. What is principally at issue here is the weekly sabbath and its observance, not the high holidays. To the details of its observance the rabbis devoted three tractates: Shabbath, Erubin, and Betzah (an egg laid on the Sabbath). The classic comment on this legislation is found in M. Hagigah 1:8: "The rules about the Sabbath, Festal-offerings, and Sacrilege are as mountains hanging by a hair, for [teaching of] Scripture [thereon] is scanty and the rules many...."

On this subject too the New Testament has much to say. The principal passages are the controversy dialogues on plucking ears of grain on the Sabbath (Mk 2:23-28par), and on the healing of the man with the withered hand (Mk 3:1-6par). Here Jesus is not shown to set aside Sabbath observance entirely, but only to offer a different *halacha* for its observance, based on different priorities. Similar stories are found in the Lucan *Sondergut* (13:10-17; 14:1-6), and in John (5:1-18; 7:19-24; 9:13-17, especially v. 16: "This man is not from God, for he does not keep the sabbath," an echo of R. Eleazar's declaration here), as well as Col. 2:16. "Mt 24:20 offers an example of the keeping of the Sabbath by Jewish Christians.... For the Jews Jesus was *sabbati destructor*, Tertullian, *De spectaculis*, 30." [126]

3. Covenant of Abraham, i.e., circumcision (see Gen 17). This precept may be voided in two ways: either one may teach, as did Paul,

---

[125] Cf. Reinhart Hummel, *Die Auseinandersetzung...* (Munich: Kaiser, 1966²), pp. 46-49, and chapter 3 below.
[126] E. Lohse, s.v. *Sabbaton*, TDNT, VII, pp. 29, and 29, n. 224. See also H. Riesenfeld, *The Gospel Tradition*, ch. 6, "The Sabbath and the Lord's Day in Judaism, the preaching of Jesus and early Christianity," (Philadelphia: Fortress, 1970), pp. 111-138.

that circumcision is not necessary in order to be an heir of the promises
made to Abraham (circumcision of the heart and proselyte baptism
sufficing), or, if one is already circumcised, one can endeavor by a
surgical operation to have a foreskin restored, the so-called Epispasmos
(see 1 Macc 1:15; 1 Cor 7:18; Martial 7:81, 6). This last was done
by some assimilated Jews to spare themselves embarrassment and
mockery at the public baths and in the gymnasia.

Here was an issue of the utmost gravity, a matter of existence or
nonexistence for mainstream Judaism. This observance, the most fundamental of the ceremonial precepts, absolutely could not be surrendered.
Circumcision, more than anything else, signified the difference, not
only between Jew and pagan, but even between Jew and God-fearer
(a man on the fringe of the synagogue). Then, as now, it was the last
observance to go when a Jew assimilated.

Jesus, so far as we can tell, did not dream of abandoning it (Lk 1:59;
2:21; Jn 7:22). It was Paul who made the decisive break, a break made
primarily, we believe, for missionary reasons (see above on Ab 3:9
(D 10)). But his decision, though it provoked protest form "some
believers who belonged to the party of the Pharisees" (Acts 15:1, 5),
was upheld by the council of Jerusalem as it is described in Acts 15.
Even the relatively Jewish-Christian Gospel according to Matthew,
respectful of the Torah as it is, though not Ebionite, seems to take
for granted the decisions in favor of Paul, since physical circumcision
and the mission to the Gentiles which led to its abandonment are no
longer burning issues for it. It too stands on one side of the great
divide. For let there be no mistake about it, in real life it is precisely
such a powerful and intimate physical symbol such as circumcision
which arouses strong emotions in people. These emotions are strong
enough to occasion the creation of whole new institutions and movements. [127]

The radical break with Jewish tradition on this point made by Paul

---

[127] For Matthew, see Hummel, *op. cit.*, p. 26, n. 54. On Jewish missionary concessions and Paul, see N. J. McEleney, "Conversion, circumcision and the law," NTS
20 (1974): 319-341. Also R. Meyer, *"peritemnō, peritomē, aperitmos,"* in Kittel
TDNT, VI, pp. 72-84, and O. Kuss, *Der Römerbrief* (Regensburg: Pustet, 1963²),
pp. 92-98. Also, arriving too recently to be used, M. Fox, "The sign of the
covenant," *Revue biblique* 81 (1974): 557-596. For modern parallels, see N. Glatzer,
American Judaism (Chicago: Univ. of Chicago, 1957) on the famous Terefah
banquet of 1878, which led to the division of Conservative from Reform Jews in
America, and the founding of Jewish Theological Seminary. Also, R. Blythe, *Akenfield*
(New York: Pantheon, 1969) on baptism by immersion as the main hindrance to conversion to the Baptist Church in a small English village.

was nevertheless not without its biblical preparation. Already in the Torah circumcision is taken in a metaphorical way as a sign of conversion and repentance. "Circumcise therefore the foreskin of your heart, and be no longer stubborn" (Dt 10:16; also 30:6; Lev 26:41). The prophets take this theme up and develop it (Jer 4:4; 6:10; 9:25; Ezek 44:7-9). It continues as a living metaphor in Qumran (1 Q S 5:5; 1 Q pHab 11:13). Philo, the supreme allegorizer, sees the danger that his disciples will press his spiritualizing tendency to untraditional extremes and tries to draw them back from the edge of the precipice (*De migratione Abrahami*, 89 f, Loeb ed., IV, p. 182 f): "Let go nothing that is part of the customs fixed by divinely empowered men greater than those of our time." He thus continued to juggle a precarious "both ... and," till a "divinely empowered man" greater than himself broke the tension. "For he is not a real Jew who is one outwardly, nor is true circumcision something external and physical. He is a Jew who is one inwardly, and real circumcision is a matter of the heart, spiritual and not literal. His praise is not from men but from God" (Rom 2:28 f, but see the entire paragraph, vv. 25-29).

4. Uncovers his own face in the Law, *hamegaleh panim bettorah*. This offense cannot be determined with certainty when stripped of its glosses. It has been interpreted as wholesale apostasy (Herford), and as irreverence or impudence toward Torah, and indeed as meaning what the glosses suggest (Marti-Beer).

5. "Even though he has good works." This admits that the heretics in question put a high store on charitable deeds, as we saw in the matter of the relationship between Ab 1:2 and 1:18. Israel has no monopoly on philanthropy. Torah is her peculiar boast.

6. "He has no share in the world to come." The formula is the same as that in M. Sanhedrin 10:1-3 where the eschatological destiny of various groups is discussed.

7. Glosses. a. "...puts his fellow to shame publicly." Wanting in several manuscripts, it probably does not fit in this context. Cf. Prov 13:5b. It could however allude to a particular situation in which an apostate Pharisee embarrasses his (former) associate (*haberô*) before a general assembly (*rabbim*) of his new coreligionists or of rabbis. [128]

b. "discloses meanings in the Torah *which are not according to the Halakah*." This case involves both a different translation of the established text and a gloss. It offers an interesting possibility. The

---

128 J. Carmignac, "HRBYM: les 'Nombreux' ou les 'Notables'?" *Revue de Qumran* 7 (1972): 575-586.

heretics in question may be masters of Torah, indeed passionately devoted to it, and yet reject the Pharisaic *halacha*. Such men were Jesus, Paul and "Matthew." This is the situation envisaged by some recent redaction criticism as lying behind the Gospel of Matthew. [129] Here it is not a matter of Torah or no Torah, but of interpretations of Torah.

c. even though [*a knowledge of*] *the Law and* good works are his." (Gloss underlined.) Marti-Beer comment: "A glossator has quite thoughtlessly introduced "torah and" before "good works," as if Eleazar could still acknowledge the possession of Torah to the groups against which he raises such gravamina and whom he especially reproaches for a shameless handling of Torah." This is not altogether convincing. Eleazar could be acknowledging their mastery of the text and indeed their missionary endeavors to extend their understanding of it. Indeed, we might paraphrase his thought with Paul's words: "I bear them witness that they have a zeal for God, but it is not enlightened." (Rm 10:2).

The saying of R. Eleazar is clearly of great importance in reconstructing the Jewish-Christian argument of the first and early second centuries. He lists the points of disagreement fairly and accurately, so far as we can confirm them from the New Testament. He acknowledges the moral rectitude and the learning of his opponents. He grants that the difference is one of interpretation. More than this one cannot ask.

3:17 (D 18)

יז   רַבִּי אֶלְעָזָר בֶּן עֲזַרְיָה אוֹמֵר: אִם אֵין תּוֹרָה, אֵין דֶּרֶךְ אֶרֶץ; אִם אֵין דֶּרֶךְ אֶרֶץ, אֵין תּוֹרָה. אִם אֵין חָכְמָה, אֵין יִרְאָה; אִם אֵין יִרְאָה, אֵין חָכְמָה. אִם אֵין בִּינָה, אֵין דַּעַת; אִם אֵין דַּעַת, אֵין בִּינָה. אִם אֵין קֶמַח, אֵין תּוֹרָה; אִם אֵין תּוֹרָה, אֵין קֶמַח. הוּא הָיָה אוֹמֵר: כָּל שֶׁחָכְמָתוֹ מְרֻבָּה מִמַּעֲשָׂיו, לְמַה הוּא דוֹמֶה? לְאִילָן שֶׁעֲנָפָיו מְרֻבִּין וְשָׁרָשָׁיו מוּעָטִין, וְהָרוּחַ בָּאָה וְעוֹקְרַתּוּ וְהוֹפַכְתּוּ עַל פָּנָיו, שֶׁנֶּאֱמַר¹: 'וְהָיָה כְּעַרְעָר בָּעֲרָבָה וְלֹא יִרְאֶה כִּי־יָבוֹא טוֹב וְשָׁכַן חֲרֵרִים בַּמִּדְבָּר אֶרֶץ מְלֵחָה וְלֹא תֵשֵׁב'. אֲבָל כָּל שֶׁמַּעֲשָׂיו מְרֻבִּין מֵחָכְמָתוֹ, לְמַה הוּא דוֹמֶה? לְאִילָן שֶׁעֲנָפָיו מוּעָטִין וְשָׁרָשָׁיו מְרֻבִּין, שֶׁאֲפִלּוּ כָּל הָרוּחוֹת שֶׁבָּעוֹלָם בָּאוֹת וְנוֹשְׁבוֹת בּוֹ אֵין מְזִיזוֹת אוֹתוֹ מִמְּקוֹמוֹ, שֶׁנֶּאֱמַר²: 'וְהָיָה כְּעֵץ שָׁתוּל עַל־מַיִם וְעַל־יוּבַל יְשַׁלַּח שָׁרָשָׁיו, וְלֹא יִרְאֶה כִּי־יָבֹא חֹם, וְהָיָה עָלֵהוּ רַעֲנָן וּבִשְׁנַת בַּצֹּרֶת לֹא יִדְאָג, וְלֹא יָמִישׁ מֵעֲשׂוֹת פֶּרִי'.

¹ ירמיה יז, ו.
² שם שם, ח.

---

129 See, for example, R. Hummel, *op. cit.*, and K. Stendahl, *The School of St. Matthew* (Philadelphia: Fortress, 1969²).

18   R. Eleazar b. Azariah said: If there is no study of the Law there is
no seemly behaviour, if there is no seemly behaviour there is no study
of the Law; if there is no wisdom there is no fear [of God], if there is
no fear [of God] there is no wisdom; if there is no knowledge there
is no discernment, if there is no discernment there is no knowledge;
if there is no meal there is no study of the Law, if there is no study
of the Law there is no meal. He used to say: He whose wisdom is more
abundant than his works, to what is he like? To a tree whose branches
are abundant but whose roots are few; and the wind comes and
uproots it and overturns it, as it is written, *He shall be like a tamerisk
in the desert and shall not see when good cometh; but shall inhabit
the parched places in the wilderness.* But he whose works are more
abundant than his wisdom, to what is he like? To a tree whose branches
are few but whose roots are many; so that even if all the winds in the
world come and blow against it, it cannot be stirred from its place,
as it is written, *He shall be as a tree planted by the waters, and that
spreadeth out his roots by the river, and shall not fear when heat
cometh, and his leaf shall be green; and shall not be careful in the year
of drought, neither shall cease from yielding fruit.*

R. Eleazar ben Azariah contributes a rather longer mishnah to the
theme of study/wisdom and its relation to life and action. The passage
falls into two parts. Each part balances positive and negative elements.
The first part balances four contrasted pairs evenly. The second part,
containing a single parable in antithetic parallelism, breaks the even
balance by making works superior to wisdom. We cannot help feeling
that the several sayings in Aboth which deal with this theme and
incline in favor of works run counter to the basic tendency of rabbinic
thought and are building up to the climactic debate on this question
which took place at Lydda, between Aqiba and Tarfon, and which
determines the question in favor of the superiority of study (see below
on M. Kid 1:10).

Though the text of this passage remains rather stable in the Mishnah
tradition (except for the omission of the prooftexts which were doubtless added later than the first stratum of the parable), the version in
ARN[A], ch. 22 (Goldin, p. 100) offers some variants. Part A lacks
the last two contrasting pairs (knowledge and discernment; study and
flour). This omission can be explained in three ways. Either the editor
knew our text of Aboth and assumed the reader would add the rest
from memory, or the longer text of Aboth betrays the accretion of
sayings produced by the self-generating formula, or the editor judged
the last two pairs muddy, banal and indistinct, and deliberately omitted
them. Also, the description of the two men illustrated by the parable

runs differently: "One in whom there are good works, who has studied much Torah, to what may he be likened?" "One in whom there are no good works, though he studied much Torah, to what may he be likened?" This version, whether earlier or later, plainly lacks the refinement of statement found in the Mishnaic version. Instead of "more abundant than" we are given "all Torah, no works," a crudeness of contrast more likely attributable to editorial carelessness than to primitiveness.

Also, the order is reversed, positive first, negative second. ARN[A] has proof texts, but the text for the positive branch of the parable is Ps 1:3, not Jer 17:8, to which of course it is closely related. Ps 1 is a wisdom psalm, close to the spirit both of Jeremiah and of Deuteronomy (themselves in some measure historically related) and of the rabbis as represented in Aboth, the continuators of the wisdom school in Israel. [130] Similar parables, attributed to Elisha ben Abuya, are found in ARN[A], ch. 24.

A. Turning now to the content of each part, the first problem which confronts us in the first half is the meaning of *derech eretz*. Literally it means *way of the land*. Some of the translations suggested are: culture, life in the world, practical life, the acting out of wisdom, seemly behavior (Danby), *Bildung*, well-bred manners, good morals (Marti-Beer), worldly occupation, *savoir-vivre* (Goldin). It will be hard to determine the meaning beyond dispute but we may suggest the following. Four of the eight contrasted elements are synonymous: Torah, wisdom, knowledge, Torah. (Note the *inclusio*.) If then there is to be any progress in thought, the other four must differ from one another. But fear of God implies good morals. Therefore that cannot be the meaning of *derech eretz*. Good manners seem too trivial, and perhaps anachronistic, an issue to be involved. By a process of elimination therefore we arrive at worldly occupation. Such a sense would also form a kind of minor *inclusio* with the meal of pair four. (For readers of the translation it should be made clear that the meal (*qemaḥ*) of this saying means flour, and thus food, and has nothing to do with

---

[130] The doctrine of the two ways found in our Aboth parable, as well as in the New Testament, Qumran (1 Q S), the Didache, the letter of Pseudo-Barnabas, and suggested in Ps 1 and Jer 17, is thought to go back to the convenant renewal ceremonies such as are described in Deut 28 and 30:15-20. See most recently W. Rordorf, "Un chapître d'éthique judéo-chrétienne: les deux voies," in *Judéo-Christianisme* (Daniélou-Festschrift; Paris: Beauchesne, 1972 = RechSR 60 [1972]: 1-320), pp. 109-128 and the literature there cited. Also Klaus Baltzer, *The Covenant Formulary* (Philadelphia: Fortress, 1971).

the eating of Ab 3:3, 6.) An obvious internal parallel may be found at 2:2, where the combination of Torah-study and *derech eretz* is also praised. (There Danby correctly renders *derech eretz* as worldly occupation.) Herford well observes that the four pairs of contrasts find their harmonious resolution in the need the inner and outer sides of man have for each other. (Potency must issue in act; action presupposes a potency or capability for action, as the Greeks might say. Our human potential needs to be realized, as we might say today.)

Discernment (*binah*) differs from knowledge (*da^cat*) as insight and application of principles into a given concrete situation differ from a knowledge of general principles. The early Christians too were interested in discernment, the discernment of spirits good and evil (*diakrisis pneumatōn*: 1 Cor 12:10; Heb 5:14; cf. 1 Thess 5:21). Paul lists it as a charism and such it is, but not without its human concomitants: knowledge and training. It is the merit of this Aboth saying and of Heb 5:14 to remind us of these presuppositions.

R. Eleazar agrees with Aristotle that the contemplative life (Torah study) presupposes a minimum of physical ease, at least food. *Primum est vivere, deinde philosophari.* Some rabbis were wealthy landowners; others worked at a trade. Many poor students were supported by the head of the academy. Jesus added mendicancy to the number of approved means of support, but all agreed that the people should contribute to the support of the missionaries/scholars. [131]

This section A, as well as section B, are parallels in content with Aboth 1:17; 3:9 (Danby 10); 5:14; the common theme is tension between study and works. But section A resolves the tension, not by opting for one or other of the two poles, as do the others, but by maintaining an evenly balanced affirmation of the indispensability of both poles. Thus it comes close to an Hegelian synthesis or *Aufhebung* of the polarized values, a fragile theory destined not to survive institutionally, and yet to survive. [132]

B. This section asserts the frailty of wisdom without much action, and the superiority of abundant works to wisdom. This teaching is illustrated by a parable. Four further parables illustrating the same point are offered by Elisha ben Abuya, who according to legend died

---

[131] For the New Testament, see Mt 10:8b-11 par; 1 Cor 9:14; 1 Tim 5:18; Didache 13:1 (all based on Num 18:31). For rabbinic material, see E. E. Urbach, *Class-status...*, and A. Büchler, *The Political and the Social Leaders of the Jewish Community of Sepphoris in the Second and Third Centuries* (London: Jews' College, n.d.). For another line of thought, see Mt 6:33; Prov 9:5, 11; Ecclus 15:1-3.

[132] The Albeck edition has *da^cat* and *binah* in the wrong order.

an apostate. Since his teaching (in ARN^A, ch. 24) could be regarded as heterodox and leading to his fall, it is all the more remarkable that it should have been preserved by the rabbis, attesting to their tolerance and breadth of mind. He compares works and Torah as (1) building with stone and bricks, (2) lime on stone and bricks; (3) a cup with and without a base, (4) a horse bridled and unbridled. The conclusion each time is that too much study of Torah with indifferent works can easily run amok. What is not said is that it can be socially divisive, though this may be implied.

The parable in Ab 3:17 teaches that Torah study, isolated from action, can hardly withstand the buffets of life (the winds). The deluge parable at the end of the Sermon on the Mount (Mt 7:24-27, par Lk 6:47-49; cf. Jas 1:22-25) employs the same illustration essentially (though it is a matter of houses rather than trees being knocked over by the wind) but makes a rather different point: "Every one then who *hears* these words of mine and *does* them will be like a wise man who built his house upon the rock.... And everyone who hears these words of mine and does not do them will be like a foolish man who built his house upon the sand...." To be sure, hearing and doing are contrasted with hearing and *not* doing, but there seem to be two further points not contained in the rabbinic parallels: (1) the contrast between building on rock and building on sand, a matter then of the right foundation, rather than of the right inner dispositions. (2) This solid foundation is to be found in "these words of mine" (Jesus), not as though they replaced, or were in opposition to Torah (*mē genoito*), but rather in that they give the right basic orientation both for the understanding and for the doing of Torah. (This presupposes, inter alia, an understanding of the six antitheses of Mt 5:21-48 as a kind of interpretation of the Second Table of the Decalogue.)

In conclusion we may say that the teaching of R. Eleazar ben Azariah and that of those who agree with him come from a time when the heritage of Pharisaic Judaism was still fluid and able to criticize itself effectively. Indeed, the dialectical interplay is at its height. And though in a short time the abyss between the church and the synagogue would open and dialogue and dialectic break down, their spirit would somehow always be present so long as these rabbinic sayings were preserved and learned.

3:18 (D 19)

יח רַבִּי אֶלְעָזָר (בֶּן) חִסְמָא אוֹמֵר: קִנִּין וּפִתְחֵי נִדָּה הֵן הֵן גּוּפֵי הֲלָכוֹת; תְּקוּפוֹת
וְגִמַּטְרִיָאוֹת – פַּרְפְּרָאוֹת לַחָכְמָה.

19   R. Eleazar Hisma said: [The rules about] Bird-offerings and the onset
of menstruation—these are essentials of the *Halakoth*; but the calcula-
tions of the equinoxes and gematria are but the savoury dishes of
wisdom.

The saying of Rabbi Eleazar Hisma provides a delightful example
of rabbinic literary style, colorful, paradoxical, terse, utterly frank about
unmentionables, bold, even saucy, in assertion, easy to remember because
vivid and bordering on the comic, attaining a maximum effect from
the simplest literary means (the double *hen* in this case). But its
content is not trivial. It attempts to answer the question: what is the
central message of Torah, what should our priorities be in Torah study,
what is really important? It works by means of a sharply pointed
contrast between two possible sets of concrete choices. It heightens
the tension between the poles we have been examining in this group
of sayings, the tension between Torah (in the sense of *halacha*) and its
rivals, and heightens this tension to an extreme. Yet the rival here does
not consist of good works. Rather, the rival here may be considered
on the one hand a wider human culture (the natural sciences, especially
astronomy, and mathematics, the crown of study for the Greeks), and
on the other hand objects of vain human curiosity such as astrology
and the discovery of esoteric meanings in the Torah by means of the
numerical values of their constituent letters, the so-called *gematria*. [133]
In the first case Eleazar would be warning against the danger of total
Hellenization. In the second, he would be urging the modest, sober,
empirical concerns of *halacha* against the hopeless quest of the essentially unknowable. Perhaps the ambiguity is intentional. If so, one is
all the more amazed at the multiple meanings compressed into so
few words.

---

[133] 1. Aristotle, *Nicomachean Ethics*, book 10, ch. 7, 1177a-1178a; *Eudemian
Ethics*, book 7, ch. 15, 1249b16-23. 2. F. V. Cumont, *Astrology and religion among
the Greeks and Romans* (New York: Dover, 1960²). 3. Wilhelm Gundel and H.
Gundel, "Planeten bei Griechen und Römern," in Paulys *Realencyclopädie der classi-
schen Altertumswissenschaft*, ed. G. Wissowa et al., XX, 2 (Stuttgart: Drucken-
müller, 1950), cols. 2017-2185. 4. P. W. Skehan, *Studies in Israelite poetry and
wisdom* (Washington: Catholic Biblical Association of America, 1971; CBQ Monograph Series, no. 1) discusses the possibility of *gematria* operating already in Old
Testament and interestamental wisdom literature.

Both Eleazar's style and his message illustrate the profound truth
of the Hegelian dictum: Neither the universal nor the particular matter
but only the concrete universal.

Let us examine some of the individual terms. *Qinnim*, bird-offerings,
are mentioned in Lev 1:14-17; 5:7-13; 12:6-8; 14:22-32; 15:14-30;
Num 6:10-12; Lk 2:24. There is a special tractate devoted to them in
the Mishnah, entitled Qinnim, in the seder Qodashim. We may ask the
question: why did Eleazar mention precisely these rather than some
other legal matter? The following considerations come to mind: bird-
offerings are treated at the beginning of Leviticus along with other
burnt offerings, cattle or sheep. Qinnim were the sacrificial offering
of the poor, who could not afford the larger feasts. They thus represent
the highest means whereby ordinary people could participate in the
priestly system of worship in the Temple. Since the characteristic
tendency of the Pharisaic halacha was to extend the application of the
purity laws, which, in the Old Testament, apply only to priests, to the
whole people of Israel, viewed now as a priestly people (Ex 19:6)
with full radicality, by mentioning the most salient element in the first
chapter of Leviticus, Eleazar may have meant to refer to the whole
book (*pars pro toto*), the book of predilection for the Pharisees. Indeed,
there is a tradition that in the classical Jewish school the children
begin their reading of Torah with Leviticus, *not* Genesis, however odd
this may seem to us. This tradition is not easy to date, but our point does
not depend on it alone. It is found in ARN^A, ch. 6 (Goldin, p. 41),
and in Leviticus Rabba 7:3 ad finem, p. 156. Since the origins of the
stars and planets are given in the opening chapter of Genesis, and these
naturally led to astrological speculation both among ancient and more
recent commentators, R. Eleazar may be intending a deliberate contrast
between the books of Leviticus and Genesis. (Note that Genesis is the
only one of the five books of Torah which lacks a tannaitic midrash.)
Genesis was beautiful, but irrelevant to the main business of living,
from this point of view. [134] Of course we should not overlook the comic
element in the saying. By fastening on two apparently trivial, not to
say preposterous, features of the halacha, and elevating them to a
position of great importance, R. Eleazar is being outrageous, even from
a rabbinic point of view. But behind the playfulness, he is saying something which both he and his colleagues took seriously, viz., that that

---

[134] If the pedagogic tradition just mentioned is in fact later than the tannaitic
period, it may have been influenced by this set of priorities, a practical application
of it to elementary education.

part of Scripture (and other sources of religious knowledge) which teaches us in detail how to live our lives in accordance with the will of God is the weightiest part.

Niddah (the menstruant woman) also has a Mishnah tractate devoted to her (seder Tohoroth), the biblical basis of which will be found in Lev 15:19-30. Though the rabbis treated of sexual matters with what seems to us utter frankness and matter-of-factness, they were not unaware of the humor often involved in such matters. Yet here the point is rather that Torah becomes important to us insofar as it affects the intimate details of our daily lives; the stars and esoteric meanings in Scripture do not.

Hen hen (these, these). The emphatic force of the double demonstrative has already been noted. They are the literary equivalent of a rising tone of voice. Perhaps R. Eleazar is so insistent because, as Danby and Herford suggest (*ad locum*), he was a diligent student of astronomy and geometry and wished to defend himself against the reproaches of his colleagues that he was guilty of the grievous sin, neglect (= contempt) of Torah (*biṭul Torah*). Does he protest too much? His humor suggests that he is sincere.

Gûphê (body; fig. essence, substance, essentials, from BH *gûphah*, corpse). [135] The endeavor to single out the essentials of the law seems to have been almost a subgenre of rabbinic literature and discussion. The Old Testament itself offers the ten commandments as the essentials. We have seen Hillel's well-known offer of the silver rule as an instance (b. Shab 31a). Close formal parallels occur in M. Hag 1:8 (already familiar to us on other grounds):

> (The rules about) release from vows hover in the air and have naught to support them; the rules about the Sabbath, Festal-offerings, and Sacrilege are as mountains hanging by a hair, for (teaching of) Scriptures (thereon) is scanty and the rules many; the (rules about) cases (concerning property) and the (Temple-) Service, and the rules about what is clean and unclean and the forbidden degrees, they have that which supports them, and it is they that are *the essentials of the Law*.

Here the criterion for importance is the amount of scriptural support the laws enjoy.

Another formal parallel may be found in b. Shab 32a/b (Soncino ed., p. 147):

---

[135] For this rabbinic word, see Marti-Beer on Ab 1:17.

> It was taught, R. Simeon b. Gamaliel said: The laws of *hekdesh*,
> *terumoth* and tithes are indeed essential parts of the law (*gûphê torah*),
> and they were entrusted to the ignorant.

Here the emphasis is somewhat similar to that of R. Eleazar Hisma.
Hekdesh refers to the laws on sacrifices, including *Qinnim*. *Terumoth*
and tithes are connected with *demai* (doubtfully untithed) produce, a
central concern of the Pharisaic *haberim*; indeed, these concerns largely
set them off from other Jews. [136]

The closest New Testament parallel, apparently not noticed prev-
iously, brings the Q saying of Mt 23:23 (= Lk 11:42) into head-on
collision with R. Eleazar Hisma:

> Woe to you, scribes and Pharisees, hypocrites! for you tithe mint and
> dill and cummin, and have neglected the *weightier matters of the law*
> (*ta barytera tou nomou*), justice and mercy and faith; these you ought
> to have done, without neglecting the others.

Here *ta barytera tou nomou* corresponds to the *gûphê halakoth* rather
closely. A bridge to the other, obvious, New Testament parallel is
provided by the Lucan parallel to this verse in Matthew (Lk 11:32):

> For you tithe mint and rue and every herb, and neglect justice and the
> love of God...

On the one hand, it omits the relevant phrase *barytera tou nomou*.
On the other hand, it mentions the love of God. This leads us directly
to Mk 12:28-34 where Jesus is asked which commandment is the
first of all (cf. Mt 22:36: "which is the *great* commandment in the
law!"). Of course he answers with the opening of the Shema (Dt
6:4 ff), to which he adds Lev 19:18, the double commandment of
love. Finally we may note again that in Mt 7:12 everything in the law
is made to depend on the Golden Rule. [137]

---

[136] See Mishnah and Tosephta Demai and J. Neusner, "The fellowship (*haburah*)
in the Second Jewish Commonwealth," HTR 53 (1960): 124-142.

[137] Marti-Beer make the easy observation: "In Christianity these questions [viz.,
qinnim and onset of menstruation] play no role; this shows the complete difference
between the Jewish and the Christian religion." But this does not quite respect the
force of Mt 23:23. And it would be foolish to suppose Eleazar Hisma had no regard
for ethics. Danby's note: "Being difficult and complicated they must be accounted the
most important subjects of study," remains unsubstantiated and unlikely. These laws,
or better, these *kinds* of laws, are important because they bring the will of God down
to the small *details* of life (*usque ad infima*) and trying to live according to the will
of God even in the details of ordinary life is not of itself a contemptible religious
goal, even if it is not completely possible. Alternatively, they are *said* to be important
because you might think them unimportant, and thus neglect them. Cf. Ab 2:16 and
4:2 and 11a.

Halakoth. Note that he does not say Torah. If our reading is correct, Ben Hisma expresses himself carefully here, unlike some of the parallels we have noticed above. Apparently he distinguishes between Torah (where the narratives and ethical precepts would have a prominent place) and *halakoth*, the ritual and ceremonial laws. When understood in this way, his saying runs the risk of losing its shock value and becoming banal, not to say tautologous. This would be so unless he meant to say that bird-offerings and the onset of menstruation were more essential than such noble *halakoth* as have to do with the greater sacrifices and the Temple ritual. But this is unlikely. We may indeed conjecture that he originally said Torah (as does M. Hag 1:8), and this was later softened to *halakoth* by the editors because they found his saying too bold and outrageous. It may be bold and outrageous, but not incorrect or absurd, if we understand its real point and take it on its own terms.

Gematria. We need add no more to what has been said than to note a trace of *gematria* in the New Testament at two points: in the numerological sense of Rev 13:17 f (the number of the beast, 666), though this numerical code is apparently not based on a word of Scripture; and in the genealogy at the beginning of Matthew's gospel, based on the number fourteen, the numerical value of David's name, alluded to in Mt. 1:17. [138]

Parperaoth. Commentators have a difficult time with the etymology and meaning of this word. We may list some of the possibilities: 1. periphery = fringes; 2. purple dress, adornment (not likely); 3. periphora = dainties, fig., intellectual delicacies; 4. small and unimportant matters; 5. plerophoria = what gives support or confirmation (so Krauss, *Lehnwörter*, but unlikely). Danby and most others opt for the third sense. This has the advantage of not disparaging the study and value of the natural sciences. They are good and important, but not the highest priority.

Summing up, we may say that in this saying we have *multum in parvo*, a saying which brings to vivid expression the special point of view of rabbinic piety, that we worship God by studying and observing his revealed will in all the details of our daily life. Here, perhaps more perfectly than elsewhere, we find both the splendor and the weakness of the whole movement.

---

[138] Albeck gives the plural form *gematriôth* and an impossible vocalization. The Marti-Beer text is to be preferred here.

4:5

ה   רַבִּי יִשְׁמָעֵאל בְּנוֹ אוֹמֵר: הַלּוֹמֵד עַל מְנָת לְלַמֵּד, מַסְפִּיקִין בְּיָדוֹ לִלְמוֹד וּלְלַמֵּד;
וְהַלּוֹמֵד עַל מְנָת לַעֲשׂוֹת, מַסְפִּיקִין בְּיָדוֹ לִלְמוֹד וּלְלַמֵּד, לִשְׁמוֹר וְלַעֲשׂוֹת. רַבִּי
צָדוֹק אוֹמֵר: אַל תַּעֲשֵׂם עֲטָרָה לְהִתְגַּדֵּל בָּהֶם, וְלֹא קַרְדֹּם לַחְפּוֹר בָּהֶם. וְכָךְ הָיָה
הִלֵּל אוֹמֵר: וְדִשְׁתַּמַּשׁ בְּתָגָא חֲלַף. הָא לָמַדְתָּ: כָּל הַנֶּהֱנֶה מִדִּבְרֵי תוֹרָה נוֹטֵל חַיָּיו
מִן הָעוֹלָם.

5   R. Ishmael his son said: He that learns in order to teach is granted
    the means to learn and to teach; but he that learns in order to perform is
    granted the means to learn and to teach, to observe and to perform.
    R. Zadok says: Keep not aloof from the congregation, and make not
    thyself like them that seek to influence the judges. Make them not a
    crown wherewith to magnify thyself or a spade wherewith to dig. And
    thus used Hillel to say: He that makes wordly use of the crown shall
    perish. Thus thou mayest learn that he that makes profit out of the
    words of the Law removes his life from the world.

This curious mishnah offers us a collection of sayings gathered
around the frequently recurring theme of financial support and remuneration for Torah work. Though it contains several problems of text
and interpretation, its main points are clear enough.

All critical editions, including the Albeck text printed here, omit
the first two sayings attributed to R. Zadok: "Keep not aloof ...
influence the judges." We may take them as later interpolations,
the first of which, derived from Ab 2:5, is irrelevant to the question
of financial support, the second of which, derived from Ab 1:8, may
have some bearing on this question, since one may influence judges
illegitimately by bribery, and this is one reason the Sages, who also
served as judges, are advised not to receive payment for their teaching.

A. The saying attributed to R. Ishmael ben Johanan ben Baroka
does not express itself with perfect clarity. Herford is led to propose a
conjectural emendation: "He that learns in order to *learn*," instead of
"he that learns in order to *teach*." The change would be one of vocalization only and thus one might be inclined to accept it, except that as
the saying stands it is redundant: "learns in order to learn." If one
then proposes to change the first word to another, e.g., "studies," the
emendation is more drastic and less acceptable. It seems we must retain
the text as it stands and understand it better. The point surely is that
one who is preparing to be a teacher of Torah is given (or should
be given) financial support both while he is a student (what we
would call a scholarship or subsidy) and when he teaches (what we
would call tuition fees). The second part of the saying, while not

perfectly clear, would then most likely mean that he would be given additional financial support for special services in the observance of Torah.

Marti-Beer have a quite different understanding of the saying. In their view, the subject of the verb *masphîqîn* (they grant, Danby "is granted") is "the heavenly powers or God." [139] Their interpretation then proceeds:

> R. Ishmael sets up guidelines for true Torah-study in his saying. 1. Learning is, so to say, the lowest grade. 2. Higher than the mere love of learning stands learning as service of others. To learning teaching must be added. 3. The last and highest goal is the application of the teaching, or doing. In this final goal, Pharisaism agrees with the Gospel, cf. Mt 7:24 ff, Lk 8:21, Rm 2:13, Jas 1:22 ff. The juxtaposition of learning, teaching and doing is similar to Ezra 7:10 (*darash*, *ᶜasoth*, *lammed*). For the liberal and richly crowned learning recommended by R. Ishmael, already Fagius recognized as parallel Mt 13:12: "For to him who has will more be given, and he will have abundance."

While this is interesting enough, it is almost certainly wrong. It does not fit the context provided by the saying of R. Zadok. Given the frequent discussion of financial remuneration for Torah-work in Aboth, other rabbinic texts and the New Testament, it seems best to take as the subject of the verb all those, whether patriarchs, wealthy citizens or paying students, who provided material support for the scholars. [140]

---

139 ARN[B], ch. 32 (not ARN[A] as Herford reads) offers a troublesome variant: "*ain masphîqîn*, they do *not* give him the means." Supposing this to be an authentic variant, it would favor the alternate view (of, e.g., Ab 2:2) that all engaged in Torah-study should be self-supporting. This kind of manipulation of texts is often found where there are contradictions in the sources and it is felt that harmony must be achieved at all costs, esp. on a matter of very practical importance. See, e.g., Mk 6:8 f on staff and sandals (permitted) and the Synoptic parallels (not permitted).

140 Among Aboth texts, besides those cited below, note 3:5, which says that scribes must be relieved of the yoke of the government (payment of taxes, b. Baba Bathra 8), and the yoke of worldly care (concern about their livelihood). Other rabbinic texts, chiefly from the Jerusalem Talmud, are collected by A. Büchler, *The Political and Social Leaders of the Jewish Community of Sepphoris in the Second and Third Centuries* (London: Jews' College Publications, no. 1, n.d.). Note further the similar sounding passage in ARN[A], ch. 29 (Goldin, pp. 119 f):

> Abba Saul ben Nannas says: There are four types of scholars: one studies himself but does not teach others; one teaches others but himself does not study; one teaches himself and others; and one teaches neither himself nor others.

What is omitted from this variation is the theme of the (financial) means with which to carry on this activity. Abba Saul goes on in the passage cited to illustrate each of the four types adduced.

B. The saying attributed to R. Zadok has a rather unusual form: first the teaching, then a citation in support of the teaching (from Hillel [Ab 1:13], not drawn from Scripture, unique in Aboth), finally a lesson drawn from the citation. 141

The main point is: do not lower Torah-study to a source of fame and fortune, a familiar protest against clerical freeloaders and spongers of all sorts. ("Digging" conjures up someone gauging devout widows out of their meagre substance.) More than this may be intended, however. Is R. Zadok laying down a rule, a *halacha*, viz., you may not receive financial rewards for expertise in Torah? We know that this was an ideal among some (Ab 1:13; M. Bek 4:6; b. Ned 37a, 62a). The realization of the ideal naturally varied with political, social, and economic circumstances.

The ideal was not foolish. There was first the general consideration that the higher goods (truth, justice) did not diminish through wide diffusion. They belonged to all. Socrates scored the sophists (teachers of rhetoric) for making a profit from the truth (e.g., in the *Gorgias*). Justin Martyr vividly describes his search among the philosophical schools of his day, his rejection of the Peripatetics for their venality, and his choice of the Platonists because they agreed to teach him gratis (*Dial.*, ch. 2). The Gospels too teach: "Freely have you received, so freely give" (Mt 10:8b, on which see further below). But the rabbis have a second reason for insisting on this principle of gratuity, as we have already seen, the very practical consideration that the sages were also judges. The integrity and independence of the magistracy was at stake. Even more fundamental was the religious consideration. Torah was the supreme gift of God to man, it was intended for all. To deny men Torah on financial grounds was to deny them the divine life, life in accord with God's will.

The ideal, like all ideals, was not always realizable. The rabbis recognized the opposite danger: if all the scholars had a trade, they might become more absorbed in their trade than in their studies, leading to neglect of Torah (Ab 2:6e; 3:18a). Political oppression also sometimes removed the economic basis for intense study.

The New Testament and early Christian literature know these tensions. Consider the contradiction between Mt 10:8b (cited above) and

---

141 On the crown as a symbol of reward see Phil 4:1; 1 Thess 2:19. Some texts give for "to dig with" a clarifying variant, "to eat with." Cf. also Ab 4:17 (R. Simeon) and its commentary in ARN^A, ch. 41; also, the comprehensive article by W. Grundmann, TDNT, VII, pp. 615-636.

10:10b: "for the laborer deserves his food (*tēs trophēs*)." Lk 10:7 reads the same, except that it replaces "his food" with "his wages" (*tou misthou*). The Didache takes up this latter problem and solves it with a distinction: "And when an Apostle goes forth let him accept nothing but *bread* (*artou*) till he reaches his night's lodging; but, if he ask for *money* (*argyrion*), he is a false prophet" (Did 11:6; cf. 13:1 f). But the conflict between Mt 10:8 and 10 remains. A similar conflict occurs in St. Paul. On the one hand, he asserts his right as a minister of the gospel to reward for it (1 Cor 9:4-12a; 2 Thess 3:7-9). On the other hand, he boasts that he did not make use of this right (1 Cor 9:12b-14; 2 Cor 11:9, cf. Acts 18:1-3; 20:33). Finally he admits that he did receive support from at least one church (Philippi) (2 Cor 11:8). Thus it may be said that Paul affirms one theory (that of Mt 10:10 and Ab 4:5a) while he (normally) lives another (that of Mt 10:8a and Ab 4:5b). [142]

From a much later period, Maimonides offers a characteristically clever, down-to-earth and frank solution.

A SPADE TO DIG WITH

I first resolved not to comment at length on this statement because it is self-explanatory. Moreover, I thought that what I had to say about it would neither please nor be feasible for most of the great scholars. Nevertheless, I do want to say certain things regardless of those who preceded me and regardless of my contemporaries. Know therefore that this statement that one should not make the Torah a spade to dig with, that is to say, that one should not treat the Torah as a source of liveli-

---

[142] D. Daube, *New Testament and Rabbinic Judaism*, pp. 394-400, treats of Ab 4:5 in relation to 1 Cor 9:8-10, but on the main issue of the right to financial support, he lacks nuance, presupposing that rabbis never took money. In this he follows Schürer, *The History of the Jewish People in the Time of Jesus Christ*, trans. S. Taylor and P. Christie (Edinburgh: Clark, 1885), II¹, pp. 317-319, who however distinguishes between nonpayment for judging and nonpayment for teaching, and G. F. Moore, *Judaism...*, II, p. 96 f. He has been well criticized by D. L. Dungan, *The Sayings of Jesus in the Churches of Paul* (Philadelphia: Fortress, 1971) ,pp. 12-14. On the relation between Paul and the Synoptic material on this question, see *ibid.*, pp. 3-80. On the whole social evolution of the scribes, see E. E. Urbach, *Class-Status and Leadership in the World of the Palestinian Sages* (Jerusalem: Israel Academy of Sciences, Proc., Vol. II, no. 4, 1966), and now my review thereof, RB 80 (1973); 138 f, but esp. the masterful pages of J. Jeremias, *Jerusalem...* (Philadelphia Fortress, 1969), pp. 111-116. Finally we may note the interesting albeit unconvincing article by M. Himmelfarb, *Commentary* 56 (Oct., 1973): 68-71 who tries to contrast a supposed Greek patrician strain of scholarship (*scholē* = leisure, thus the privilege of the leisured classes) with a rabbinic plebeian strain. The fact is of course that both cultural streams had both patrician (e.g., Aristotle, Judah ha-Nasi) and plebeian (e.g., Epictetus, Honi) representatives.

hood ... against this clear statement, many men have blinded themselves, rejected it, have paid it only the most superficial attention and
not gone to the heart of the matter.—I will give the correct explanation.
Many have imposed on individuals and communities ... have led men
to think—wrongly so—that it is altogether proper, even obligatory to
give financial assistance to sages, to scholars, to disciples, to all those
engaged in and devoted to the study of Torah. This is entirely wrong.
There is no basis at all for this in the Torah. Indeed, if we examine
the words of the Sages, of blessed memory, we never find individuals
seeking financial help for scholars.... On the contrary, in all their
communities there were some scholars who were utterly poor and some
who were extremely rich. And God forbid! that we say the contemporaries of those scholars were not charitable, that had a poor scholar
asked for help, his contemporaries would not have filled his house
with gold and diamonds. The fact is that the poor scholar refused
such gifts, but preferred to be content with income from his own work,
be it much or little. The scholar scorned what one can get from human
hands, because the Torah forbade accepting such help. You know that
Hillel the Elder was a woodchopper ... that of Rabbi Hanina ben Dosa
a heavenly voice declared, "The whole world is nourished only for the
sake of my son Hanina, while my son Hanina is content with a small
portion of dried-out dates from one end of the week to the other"—
he never asked anyone for charity.... Not one of the Sages who was
poor spoke disparagingly of his contemporaries or of others that they
did not make scholars rich. The Sages were true saints ... they believed
in the Lord, blessed be He, and in the Torah of Moses, that through
devotion to it a man will merit the life of the world to come. They
never permitted themselves this begging for money. They saw, indeed,
that this taking funds would be profaning the Name of God in the
sight of the masses—because then people come to regard the study
of Torah as no more than another occupation by means of which a man
makes a living. Thus Torah study would become contemptible in their
eyes.... What the Torah does permit scholars is this: they may give
their money to some person for him to do business with it for them
as he sees fit. A person who helps a scholar in this fashion will be
rewarded.... The Torah also permits the merchandise of a scholar to
be sold first, before anyone else's.... Such privileges the Lord, blessed
be He, allowed, the way he sets up gifts for the priest and tithes for
the Levite.... So too the Torah has relieved scholars from various
taxes ... and this, even if the scholar happens to be a wealthy person. [143]

We note first his assumption that Torah does not permit remuneration for teaching. Second, he notes that this prohibition has frequently
been violated. Third, he offers a casuistic solution which saves the
difficult principle while allowing indirect subsidies. It is curious that

---

[143] Goldin, *ad locum*, pp. 161 f.

he speaks of the prohibition as Torah. Neither he nor Aboth offer a scriptural basis for it. He probably thinks of Aboth as Torah. On the other hand, the New Testament's choice of Old Testament support is indirect at best, viz., Num 18:31, possibly alluded to in Mt 10:10, and Paul's quote from Dt 25:4: "You shall not muzzle an ox when it is treading out the grain."

In conclusion, it is clear that once again we have an example of the dialectic which characterizes so much of Aboth, the juxtaposing of opinions which contradict one another, in this case a dialectic which has been painted over by harmonizing interpretations for a long time. This mishnah treats of one of the more humble but unavoidable aspects of a religious life ideal, the ceaseless study of Torah, "the crown," viz., how do you live while doing it?

4:9

ט רַבִּי יוֹנָתָן אוֹמֵר: כָּל הַמְקַיֵּם אֶת הַתּוֹרָה מֵעֹנִי, סוֹפוֹ לְקַיְּמָהּ מֵעֹשֶׁר; וְכָל הַמְבַטֵּל אֶת הַתּוֹרָה מֵעֹשֶׁר, סוֹפוֹ לְבַטְּלָהּ מֵעֹנִי.

9   R. Jonathan said: He that fulfils the Law in poverty shall in the end fulfil it in wealth; and he that neglects the Law in wealth shall in the end neglect it in poverty.

As we draw our study of Aboth to a close, we may be briefer, as themes with which we are already familiar recur. The saying of R. Jonathan (or Nathan) is a single proverb expressed in two perfectly balanced and contrasting parallel sentences. Its content may be described, on the one hand, as the effect of economic shifts on Torah observance, on the other hand, and less explicitly, as the effect that habits in one's youth will have on one's old age. Fundamentally, the saying intends to unmask the most common excuses for postponing Torah-study, the pleas of poverty or press of business, as the rationalizations they are (cf. Ab 2:5: "Say not, When I have leisure I will study....") A theme which links this mishnah with the following one, as well as with Ab 1:5, is concern for the sin of *beṭul Torah*, the neglect, and thus implicity, the despising of Torah. [144]

Perhaps the real point of the saying is that love of Torah (implicitly, a or *the* condition of salvation) is a gift, a gift which does not depend on economic or material conditions or on age. Conversely, folly, i.e.,

---

[144] The saying is reproduced with slight variations in ARN[A], ch. 30 (Schechter ed., p. 89; Goldin, p. 123), and in ARN[B], ch. 35 (Schechter ed., p. 82).

neglect of Torah, hardening one's heart so as not to hear the word of God, the voice of wisdom, is possible in any state of life.

We may note two further points. (1) The verb "to fulfill" the Law is *meqayyem* (from the root *qwm*). This sheds light on the Semitic substratum of the Greek verb *plēroō* as used in Mt 5:17, Rom 3:31; 13:8, 10 (*plērōma*). [145]

(2) The rich man here (*me°sher*) is contrasted with the poor man (*me°oni*), as he is in Lk 6:20-21, 24-25 (blessings and woes) but without any explicit bias in favor of the poor man. This passage is neutral on the religious value of wealth. [146]

4:10

רַבִּי מֵאִיר אוֹמֵר: הֱוֵי מְמַעֵט בָּעֵסֶק, וַעֲסֹק בַּתּוֹרָה; וֶהֱוֵי שְׁפַל רוּחַ בִּפְנֵי כָל אָדָם; יְ
וְאִם בִּטַּלְתָּ מִן הַתּוֹרָה, יֶשׁ לְךָ בְּטֵלִים.

10 R. Meir said: Engage not overmuch in business but occupy thyself with the Law; and be lowly in spirit before all men. If thou neglectest the Law many things neglected shall rise against thee; but if thou labourest in the Law He has abundant reward to give thee.

This teaching of the great Rabbi Meir comprises two separate sayings. The first (A) is in the form of a triplet of the kind familiar to us from chapter one of Aboth. The first two parts of the triplet involve (1) a play on the stem *°asaq* (business, be busy), (2) a step or hook construction based on the link word *°asaq*, a literary ornament familiar to us from Rm 5:3 ff, Jas 1:3 f, etc., (3) a unified theme. The third clause ("be lowly in spirit...") is a kind of outrider, added to fill up the measure but unrelated in content to the first two. [147]

The emphasis on humility (*shephal-ruach*) is however an important addition, because it connects zeal for Torah study with an attitude which is the very opposite of the proverbial Pharisaic (and generally intellectual) arrogance. It thereby shows that alongside of the Christian

---

[145] We (along with Bacher, Fiebig, Dalman, Strack-Billerbeck, et al.) affirm this on the basis of the rather strong similarity of idiom and context, despite the challenge of G. Delling, TDNT, VI, p. 293 f, s.v. *plēroō*, based on H. Ljungman, *Das Gesetz Erfüllen* (Lund: Gleerup, 1954), pp. 26-33. How the root meaning of the hifil of *qwm* (lit., to cause to arise, to establish) sheds light on the meaning of the New Testament passage is treated elsewhere herein.

[146] Cf. Ab 6:9: "At the time of a man's departure, neither silver nor gold nor precious stones go with him, but only [his knowledge of] the Law and good works" (see the entire passage). See further F. Hauck and W. Kasch, s.v. *ploutos*, etc., TDNT, VI, pp. 318-332.

[147] Note the slight textual problem in the opening words. The Albeck and the Herford texts are clearer than that of Marti-Beer and are followed here.

critique of Pharisaic arrogance and hypocrisy, there was an inner-Pharisaic critique as well. All along we have found thus far that many early Christian criticisms of the Pharisaic movement have been either anticipated or seconded by the rabbis themselves, but without breaking the internal dialectic, without a rejection of their peculiar (and burdensome) oral law, and without Christology. [148]

(B) The second saying of R. Meir expresses itself in two balanced conditional sentences and returns to the theme of neglect of Torah (*beṭul Torah*) which we have already encountered in Ab 1:5 and 4:9. But the subject of the apodosis changes from the first sentence ("many neglected things") to the second ("He," i.e., God). This disturbance in the perfect symmetry of the parallelism may have been motivated by a desire to avoid presenting God as the direct cause of punishment and misfortune. [149]

Once again the motive of Torah study is divine reward (*śakar harbeh*) both in this world and in the world to come. The reward for choosing the right priorities in the Gospel (e.g., the kingdom of God and his righteousness, Mt 6:33, cf. Lk 12:33; Col 3:2) is the same. [150]

4:12

יב רַבִּי אֶלְעָזָר בֶּן שַׁמּוּעַ אוֹמֵר: יְהִי כְבוֹד תַּלְמִידָךְ חָבִיב עָלֶיךָ כְּשֶׁלָּךְ, וּכְבוֹד חֲבֵרָךְ –
כְּמוֹרָא רַבָּךְ, וּמוֹרָא רַבָּךְ – כְּמוֹרָא שָׁמַיִם.

12 R. Eleazar b. Shammua said: Let the honour of thy disciple be as dear to thee as thine own and as the honour of thy companion, and the

---

148 On undue involvement in worldly business see Heb. Sir 38:24b: "*veḥasar ʿasaq huʾ yithakam*, the one who lacks a trade, he will become wise." This verse begins the important section in Sirach (38:24-39:11) termed the Praise of the Scribe, which proceeds in the first place (38:24-34) with a satire on various craftsmen. Cf. also Ab 2:2.

On humility see further Ab 4:4a (itself based on Heb. Sirach 7:17, on which see H. Duesberg and I. Fransen, *Ecclesiastico* [Turin: Marietti, 1966], pp. 122 f.) and 5:19.

149 At this point we may note the range of vocabulary employed in Ab 4:9 and 10 for labor in the Torah: (1) *qayyem* (fulfill, establish), (2) *ʿasaq* (be busy), (3) *ʿamal* (labor, toil). This saying is given with some variations in ARN[A], ch. 29 (Goldin, p. 119), and in ARN[B], ch. 33.

150 On this theme see especially Strack-Billerbeck, IV, pp. 484-500, excursus 20, and Würthwein-Preisker, s.v. *misthos*, in Kittel, TDNT, IV, pp. 695-728, and their bibliography for further literature, to which add the valuable correctives in Morton Smith, *Tannaitic Parallels to the Gospels* (Philadelphia: SBL, 1968[2]), JBL Monograph Series, no. 6, pp. 49-73, 161-184; also G. Bornkamm, "Der Lohngedanke im N.T.," *Studien zu Antike und Urchristentum*, pp. 69-92, and W. Pesch, *Der Lohngedanke in der Lehre Jesu verglichen mit der religiösen Lohnlehre des Spätjudentums.*

honour of thy companion as the fear of thy teacher, and the fear of
thy teacher as the fear of Heaven.

This mishnah concerns the relations of great respect which should
obtain between a disciple and his teacher.

Form: The saying is constructed on the pattern of escalating steps;
the three stages are linked by the hook words *kabod* (honor, glory)
and *morah* (fear, reverence). The words shift from honor to fear when
the person involved is not an equal but superior, a little essay in the
sociology of knowledge. [151]

Content: Three points may be extracted from the saying: (1) In
matters of Torah study, always overesteem your colleagues; err on the
side of generosity. (2) Hold everyone *connected with study* in honor
and *esteem*. (3) Your teacher (here the word *rabbi* is used) is comparable only to God. The last point is of importance to us, as meta-
phorically expressing, with great force, the close connection, in rabbinic
religion, between everything connected with study and divine things.
It would not be unfair to say that the early Christians took the last
part of this mishnah with radical seriousness, regarding their unique
teacher as the Messiah (Mt 23:8-10) and even as divine (Jn 1:1).
We might almost say that a potential Christology lies implicit in this
mishnah, however foreign, indeed abhorrent, this might be to the
intent of Eleazar ben Shammua. Aknin explains that the teacher is
like God because he brings a man to the life of the world to come. [152]

Rabbinic parallels: (1) M. Baba Metzia 2:11, where the precedence
of one's teacher over one's father is discussed. (2) Tos. Baba Metzia
2:28 deals with the same point; (3) M. Kerithoth 6:9; (4) b. Kid 33b;
(5) b. Sanh 110a; (6) b. Pes 22b, where Akiba's interpretation of
Dt 6:2 is given; (7) Mek. Ex. ad 17:9; 18:12 (ed. Lauterbach, II,
pp. 140 (= ARN[A], ch. 27) and 177f respectively); (8) Sifre Deut.
ad 6:9 and *passim*, etc., etc. According to Taylor, *in loco*, "God himself
is the great Chief Rabbi, and diligently studies and teaches Torah,"
in the rabbinic view. He supports this with citations from Targum
Cant 5:10 and Targum Jerus. Deut. 32 (par. b. AZ 3b).

---

[151] The intrusion of the phrase "and thine own as" represents a textual corruption,
explainable as an attempted assimilation of our mishnah to the pattern of Ab 2:10.
Albeck and Danby both offer contaminated texts, as does ARN[A]; Taylor, Herford and
Marti-Beer provide a clean text. The versions in ARN[A], ch. 27 (Goldin, p. 115)
and ARN[B], ch. 34, both offer in addition to the above corruption, glosses in the form
of biblical proof texts, the A version citing Ex 17:9, Num 12:11, Num 11:28; the
B version, Ex 17:8 and 7:2.

[152] Goldin, *in loco*.

59618

New Testament parallels: Mt 10:20 (to which see Jn 14:26; 1 Cor 2:4); Mt 10:40; Eph 6:7; Mt 23:5-8. [153]

On Ab 4:13, see on 3:8 and 9 above.

4:20

כ אֱלִישָׁע בֶּן אֲבוּיָה אוֹמֵר: הַלּוֹמֵד יֶלֶד, לְמָה הוּא דוֹמֶה? לִדְיוֹ כְתוּבָה עַל נְיָר חָדָשׁ. וְהַלּוֹמֵד זָקֵן, לְמָה הוּא דוֹמֶה? לִדְיוֹ כְתוּבָה עַל נְיָר מָחוּק. רַבִּי יוֹסֵי בַר יְהוּדָה אִישׁ כְּפַר הַבַּבְלִי אוֹמֵר: הַלּוֹמֵד מִן הַקְּטַנִּים, לְמָה הוּא דוֹמֶה? לְאוֹכֵל עֲנָבִים קֵהוֹת וְשׁוֹתֶה יַיִן מִגִּתּוֹ· וְהַלּוֹמֵד מִן הַזְּקֵנִים, לְמָה הוּא דוֹמֶה? לְאוֹכֵל עֲנָבִים בְּשׁוּלוֹת וְשׁוֹתֶה יַיִן יָשָׁן· רַבִּי אוֹמֵר: אַל תִּסְתַּכֵּל בַּקַּנְקַן, אֶלָּא בַמֶּה שֶׁיֵּשׁ בּוֹ· יֵשׁ קַנְקַן חָדָשׁ מָלֵא יָשָׁן, וְיָשָׁן – שֶׁאֲפִלּוּ חָדָשׁ אֵין בּוֹ·

20 Elisha b. Abuyah said: He that learns as a child, to what is he like? To ink written on new paper. He that learns as an old man, to what is he like? To ink written on paper that has been blotted out. R. Jose b. Judah of Kefar ha-Babli said: He that learns from the young, to what is he like? To one that eats unripe grapes and drinks wine from his winepress. And he that learns from the aged, to what is he like? To one that eats ripe grapes and drinks old wine. Rabbi said: Look not on the jar but on what is in it; there may be a new jar that is full of old wine and an old one in which is not even new wine.

Three separate sayings are given here, each ascribed to a different sage, but all related to the theme of learning in connection with youth and old age. The first two sayings match one another closely, the third may be understood as a playful retort of the young Rabbi to the main point of the second saying. The point of saying A is that learning early in life is better than late in life, of saying B, that a mature teacher is better than a green one, of C that the age of the teacher is not of itself a reliable guide to his excellence. There are also old fools. All three of the sayings are expressed in terms of brief similitudes, the first drawn from the experience of scribes, the second and third from the world of wine.

The metaphors of new and old wine and their containers remind us immediately of Mk 2:22 and its parallels, each with interesting variations, in Mt 9:17 and Lk 5:37-39. Lk 5:39, "And no one after drinking old wine desires new; for he says, 'The old is good,' " reminds us of the saying (B) of R. Jose b. Judah. The variant readings to the final word "good" in this verse (*better*: Alexandrinus, etc.; omit

[153] See Gerhardsson, *Memory and Manuscript*, p. 182, n. 5, and D. Daube, "Responsibilities of master and disciples in the Gospels," NTS 19 (1972): 1-15, as well as part 3, ch. 5 of his *New Testament and Rabbinic Judaism*, pp. 266-8.

v. 39: Bezae, etc.) remind us of Rabbi's corrective in saying C. (Rabbinic dialectic is sometimes achieved in the New Testament by textual variation.) But the metaphor in saying C is not without its New Testament parallel either. In 2 Cor 3:2 and 3 Paul compares his converts to a letter of recommendation from Christ, written on their hearts, not with ink but with the Spirit of the living God. Rabbi's praise of gifted young minds may also be compared with the more radical praise of *nēpioi* ("babes") in the Gospel (Mt 11:25, par Lk 10:21), undoubtedly referring to some of the *am ha-aretz* (see ch. 3). See further the citation of Ps 8:3LXX ("Out of the mouth of babes and sucklings thou hast brought perfect praise") in a passage of carefully understated but important anti-Pharisaic polemic, Mt 21:10-17, esp. v. 16. Of the many Gospel passages where people express astonishment at the improbability that Jesus could teach so well, see especially Jn 7:15 and Lk 2:46 f. [154]

Rabbinic parallels. Marti-Beer suggest that originally saying A may have been an attack on R. Akiba, a notoriously late vocation, of whom it was well said: "At the age of forty he went to study Torah; at the end of thirteen years he taught Torah to multitudes." [155]

Rabbi Jonah cited the fine text of Job 32:6-9 on this passage. It is worth quoting:

> I am young in years and you are aged; therefore I was timid and afraid to declare my opinion to you. I said, "Let days speak, and many years teach wisdom." But it is the spirit in man, the breath of the Almighty, that makes him understand. It is not the old that are wise, nor the aged that understand what is right.

ARN[A], ch. 23 (Goldin, p. 102), offers further parables to saying A while the other two sayings are further illustrated in ARN[B], ch. 34, where the parts are attributed to different authors. See also Sifre Deut 11:22.

---

[154] On *nēpioi* and cognates, see S. Légasse, *Jésus et l'enfant* (Études bibliques; Paris: Gabalda, 1969).

[155] ARN[A], ch. 6, Goldin ed., p. 42.

M. Kiddushin 1:10

י   כָּל הָעוֹשֶׂה מִצְוָה אַחַת, מְטִיבִין לוֹ, וּמַאֲרִיכִין לוֹ אֶת יָמָיו, וְנוֹחֵל אֶת הָאָרֶץ. וְכָל
שֶׁאֵינוֹ עוֹשֶׂה מִצְוָה אַחַת, אֵין מְטִיבִין לוֹ, וְאֵין מַאֲרִיכִין לוֹ אֶת יָמָיו, וְאֵינוֹ נוֹחֵל אֶת
הָאָרֶץ. כָּל שֶׁיֶּשְׁנוֹ בַּמִּקְרָא וּבַמִּשְׁנָה וּבְדֶרֶךְ אֶרֶץ, לֹא בִמְהֵרָה הוּא חוֹטֵא, שֶׁנֶּאֱמַר¹:
׳וְהַחוּט הַמְשֻׁלָּשׁ לֹא בִמְהֵרָה יִנָּתֵק׳. וְכָל שֶׁאֵינוֹ לֹא בַמִּקְרָא וְלֹא בַמִּשְׁנָה וְלֹא בְדֶרֶךְ
אֶרֶץ, אֵינוֹ מִן הַיִּשּׁוּב.

¹ קהלת ד, יב.

10   If a man performs but a single commandment it shall be well with him
and he shall have length of days and shall inherit the Land; but if
he neglects a single commandment it shall be ill with him and he shall
not have length of days and shall not inherit the Land. He that has a
knowledge of Scripture and Mishnah and right conduct will not soon
fall into sin, for it is written, *And a threefold cord is not quickly
broken.* But he that has no knowledge of Scripture and Mishnah and
right conduct has no part in the habitable world.

Mishnah Kiddushin 1:10 transmits an anonymous saying; according
to the letter of Goan Sherira (A.D. 987) to Jacob b. Nissim and the
men of Kairwan, anonymous traditions in the Mishnah are ascribed
to R. Meir. [156] This is not always a safe rule, but it remains a possibility
here. In any case, we notice the saying's somewhat haggadic character.
It has nothing whatever to do with betrothals, the main subject of the
tractate. The preceding mishnah had made an important distinction
between laws which depend on the Land of Israel and those which
do not. The mention of the Land led to the Deuteronomic thought of
inheriting the Land, conditions for which are given in the first half
of our mishnah (cf. Deut 4:40). It is common to conclude tractates
with a bit of haggada. Here we have one, not at the end of a tractate,
but at the end of a chapter.

With regard to the structure, we note at once its division into two
parts, each composed of two evenly balanced antithetical parallels.
All four are interrelated, after the fashion of 1:1; 2:2. Part A deals
with performing or not performing one commandment, for which a
threefold reward or punishment is given. Part B treats of the possession
(i.e., knowledge) or nonpossession of Scripture, Mishnah, and right
conduct (or, a decent trade). But at this point, the symmetry of form
breaks down. The results are: (1) he will not quickly sin (or, be a
sinner). Then follows Qoh. 4:12. (2) "He has no part in the habitable

---

[156] E. B. Lewin (Haifa, 1921) (non vidi). French translation L. Landau, *Épître
historique du R. Sherira Gaon* (Antwerp: Bary, 1904).

world," literally, he is not from the inhabited world, or, civilization.
We may note further the possibility of a chiasmic pattern: (a) one
good/bad deed, (b) three blessings/curses, (b) three good/bad deeds,
(a) one blessing/curse (= abba).

An exact determination of the content of the mishnah depends on
the understanding of two matters. The first is the meaning of the
term "habitable world (hayyishshûb). We may note: (a) that it is the
perfect equivalent of the Greek hē oikouménē, a participle used as a
noun, with which should be supplied either eretz (land) or 'ôlam
(world). 157 (b) Literally it means the inhabitable or inhabited world
(land), and as such is contrasted with the desert (so Albeck in loco)
or the sea. (c) By extension, the word means civilization, the civilized
world (as opposed to the barbarians?). (d) In two passages Qoh. R.
ad 1:15; Ruth R. ad 1:17) it means this world as opposed to the
hereafter (desert), but does not refer to the hereafter itself. 158
(e) Here one might propose that, in our passage, hayyishshûb does
mean the hereafter, the world to come. The contrasting term in context,
"not falling quickly into sin," remains somewhat inconclusive in determining the sense (cf, M. Sanh 10:1 ff). The strongest support for this
way of taking this term may be Hebrews 2:5, tēn oikoumenēn
tēn mellousan, the exact equivalent, it would seem, of ha-'ôlam ha-ba,
but with the denotation "inhabited," used as we find in hayyishshûb.
Rashi and Maimonides, in their commentaries in loco, take the Land
of the first half as referring to the future life, but this medieval interpretation cannot be made decisive for the tannaitic understanding. 159
The second issue on which an exact interpretation hinges is the inserted
quotation from Qoh. 4:12. Often, biblical quotations are later additions
to Mishnah passages, as we have seen in Aboth, but here the possibility
arises that the O.T. text generated the mishnah, B. The crucial word,
linking all three clauses, is bimeherah, quickly, soon. A plausible
genesis for the entire mishnah might then be: (a) mishnah A, formulated on the basis of M. Kid 1:9 and Deut 4:40; (b) its mention of
three blessings leads to a reminiscence of Qoh. 4:12 and (c) the
formation of mishnah B. Cf. also Ab 2:2.

For our purposes, the importance of the passage lies in B. Here it
is made explicit that knowledge of Torah, including Mishnah, is
necessary for salvation, a condition thereof, an ethical requirement on

---

157 See O. Michel, s.v. oikoumenē, in TDNT, V, pp. 157-9.
158 See M. Jastrow, A Dictionary of the Targumim..., s.v., p. 599.
159 Cf. Strack-Billerbeck, Kommentar..., I, p. 200.

a par with keeping the commandments. This gives to detailed mastery
of a religious tradition a religious significance of the highest order,
a phenomenon peculiar to rabbinic religion, at least in this precise sense.

The saying leads quite naturally into that famous debate at Lydda
which has come down to us in manifold recensions, the debate on
which is greater, study or doing. The classic account of this debate
occurs in the Babylonian Talmud precisely as a kind of Haggadic
commentary on our mishnah, at b. Kiddushin 40 b (Soncino ed.,
p. 202).

וכבר היה רבי טרפון וזקנים מסובין בעלית בית נתזה בלוד נשאלה שאילה זו בפניהם
תלמוד גדול או מעשה גדול נענה רבי טרפון ואמר מעשה גדול נענה רבי עקיבא ואמר
תלמוד גדול נענו כולם ואמרו תלמוד גדול שהתלמוד מביא לידי מעשה:

> R. Tarfon and the Elders were once reclining in the upper storey of
> Nithza's house, in Lydda, when this question was raised before them:
> Is study greater, or practice? R. Tarfon answered, saying: Practice is
> greater. R. Akiba answered, saying: Study is greater, for it leads to
> practice. Then they all answered and said: Study is greater, for it
> leads to action.

Note in this version the circumstantial detail. The principals and
place are named. It is further made clear that Akiba's decision is no
mere private opinion, but approved by a majority vote and hence
normative.

There are eight other versions of this story. We will discuss the two
most important variants below. Here we note that elsewhere in the
Babylonian Talmud (b. Megillah 27a, Soncino ed., p. 162 and b. Baba
Kamma 17a, Soncino ed., p. 75) only the concluding principle, along
with its reason, is cited, without the narrative, as though it were
accepted doctrine. It is attributed to the Master (R. Judah ha-Nasi),
as it is in the next version.

The most important variant comes from the Palestinian Talmud, j.
Pesachim 3:7, Krotoschin ed. 30b (Schwab ed., p. 45). What follows
is a literal translation from the original, as Schwab is very paraphrastic.
As this version is more complex than the Babylonian, it will be broken
down into parts for convenience of analysis.

> 1. Rabbi repeated thus: Practice comes before (precedes) study (ha-
> ma°aseh qôdem le-talmud).
> 2. They voted in the upper storey of Arum's house in Lydda: Study
> comes before practice.
> 3. Rabbi Abahu sent his son to R. Haninah at Tiberias [to study
> Torah]. They came and said to him: He does good works [lit., ḥesed,

e.g., burying the dead]. He sent for him and said...: Is it because there are no grave-diggers in Caesarea that I sent you [to study] in Tiberias?

4. For they debated and voted and decided in the upper storey of Arum's house in Lydda that study came before practice.

5. The rabbis at Caesarea said: That which you say [is true] when there is someone there who will act [i.e., will take care of the good deeds]. But if there is no one there who will act, practice precedes.

6. Here is a confirming illustration. Once Rabbi Hiyya, Rabbi Jose, and Rabbi Immi were late in arriving at [the school of] Rabbi Eleazar. He said to them: Where were you? They told him of their good deed. He said to them: And were there not others there? They said to him: He was a traveling stranger.

We note: (1) the principle is given, with *qôdem* rather than *gedôl* as the main verb, and Rabbi is mentioned as the tradent, though not as the originator. (2) The story is given in bare form; no debaters are mentioned; the voting takes place in Arum's, not Nithza's, house, but at Lydda. (3) A story of R. Abahu's son is introduced. (4) The Lydda debate story is repeated as the climax or coda of the Abahu story, in the same form as no. 2, but with the addition of the verbs *debate* and *decide to vote*. The rabbis of Caesarea qualify the principle by adding a proviso, and thereby domesticate, indeed, trivialize, the issues involved to a matter of burying the dead. They miss both the original historical context, viz., the Hadrianic persecution, and the universal intent of the principle, with its attendant grandeur and singularity. Perhaps it would be truer to say that they do recognize its shocking, to some abhorrent, singularity, and simply oppose it. (6) A third story is given in confirmation of no. 5.

This Palestinian version is decidedly secondary and has as its chief effect to soften, to minimize, the force of the original principle. The change in wording of the principle (*is greater* changes to *comes before*) may indicate a shift in understanding of the principle. The shift would involve moving from a priority of nature (intrinsic superiority) to a priority of time (mere temporal precedence). [160]

The third main version comes from Cant. R. 2:14, section 5 (Soncino ed., p. 131 f):

> Once they had a discussion in the house of Aliyath Arim at Lydda on the question: Which is more important, study or action? R. Tarfon maintained that action was more important; R. Akiba maintained that study was more important. They took a vote and decided that study was more important because it leads to action.

---

[160] The version in j. Hagigah 1:7, 76c offers slight textual variants from j. Pes 3:7, but represents substantially the same tradition.

We perceive at once that this story is a conflation of the two earlier forms. It is primarily dependent upon the Babylonian recension: there are no intervening narratives; the classic simplicity of outline is preserved; the names of the protagonists are given and they are in accord with those in b. Kid. On the other hand, the name of the householder derives from the Palestinian tradition. [161]

Many modern commentators endeavor to give the anecdote a meaningful historical context. They point out that the debate probably took place during the Hadrianic war (A.D. 132-135), during a time of persecution, when the study of Torah was officially outlawed. Thus, they imply, the decision was not intended to assert a general principle, but only as an emergency measure. Others however assume that the decision was not merely an ad hoc reaction to a challenge, but a decision in principle as to the chief responsibility of the sages themselves. It has further been argued (by J. Neusner, orally) that the force of the subordinate clause ("because study leads to practice") is that study is only a means to the end. The end is always intrinsically greater than the means because it dictates and governs them. This seems oversubtle in view of the main assertion: study is greater. If anything, the subordinate clause endeavors to keep the two poles in fruitful tension, while affirming and justifying the superiority of study. It was important not to break the dialectic. [162]

The importance of the debate and resolution at Lydda, it seems to us, stems from its providing the formula (study is greater than practice, because study leads to practice) which brings to a climax and epitomizes in a phrase the logic, the inner tendency, of an entire era, of the whole

---

[161] The version of the debate preserved in Sifre Deut. 11:13, section 41 (Finkelstein ed., 1939, 1969², p. 85), brought in as a comment on Deut 5:1 (q.v.), need not receive separate analysis. It is brief, preserves the *gadol* form, the house belongs to Aris, and Rabbi Jose the Galilean is named along with Tarfon and Aqiba. The two other occurrences of the story in the sources I have been unable to compare. They are: (1) the Mekilta de R. Simeon b. Yohai, 19:17, Melamed ed., p. 100; (2) Midrash Tannaim 1:7, Hoffmann ed., p. 34.

[162] Typical of the historicizing interpretation is L. Finkelstein, *Akiba* (New York: Atheneum, 1970³), pp. 258-260. He also applies his patrician versus plebian distinction to the positions of Tarfon and Akiba. This seems implausible here. The view that the issue was the responsibility of the sages themselves is held by G. Allon, *Toldot*, 3124, cited in J. Neusner, *History and Torah* (New York: Schocken, 1965), p. 102, n. 56, where further references are given. To them add W. Bacher, *Die Agada der Tannaiten* (Strasburg: K. Trübner, 1884, p. 300; 2nd ed., 1903, p. 296). See further now the delightful note in J. Goldin, "Several sidelights of a Torah education in tannaite and early amorical times." *Ex orbe religionum* (Studia Geo Widengren), I, (Leiden: Brill, 1972), pp. 176-191; the note is no. 4 on p. 179.

movement from Pharisaic associations to tannaitic rabbinism. This
movement extends roughly from 200 B.C. to A.D. 200, more precisely,
from Hillel to A.D. 135, or at least from Rabban Johanan ben Zakkai
to A.D. 135. This formula was to be sure produced under the excru-
ciating pressure of a particular moment in history, the revolt against
the Emperor Hadrian and the ensuing persecution. The rabbis formulated their momentous principle in a *status confessionis*. The situation
forced a decision they would otherwise have preferred to avoid. But
the decision they made was no mere accident or quirk of the moment,
subsequently revoked. No, the decision lived on, as a fundamental
shaping principle of all future Judaism, and is quoted as such in the
Talmud and elsewhere. In this formula, there can be no doubt, one,
if not *the*, specific difference of later Judaism among the religions of
mankind has come to definitive expression. [163]

What does the formula mean? Certainly it does *not* mean that
rabbinic Judaism was indifferent to ethical conduct, or relegated it to
a minor place. The subordinate clause is enough to rule out such
perverse misunderstandings. Everything turns, as we have already stated
several times in the course of our commentary on the relevant Aboth
passages, on what is meant by ethical conduct ("practice"). To the
early rabbis ethical or righteous behavior consisted in fulfilling the
will of God as it had been made known in the ramarkably detailed
prescription of the Hebrew Scriptures. No distinction between more
and less important commandments could be made since no such
distinctions were made in the Scriptures themselves. Besides, when
dissident groups such as the early Christians began to make such
distinctions, the whole pattern of observance unraveled, as was plain
to see.

But this was not all. The rabbis also accepted as revelatory of
God's ethical will the whole complex of Palestinian customary laws
which had grown up as hedge around the Torah and which was
eventually enshrined in the Mishnah, the Tosephta and the *baraithot*
of the two massive Talmuds. More basic still was the decision to extend
the prescriptions of ritual purity, intended in the original Torah
exclusively for priests (*cohanim*), to all the faithful people, thereby
making them a priestly kingdom, a holy nation (Ex 19:6). The origins
of this decision were doubtless lost to the rabbis, as they remain largely

---

[163] See the as yet unpublished essay on this point by J. Neusner, "The study of
tradition as religion in Judaism," delivered at a symposium at the University of Iowa
School of Religion, 15-17 April, 1974.

unknown to us, though we may be sure that they emerged from the annealing urgency of an earlier *status confessionis*, the agonies of the Hasmonean revolt against the Seleucid kings, and their aftermath. They may not have known how, when or why the decision had been made, but the rabbis accepted it as a legacy from their forebears, and they tried to work out its implications in everyday life with the greatest fidelity and zeal.

Once these earlier decisions were taken as first principles, the formula of Lydda followed naturally enough. For it was plain to all that one could not observe all those detailed precepts without a *detailed* knowledge of them and their right application to individual cases and circumstances. By this principle, the rabbis gave detailed knowledge of holy law a religious importance and salvific unique and unprecedented in world history.

Conclusion

From our study of the early rabbinic tractate Aboth certain main conclusions will by now have emerged with great clarity. The first and most obvious of these is that the editors of the tractate, as well as most of the authorities they cite, placed a major emphasis on the lifelong and diligent study of Torah, in all its many expressions, among the religious values which they cherished and upheld. They expressed their high evaluation of Torah-study in an endless variety of ways: proverbs, precepts, parables, whatever literary means were available to them.

The second conclusion follows hard upon the first: many of the early rabbis were perfectly well aware of the dangers such a great emphasis on study entailed and frankly admitted and faced them. The danger that one would isolate oneself with a likeminded coterie and neglect the poor was noted and opposed (Ab 1:4 and 5). So too, the danger that endless debate would drown the merits of silence and that endless study would lead to neglect of practice (1:17). The dangers of pride and arrogance were noted and gently chided (2:8), and those who were tempted to stray over to side issues were nudged back into line (3:18, D 19). Even the serious danger of social division between the studious and the, for whatever reason, unlearned *am ha-aretz* was noted and somewhat inconsistently both opposed and accepted (2:5 and 6).

It need hardly be emphasized that the texts we have examined by no means exhaust the literary expression of the rabbinic praise of study.

But they are representative texts, from the central sources, and they continued to live on in the tradition: the Talmuds, haggadah, the prayer book and the elementary school tradition. [164]

Once we have isolated the phenomenon, several questions arise. Where did this high evaluation of Torah study come from? Does it stem directly from the Old Testament, and if so, from where in the Old Testament? Or does it only emerge in the intertestamental period, as a result of contact with Hellenistic culture? Did this religious ideal exist at the time of Jesus and Paul, or did it first emerge in its fullness after the debacle of A.D. 66-73? If it existed before A.D. 70, was it shared by other movements within Judaism, or was it a peculiarity of the sect called Pharisees? These questions will occupy us in the next chapter.

---

[164] For a more wide-ranging (both textually and chronologically) selection of texts, see C. J. Montefiore and H. Loewe, *A rabbinic anthology* (New York: Schocken, 1938), chapters five and six, pp. 116-190, and the corresponding sections of Bialik and Ravnitzky's *Sefer ha-Aggada*. One might also consult the general index to the Soncino translation of the Babylonian Talmud, s.v. study, p. 399, and Torah, study of, pp. 426 f. A small collection of interesting passages is all that can be provided here. B. Shab 33b; 88a; j. Peah 1:1; b. Hul 43b; b. Nid 46; b. Sanh 111b; b. AZ 50b; b. BK 91a; b. Sotah 40a; b. Pes 50b; b. Men 99b; Sifre Deut, section 41, 48, 321.

CHAPTER TWO

THE BACKGROUND OF THE RABBINIC IDEAL OF TORAH-STUDY AS A FORM OF WORSHIP

The rabbinic ideal of Torah study as one of the highest religious values arose as one possible development of the religion of the Old Testament. In this chapter we will attempt to trace the main lines of that development, insofar as they are recoverable. There are gaps in the story. We wish, for example, we knew more in detail about the positive influences of Hellenism upon the religious thought of Israel after 333 B.C., since the books of the Maccabees, while themselves betraying Hellenistic influences (esp. 4 Macc.), are primarily concerned with narrating the heroic resistance of a faithful remnant in Judea to total assimilation to the Hellenistic cultural wave and thus hardly emphasize the partial, healthy assimilation of Hellenism. We will seek the traces of this development in the Old Testament, Hebrew and Greek, the pseudepigraphic writings, the rule of the Qumran community, Philo, and Josephus.

On the other hand, our presentation of the materials intends to be selective and representative rather than exhaustive here, since our primary concern is not with the origins of the Aboth ideal itself so much as with the New Testament reaction, positive and negative, to it.

Old Testament

I. Historical Books. Perhaps the oldest source for the rabbinic line of thought about the importance of Torah is the book of Deuteronomy. (Some of the prophetic texts may be older still, but they are less clear, as we shall see.) We read, for example, in the eloquent hortatory formula of Deut 4:5 and 6:

> Behold, I have taught (*limmadtti*) you statutes and ordinances, as the Lord my God commanded me, that you should do them in the land which you are entering to take possession of it. Keep them and do them; for that will be your wisdom (*ḥŏkmatkem*) and your understanding (*bînatkem*) in the sight of the peoples, who, when they hear all these statutes, will say, "Surely this great nation is a wise (*ḥakam*) and understanding (*nabôn*) people."

Here the laws are singled out as the peculiar glory of the Israelites, their distinctive mark, while the law is virtually identified with wisdom, and the ideal of a learned people is set forth.

But sociohistorically more revealing than isolated texts are texts which were taken up into the daily liturgy of the synagogue and so lived in the popular imagination in a special way. Such are the texts which make up the *Shema*[c], the recitation of Dt 6:4-9. [1] Here we find (Dt 6:6) the command to memorize the law and to teach it.

> And these words which I command you this day shall be upon your heart [that is, learn it by heart]; and you shall teach (*shinnanttam*, literally, "repeat") them diligently to your children, and shall talk of them when you sit in your house, and when you walk by the way, and when you lie down, and when you rise.

Von Rad comments: "The demands made in vv. 6-9 attract attention by the intensity of their spirituality, and also by a certain intellectualization. For here the concern with Moses' words appears already almost as an end in itself, as something which ought to claim the whole of a man's mental and spiritual powers and to occupy him completely." [2]

These verses are perhaps the most ancient, in any case, certainly the most influential, source of the learned rabbinical tradition. [3]

---

[1] The synagogue's origins are commonly set at the time of the exile, though this remains somewhat uncertain. See W. Schrage, s.v. *synagōge*, TDNT, 7, pp. 798-852 and the literature there cited, to which add Kurt Hruby, "La synagogue dans la littérature rabbinique," *L'orient syrien* 9 (1964): 473-514. The origins of the Shema[c] prayer and the evolution of its components is likewise disputed. The opinion of Ludwig Blau is commonly followed: the first two sections, which arose out of the public reading of Torah which goes back to Ezra (Neh 8:8, 18), go back same time before Antiochus Epiphanes (reigned 175-164 B.C.). These consist of Dt 6:4-9 and Dt 11:13-21 (at least; the Decalogue was also included before the rise of the Christian movement (j. Ber 1:8; b. Ber 12a)). The third passage (Num 15:37-41) was probably added in the period of Roman rule. See L. Blau, "Origine et histoire de la lecture du Schema," *Revue des études juives* 31 (1895): 181-201, followed by, e.g., C. W. Dugmore, *The Influence of the Synagogue upon the Divine Office* (London: Faith, 1964²), pp. 16-22, and H. H. Rowley, *Worship in Ancient Israel* (Philadelphia: Fortress, 1967), p. 234. See further Strack-Billerbeck, *Kommentar...*, IV, ninth excursus, Das Shema[c], pp. 189-207, esp. p. 191.

[2] *Deuteronomy: a commentary* (Philadelphia: Westminster, 1966), p. 64. Note further the word translated "teach" in v. 7 from the root *šanah*, to repeat, to memorize, (later) to learn the *Mishnah*. Inner-Deuteronomic parallels may be noted at 11:19; 31:10-13.

[3] On the profound influence of the *Shema*[c] and its early exegesis (M. Ber 9:5) on the structure of Matthew's gospel, see the remarkable series of articles referred to and summarized in B. Gerhardsson, "Du Judéo-christianisme à Jésus par le Shema[c]," in *Judéo-christianisme* (Mélanges Daniélou; Paris: Recherches de science religieuse, 1972), pp. 23-36. In emphasizing the antiquity and influence of Deuteronomy, we do not intend to exclude the possibility of wisdom influence on the composition and

At this point we might mention another liturgical text, doubtless much later in date but joined to the preceding in the worship of the synagogue. In the Shemoneh Esreh (Eighteen Benedictions), recited daily (with some variations) by the devout, this deuteronomic thirst for knowledge finds renewed expression. The fourth blessing runs (in the Palestinian recention recovered from the Cairo Geniza): "O favor us, our Father, with knowledge from Thyself, and understanding and discernment from Thy Torah. Blessed art Thou, O Lord, gracious Giver of knowledge." [4]

Note finally that in Deuteronomy, as generally in the Old Testament, there is no technical terminology for learning activity. The verb root *lamad* (*Qal*, learn, study; *Piel*, teach) is used frequently enough but the derivative noun *talmid* (student, learner, disciple) only once (1 Ch 25:8), and the noun *melamed* (teacher) twice (Prov 5:13; Ps 119:99) in the Hebrew canon of the Scriptures. [5]

Rather, v. 7 supposes that father teaches son, and these terms, father and son, continue to express the teacher-pupil relationship not only in

---

thought of Deuteronomy itself. Recently the tracing of such influence has become an important part of Deuteronomic studies. See especially Moshe Weinfeld, *Deuteronomy and the Deuteronomic School* (Oxford: Clarendon, 1972), pp. 244-319, and for its "didacticism," pp. 298-306. For earlier literature on this subject, see the list in J. W. McKay, "Man's love for God in Deuteronomy and the father/teacher son/pupil relationship," VT 22 (1972): 426-435, n. 2.

[4] Reprinted from Schechter in Dugmore, *op. cit.*, appendix. See further Strack-Billerbeck, IV, tenth excursus, pp. 208-249.

[5] Actually the root *lamad* is of medium frequency. It occurs in verbal forms eighty times in the Hebrew Old Testament, as well as six times in the nominal form *limmud*. In four of these six instances, *limmud* can have the meaning *taught* or *disciple* (Is 8:16, 50:4 (bis), 54:13). The noun *melamed* (teacher) is also recorded in Sirach 51:17 as preserved in the 11 Q Psalm scroll. See Vattioni, *Ecclesiastico*, p. 281. The New American Bible is the first English Bible to take this important reading into account. The verbal instances of *lamad* are found primarily in four books: Psalms (24 times, esp. in Ps 119), Deuteronomy (17 times), Jeremiah (14 times), Isaiah (12 times). Cf. S. Mandelkern, *V.T. Concordantia*, p. 644.

Our knowledge of schools and education in biblical Israel remains imperfect. But schools there must have been. See G. von Rad, *Wisdom in Israel* (Nashville: Abingdon, 1972), p. 17, and the literature there cited. Also W. McKane, *Prophets and Wise Men* (London: SCM, 1966²), pp. 36 ff; Lorenz Dürr, *Das Erziehungswesen im Alten Testament und im antiken Orient* (Mitteilungen der Vorderasiatisch-aegyptischen Gesellschaft, 36. Bd., 2. Heft; Leipzig: Hinrichs, 1932); more briefly, R. de Vaux, *Ancient Israel* (New York: McGraw-Hill, 1961), pp. 48-50. A school (*beth hamidrash*) is mentioned only late (Sir 51:23). On "teacher" (*môreh* and *melammed*) in biblical Hebrew, see R. N. Whybray, *The Intellectual Tradition in the Old Testament* (BZAW, 135; Berlin: de Gruyter, 1974), pp. 45 ff, and, on the larger question, pp. 32-43.

8

Deuteronomy, but also in the wisdom literature and even into rabbinic times. The first school was undoubtedly the home. 6

At the beginning of the book of Joshua we find a striking and seminal text:

> This book of the law (*sepher-ha-torah*) shall not depart out of your mouth, but you shall meditate (hagitha) on it day and night (*yômam valaylah*), that you may be careful to do according to all that is written in it; for then you shall make your way prosperous, and then you shall have good success (Josh 1:8).

We note the following: (1) The entire verse has affinities with Psalm 1, a wisdom psalm (see below). This is especially evident in two common features: a) the use of the same rather uncommon verb *hagah* (meditate) in relation to Torah. This verbal root will reappear with greater emphasis in the somewhat mysterious Qumran "book of Hago"; b) that study should take place both *day and night* is also emphasized in Ps 1 and Qumran (see below); c) on the other hand, Josh 1:8 differs from Ps 1:2b in that while the latter speaks of meditating on Torah simply, Joshua speaks of meditating on "this *book* of the Torah," giving an impression of greater specificity and precision. (2) The final verb of the verse, translated "have good success" by RSV, is *taśkkîl* in the original, a word which could just as easily be translated "have insight, understanding," thus giving the verse an even stronger intellectual coloration. (3) For theological interpretation we can hardly hope to better J. A. Soggin's recent commentary:

> It is clear that in this passage we are rapidly tracing the course taken by postexilic Judaism, leading from the word of God to the identification of this word with the book, and then with the very letter of the book. But we must take care not to think at once, as is too often done, of a substitution of the book for the living word of God. Certainly this danger is always present in passages such as this; but we are faced here with something which rather resembles the *sola scriptura* of the Reformation, in the sense of a concrete basis, really and wholly in-carnate, but inspired by faith, and opposed to all romantic and mystical enthusiasm and to all human traditionalism. 7

---

6 Originally the father-son relationship in an instructional context was meant literally, according to H. W. Wolff, who imagines that one origin at least of the wisdom movement in Israel was the folk-wisdom of the clan (*Sippenweisheit*). See his *Amos the Prophet* (Philadelphia: Fortress, 1973). On Deuteronomy, see J. W. McKay, *art. cit.*, VT 22 (1972): 426-435. Later the terms became stereotyped and metaphorical only (e.g., Prov 1:8, 10; 2:1; 3:1). On rabbinic usage, see G. Schrenk, s.v. *patēr*, TDNT, V, pp. 977 f.

7 J. A. Soggin, *Joshua, a commentary* (Philadelphia: Westminster, 1972), p. 32.

Moving rapidly now through the historical books of the Old Testament, we pause briefly at the book of Ezra. The rabbinic movement traces its biblical origins particularly back to Ezra the Scribe (Ab 1:1). In chapter seven of the book which bears his name, Ezra is described by King Artaxerxes (in v. 14) as having *the law* of God in his hand (in Aramaic *bedat ʾelahak di bîdak*). In v. 25 of the same chapter he is said to have the wisdom of God in his hand (*kehakmat ʾelahak di bîdak*). But how can one have the wisdom of God in one's hand? Only by identifying the wisdom of God with the Torah given to Moses. It seems then that this identification was already made by the Jews in the third or even the fourth century B.C., if not already in Deuteronomy, then certainly here in Ezra, even though it is often said that Jesus ben Sirach (180 B.C.) was the first to make this crucial identification. Thus in Greek Sirach (the Hebrew is wanting here) we read (24:23): "All this (viz., wisdom) is the book of the covenant of the Most High God, the law which Moses commanded us as an inheritance for the congregations of Jacob." We see in all this a convergence of several currents of Old Testament thought: the priestly legal tradition, the scribal wisdom tradition, and even the prophetic tradition.

II. The *prophets* too, it seems, were interested in teaching and applying law, in raising up disciples (the "sons of the prophets," who formed prophetic guilds), and in increasing wisdom. Let two texts suffice. In Hosea 4:6 a b we read: "My people are destroyed for lack of knowledge; because thou hast rejected knowledge, I will also reject thee, that thou shalt be no priest to me." The context (4:1-10) gives us the picture of a controversy or lawsuit (*rib*) of God with his people. He first charges the inhabitants of the land (4:1-3). Among the charges is lack of the knowledge of God (v. 1) and the abuses listed (in v. 2) indicate that this knowledge is primarily moral in scope. But because of the sound principle enunciated (in v. 9), "like people, like priest," his real contention is with the priests (vv. 4-6), as well as with the professional prophets (v. 5). God's people perish for lack of knowledge (*daʿat*, v. 6 a), and from the parallel (in 6 c) we see that this knowledge is equivalent to the (written: so Wolff) Torah. The charge having been proven, the verdict follows inevitably, and is stated in talion-fashion: "because you have rejected knowledge, I reject you from being a priest to me." Here Hosea appeals to the early tribal ideal of priesthood (May), a high ideal of a "priesthood of knowledge" (G. A. Smith), that is, a priesthood which finds its chief glory in instructing the people in the loving service of God, and in fulfillment of their moral duties to their neighbors, rather than in an exploitation of popular superstition and pettifogging rubricism. As André Neher has well said: "Les prêtres ne sont pas attaqués par les prophètes parce qu'ils sont prêtres, mais parce qu'ils ne le sont plus." The truth of this remark is (even more) strikingly verified in a passage from Malachi. [8]

Our second prophetic text comes from the end of the prophetic era: "For the lips of a priest should guard knowledge, and men should seek instruction (*torah*) from his mouth, for he is the messenger of the Lord of hosts" (Malachi 2:7). This verse occurs in the context of a critique of the priests (Mal 1:6-2:9), and gives the prophet's portrait of the ideal priest. Verses 4 to 8 are unusual in that they offer rare praise of Levi as patron and eponym of all priests; they are a kind of midrash on his name (cf. Dt 31:9-13; 33:8-11, esp. v. 10; Ezek 44:15-31, esp. v. 23). [9]

As is known, the name Malachi, which means "my messenger," may hide the identity of the prophet, who otherwise remains anonymous. But the rabbis and others since them have suggested that the author of the prophecy was none other than Ezra the Scribe, the great patron of the rabbinic tradition (b. Megillah 15 a, Soncino ed., p. 87). Though this suggestion is not generally accepted today, it does have its value. It points to the real kinship of concerns between Malachi and Ezra, especially the knowledge of Torah and the elimination of mixed marriages. [10] Whoever the author, our verse may be

---

[8] *L'essence du prophétisme* (1955), p. 295, cited in H. W. Wolff, *Hosea* (BK/AT, vol. 14/1; Neukirchen: Neukirchener Verlag, 1961), p. 97. Cf. further J. L. Mays, *Hosea. A Commentary* (Philadelphia: Westminster, 1969), pp. 68-70, and the old eloquent chapter 21 in G. A. Smith, *The Book of the Twelve Prophets* (New York: Doubleday, 1929[2]), pp. 347-359. On the knowledge of God in Hosea, see further J. L. McKenzie, "The knowledge of God in Hosea," JBL 74 (1955): 22-7; H. W. Wolff, " 'Wissen um Gott' bei Hosea als Urform von Theologie," *Ev. Theologie* 12 (1952/3): 533-54; reprinted in his *Gesammelte Studien zum Alten Testament* (Munich: Kaiser, 1964), pp. 182-205. On Torah, see G. Östborn, *Tora in the Old Testament* (Lund: Häken Ohlsom, 1945), and J. Jensen, *The Use of Tora by Isaiah* (CBQ Monograph Series, no. 3; Washington: CBAA, 1973).

[9] On the priesthood in Israel, see most recently the works by A. Cody, *A History of Old Testament Priesthood* (Rome: PBI, 1969; An. Bib., no. 35) and L. Sabourin, *Priesthood: a comparative study* (Leiden: Brill, 1973; Suppl. to *Numen*, 25).

[10] On the rabbis as heirs of the prophets, see the full discussion in W. D. Davies, "Reflexions on tradition: the Aboth revisited," *loc. cit.*, pp. 129-137; cf. also L. Finkelstein, *New Light from the Prophets* (London: Vallentine, Mitchell, 1969). While one need hardly agree with Finkelstein's rather alarming thesis in detail, there is no doubt that the prophets did sometimes act as teachers of Torah and were consulted by the people as such.

autobiographical in that it refers to the *maleach* (messenger, angel) of Yahweh (cf. 3:1 and Hag 1:13). Its point is that priests should be teachers; as such they are representatives (angels!) of God to the people. From this sacred charge their dignity derives. [11]

There can be no doubt that both prophetic texts, linked as they are by their placing knowledge and Torah in parallelism, boldly set forth the importance of learning, of Torah-knowledge, for both the religious leaders and for the people of Israel. By listing *da^cat* along with *^emet* and *ḥesed* (Hos 4:1; cf. Mal 2:6) and in a context of moral urgency, they make of knowledge a *religious* value of a high order, a part of the cure for the moral evil and decay of their day. In this they were undoubtedly forerunners of the rabbinic ideal.

III. Turning now to the *Wisdom literature* of the Old Testament, we are faced with several problems. One is methodological. In tracing the roots of the Aboth ideal in the Old Testament, and particularly in the Wisdom literature, how do we distinguish all those cases of using one's brains, e.g., proverbial folk wisdom, from a specific theological view, viz., that study of Torah is a *religious* duty of the highest importance, well pleasing to God, and thus a form of worship, even, so to speak, a condition of salvation? Only this latter would form a precise background and biblical basis for the scribal-rabbinic ideology of Aboth, a distinctly intellectualist strain. [12] If no such

---

11 G. A. Smith's comment, *The Book of the Twelve Prophets*, vol. II, pp. 352 f, while sermonic, retains its value: "What a remarkable saying from the legal age of Israel's religion, and from a writer who emphasizes the ceremonial law! In all prophecy there is none more in harmony with the prophetic ideal. How needed in our age!—against those two extremes from which we suffer, the limitation of the ideal of priesthood to the communication of a magic grace, and its evaporation in a vague religiosity from which reason is excluded as if perilous, worldly and devilish. 'Surrender of the intellect,' indeed! This is to bury the talent in the napkin, and still preached and practiced by men of one talent. Religion needs all the brains we mortals can put into it. There is a priesthood of knowledge, a priesthood of the intellect, says 'Malachi,' and he makes this part of God's covenant with Levi. Every priest of God is a priest of truth...."

12 Recently this problem has been taken up in a lucid and careful monograph by R. N. Whybray, *The Intellectual Tradition in the Old Testament*, to which we have already called attention (n. 5). We will depend heavily upon his work in this section. But we should note that the problem he poses is somewhat different from our own. His might be put in this way: present Old Testament studies attest to a fashion of finding "wisdom" influence everywhere in the Old Testament. Are there any objective criteria, asks Whybray, for distinguishing "wisdom" from every manifestation of the ability to use one's brains in ancient Israel (p. 3)? He then proceeds to establish such criteria, particularly the isolation of distinctively sapiential/intellectual terminology.

Having concluded in his second chapter that "there is no evidence in the Old Testament for the exitsence of a class of writers known as 'the wise men,' or indeed

distinction could be made, we would have to assign practically the
whole of the biblical wisdom literature to the proximate background
of the Aboth ideal, and this would not be very helpful. Another
problem we face in this section is of a historical character. Israel's
intellectual traditions modified the course of their development especially in reaction to two major historical challenges. The first took
the form of a response to the crisis of the exile and the return to
Judea under Persian hegemony. The second corresponded to the shift
in Israel's fortunes which occurred with the Greek conquest of Judea
under Alexander the Great. Though problems of dating texts remain,
we will attempt to distinguish between early and late wisdom texts
and to place a brief passage on the influence of Hellenism between
them.

Taking the words contained in the Hebrew canon as representative
of early wisdom texts, we may begin by noting that the root *ḥkm*
occurs 346 times (this includes the Aramaic equivalent in Daniel and
Ezra), of which Proverbs, Job and Ecclesiastes account for 189. These
books then are in a class by themselves, so far as wisdom literature
goes. Other words characteristic of this literature are: *bina, baʿar, kesil,
leṣ, leqah, nabon, sakal, ʿarum, tušiyya*—eight terms in all. [13]

> An examination of the vocabulary of Proverbs, Job and Ecclesiastes
> shows that these books ... contain a large number of words which refer
> to the problems of the individual and his place in society. This
> distinctive terminology comprises, in general terms, the following range
> of topics:
> i. Wisdom and folly; virtue and wickedness; human conduct in
> general.
> ii. The consequences of the possession of these qualities, e.g., pros-
> perity, happiness, friendship; disaster, poverty, punishment.
> iii. The search for knowledge and for prosperity: intelligence,
> knowledge, education, advice, thought, planning. [14]

It will be obvious from this broad description that the circle of
concerns characteristic of Israelite wisdom literature, while occasionally
evincing a rudimentary interest in the scientific classification of natural

---

of *any* class of men so designated" (p. 54), Whybray then proceeds (p. 55, n. 1)
to substitute the phrase "intellectual tradition" for "wisdom tradition," thereby replacing
one modern phrase with another. It is not at all clear to me how this helps to clarify
the discussion. Such a procedure has the disadvantage of using a non-biblical word to
designate biblical realities, and does not break free of the danger of circularity which
he admits (pp. 154 f) continues to bedevil the discussion.

[13] Whybray, *op. cit.*, pp. 142-49.
[14] *Ibid.*, pp. 122 f.

objects, [15] tends on the whole to have a practical, humanistic orientation, as ethical as Israelite monotheism.

Besides the three great collections in Job, Proverbs and Ecclesiastes, the characteristic vocabulary and circle of concerns of this tradition have been detected by Whybray in the following places in the Old Testament.

1. Gen 2 f. (possibly also 11:1-9);
2. Gen 37-50 (the Joseph story);
3. Dtn 1-4;
4. Dtn 32 (the Song of Moses);
5. II Sam 9-20 I Reg 1 f. (the Succession Narrative);
6. I Reg 3-11 (the History of Solomon);
7. Ps 1, 19:8-15, 37, 49, 51, 73, 90, 92, 94, 104, 107; 111, 119,
8. Isa 1-39, both in the genuine utterance of Isaiah and in a number of later additions and glosses;
9. Jer, also with some later additions and glosses;
10. Ez 28;
11. Dan;
12. 2 late additions or glosses to the Minor Prophets (Hos 14:10; Mi 6:9). [16]

We will not stay to examine all these texts but only a few characteristic passages. First, however, we should make the general point that the people of ancient Israel, by giving such a prominent place to wisdom books and themes in their religious literature, and thereby erecting wisdom into a high and central religious value, had already laid the groundwork for their later reputation as a wise, learned, studious and reflective body among the peoples of antiquity. [17]

---

[15] A. Alt, "Die Weisheit Salomos," *Kleine Schriften...* (Munich: Beck, 1959), vol. 2, pp. 90-99.

[16] Whybray, *op. cit.*, p. 154. On the number of wisdom psalms there is considerable variation and disagreement among specialists. See the survey of research and opinion in R. E. Murphy, "A consideration of the classification, 'Wisdom Psalms,'" *Suppl. VT* 9 (Leiden: Brill, 1963), pp. 156-67. He advances a short list of seven: 1, 32, 34, 37, 49, 112, 128, which agrees in only three cases with Whybray's list, viz., 1, 37, 49.

[17] To be sure, the Jews were also viewed by their neighbors as a proud, upstart, separatist little people with peculiar and even repugnant religious practices, as well as grievous political blunders and misfortunes. Cf. the material gathered in Menahem Stern, *Greek and Latin Authors on Jews and Judaism*, vol. I (Jerusalem: IASH, 1974). But they could not withhold their admiration from the Bible forever (cf. Pseudo-Longinus, *On the sublime*, Loeb edition with Aristotle, *Poetics*, ed. W. Hamilton Fyfe). Nor could they fail to be impressed by the kind of intellectual courage

Proverbs, chapters 1-9, is a wonderful collection of poetry every word of which is directed to the praise of wisdom. It is thus a kind of mighty manifesto at the gateway to this literature, including within itself most of the characteristic vocabulary and many of the themes of the tradition, while simultaneously subordinating the inheritance of international wisdom to a pure Yahwistic and even Deuteronomistic faith. A typical passage runs:

> 1My son, if you receive my words (ʾamarei)
>   and treasure up my commandments (mitzvotai) with you,
> 2making your ear attentive to wisdom (ḥokmah)
>   and inclining your heart to understanding (tebûnah);
> 3yes, if you cry out for insight (binah)
>   and raise your voice for understanding (tebûnah),
> 4if you seek for it like silver
>   and search for hidden treasures;
> 5then you will understand (tabîn) the fear of the Lord (yirʾat Yhvh)
>   and find the knowledge of God (daʿat elohim),
> 6For the Lord gives wisdom (ḥokmah);
>   from his mouth come knowledge (daʿat) and understanding
>   (tebûnah) (Prov 2:1-6).

Here we find a paternal invitation to wisdom in the form of a conditional sentence: if you seek wisdom, the wisdom of the commandments, then the highest spiritual goods are yours. In v. 6 ff. an explanatory rider gives the source of wisdom. In the protasis v. 1 uses terms which send us back to the Deuteronomic Torah, and in the following verses these are identified with, or are regarded as the content of, the main expressions of wisdom. The author(s) never tire of repeating these terms, though they arrange them in ever new combinations and reflect them with ever-varied metaphors (v. 4).

Another beautiful praise of wisdom in a different literary form, the makarism, is found in Prov 3:13-18:

> 13Happy is the man who finds wisdom,
>   and the man who gets understanding,
> 14for the gain from it is better than gain from silver
>   and its profit better than gold.
> 15She is more precious than jewels,
>   and nothing you desire can compare with her.

---

represented by the Hellenistic Judaism which came to expression most notably in the book of Wisdom and in the many works of Philo. These works reflect a capacity for mastering the best of Greek thought while keeping it in ethical and religious subordination to the heritage of Israel, a capacity matched in antiquity only by the Romans. See further below.

16Long life is in her right hand;
    in her left hand are riches and honor.
17Her ways are ways of pleasantness,
    and all her paths are peace.
18She is a tree of life to those who lay hold of her;
    those who hold her fast are called happy.

The passage is bounded by an *inclusio*: the first and last word is happy (*ʾasherē*). The point is plainly that wisdom is the highest human value. The synagogue was quick to seize upon the metaphor in verse 18a and apply it to Torah, though it harks back to the Garden of Gen 2-3. [18]

A peculiarity of some passages in this literature is the personification of wisdom as a heavenly being in terms which come dangerously close to mythology, but which very likely have an antimythological intent. That is, it has been suggested that this personification began as a syncretistic invasion of Near Eastern religions (Babylonian Astarte-Ishtar, Egyptian Maat, Greco-Egyptian Isis) and then was successively mastered and purified by biblical and postbiblical Jewish authors in such a way as to maintain the absolute sovereignty of Yahweh. Nevertheless, it can hardly be doubted that this wisdom-hypostasis contributed materially to the New Testament qualification of Israelite (especially Deutero-Isaianic) monotheism, a qualification whose later doctrinal precipitate was the doctrine of the Divine Trinity. [19] The significance of these personifications for the New Testament is more Christological than intellectual and scholastic, yet the two currents cannot be altogether disentangled since there exists the possibility of a Wisdom Christology

---

[18] See the prayer in the Siddur as the scrolls are returned to the ark, e.g., the *Prayer book*, ed. B. Z. Bokser (New York: Hebrew Publishing Co., 1961), p. 74. It should be noted, however, that this prayer does not occur in the oldest known Jewish prayerbook, *Seder R. Amram Gaon*, Part I, ed. David Hedegard (Lund: Lindstedts, 1951), p. 183.

[19] See, out of the enormous literature, G. Boström, *Proverbiastudien: die Weisheit und das fremde Weib in Spr. 1-9* (Lund: Gleerup, 1935); H. Ringgren, *Word and Wisdom* (Lund: Gleerup, 1947); W. F. Albright, "Canaanite-Phoenician Sources of the Hebrew Wisdom," *Suppl. VT* 3 (1955), pp. 1-15; W. L. Knox, "The Divine Wisdom," JTS 38 (1937): 230-237; *idem, Paul and the Church of the Gentiles* (Cambridge: U.P., 1939), pp. 55-89; R. N. Whybray, *Wisdom in Proverbs* (London: SCM, 1965), SBT, no. 45; H. Conzelmann, "The Mother of Wisdom," in *The Future of our Religious Past* (Bultmann-Fs.) (New York: Harper, 1971), pp. 23-43; B. L. Mack, *Logos und Sophia* (Göttingen: Vandenhoeck & Ruprecht, 1973), *Studien zur Umwelt des N. T.*, 10; also the commentaries, works to be cited further on, and Fohrer-Wilckens, s.v. *sophia* in TDNT, 7, pp. 465-528; note esp. the neglected article by R. M. Grant," "The Book of Wisdom at Alexandria," *After the New Testament* (Philadelphia: Fortress, 1967), pp. 70-82.

in the New Testament. Such a Christology could provide the highest possible support for the kind of school activity which especially interests us.

Personifications of wisdom in the proto-canonical literature occurs especially in Proverbs 1:20-33; 8; and Job 28. The first text presents Wisdom as a woman who preaches in public places:

> 20Wisdom cries aloud in the street;
>   in the markets she raises her voice;
> 21on the top of the walls she cries out;
>   at the entrance of the city gates she speaks:
> 22How long, O simple ones, will you love being simple?
>   How long will scoffers delight in their scoffing and fools hate
>   knowledge...?

Because the simple reject the invitation which Lady Wisdom extends to them, they will suffer dire consequences:

> 29Because they hated knowledge
>   and did not choose the fear of the Lord,
> 30would have none of my counsel,
>   and despised all my reproof,
> 31therefore they shall eat the fruit of their way
>   and be sated with their own devices.
> 32For the simple are killed by their turning away,
>   and the complacence of fools destroys them;
> 33but he who listens to me will dwell secure
>   and will be at ease, without dread of evil.

We notice at once that rejection of evil is described as hatred of knowledge (śanᵓû daᶜat), strong language. This is evidently the great sin, as neglect-contempt of Torah (beṭul Torah) will be for the rabbis later. As yet there is no eschatological punishment for folly; vice is its own punishment. The killing and destroying mentioned in v. 32 are not further specified. Recently the purity of this passage as a wisdom text has been called into question. Distinctly prophetic features of rebuke and threatening have been detected. We have here then a mixed form, suggesting that this is a transitional text in the development from prophetic to scribal and then to later rabbinic literature. [20] As background to Prov. 1 we may discern (at least indirectly) the following

---

[20] On the address's character as prophetic *Schelt-und Mahnpredigt*, see Christa Kayatz, *Studien zu Proverbien 1-9*, WMzANT, no. 22 (Neukirchen-Vluyn: Neukirchener Verlag, 1966), pp. 119-122, and the further discussion in Felix Christ, *Jesus-Sophia*, ATANT, no. 57 (Zurich: Zwingli, 1970), pp. 16-23.

typically sapiential thoughts: Wisdom calls the simple, the scoffers and the foolish to herself, but finds no hearing and announces her disappearance (v. 28). Only a few chosen souls listen to her (v. 33). [21]

In chapter 8 of Proverbs, a more elaborate and complex hypostatic text, the introduction remains familiar:

> 1Does not wisdom call,
>   does not understanding raise her voice?
> 2On the heights beside the way,
>   in the paths she takes her stand;
> 3beside the gates in front of the town,
>   at the entrance of the portals she cries aloud:
> 4To you, O men, I call,
>   and my cry is to the sons of men.
> 5O simple ones, learn prudence (*ᶜarmah*);
>   O foolish men, pay attention.

After a brief command to listen (6a) there follows a lengthy self-recommendation of wisdom (6b-31), of which the most remarkable part is a self-legitimation by means of a reference to wisdom's age and experience (22-31). The chapter concludes with a renewed invitation (32-36) containing two makarisms. [22] Once again, wisdom is asserted to be the highest value, in the plainest terms:

> 11for wisdom is better than jewels,
>   and all that you may desire cannot compare with her.
> 35For he who finds me finds life
>   and obtains favor from the Lord;

Yet it is not said that wisdom is a gift of God; it is directly accessible to the diligent man:

> 17I love those who love me,
>   and those who seek me diligently find me.

The implication remains that only a few seek. Moreover, the accessibility of wisdom suggested in v. 17 may not be taken to mean that wisdom is independent of God. Verse 22 makes that clear enough:

> 22The Lord created [or: acquired; *qanani*] me at the beginning
>   [*reᵓšit*] of his work,
>   the first of his acts of old.

On the other hand, we may question the literary unity of the chapter. If, as has been suggested, verses 22-31 were originally a separate

---

21 See Christ, *op. cit.*, p. 23.
22 Compare the analysis in Christ, *op. cit.*, p. 24.

hymn, we may then distinguish between verses 1-21, which possess a general sapiential-religious character wherein Yahweh (except for 13a) does not figure, and verses 22-31 which praise Yahweh's wisdom.

Job 28 contrasts man's search for precious metals and stones through mining with the quest for wisdom. Wisdom is elusive and unpurchasable, hidden from the eyes of all living (v. 21). Only "God understands the way to it, and he knows its place. For he looks to the ends of the earth, and sees everything under the heavens. When he gave to the wind its weight and meted out the waters by measure; when he made a decree for the rain, and a way for the lightning of the thunder; then he saw it and declared it; he established it, and searched it out" (vv. 23-27). That is, God's wisdom is revealed in his creation, yet it cannot be grasped. The world does not reveal the mystery of its order. The deep resignation of this poem was unbearable to a later editor, who added verse 28:

> And he said to man, "Behold, the fear of the Lord, that is wisdom;
> and to depart from evil is understanding."

This maxim leads man abruptly from cosmological speculations to ethical questions which are more within his ken. This sudden shift in meaning at the end of the poem "no doubt impairs its ancient grandeur, but it is obviously dictated by a pastoral concern—thou too, O man, hast a portion in the divine wisdom: thy wisdom is the fear of God." [24]

Turning now to some wisdom psalms, we find an interesting example in Ps 111, an acrostic.

> 1Praise the Lord.
>   I will give thanks to the Lord with my whole heart, in the company
>   of the upright, in the congregation.
> 2Great are the works of the Lord,
>   studied (drûshim) by all who have pleasure in them.
> 3Full of honor and majesty is his work,
>   and his righteousness endures for ever.
> 4He has caused his wonderful works to be remembered;
>   the Lord is gracious and merciful.
> 5He provides food for those who fear him;
>   he is ever mindful of his covenant.
> 6He has shown his people the power of his works,

23 Christ, op. cit., p. 26.

24 G. von Rad, Old Testament Theology, vol. 1 (Edinburgh: Oliver & Boyd, 1963), pp. 446 f; idem, Wisdom in Israel (Nashville: Abingdon, 1972), pp. 145-149.

in giving them the heritage of the nations.
7The works of his hands are faithful and just;
    all his precepts (*piqqûdayw*) are trustworthy,
8they are established for ever and ever,
    to be performed with faithfulness and uprightness.
9He sent redemption (*pidut*) to his people;
    he has commanded (*tziwwah*) his covenant (*britô*) for ever.
10The fear of the Lord is the beginning of wisdom;
    a good understanding (*śekel*) have all those who practice it.
    His praise endures for ever!

This psalm amazes us by its capacity to combine themes and tendencies of Israel's various religious inheritances with the greatest ease and naturalness while maintaining its artificial acrostic form and a diction which remains poetically free to express conventional ideas in less common words and to express less conventional ideas in common biblical phrases. The obvious central focus of the psalm is the praise of God in his *works* (vv. 2, 3, 4, 6, 7, employing three terms: *maᶜaśeh, pōᶜal, niphleʾot*). What is important for us is the nature of these works and the appropriate reaction to them. The works are redemption (v. 9), the gift of the land (v. 6b), the material blessings of creation (v. 5), the covenant (vv. 5 and 9), and finally his precepts (v. 7), the commandments contained in the covenant (v. 9). One could almost speak of an escalating particularization, a movement from praise for creation to praise for Torah, the movement which characterizes the evolution of rabbinic Judaism from the religion of the Old Testament. And what is the appropriate response to God's works? Study (*darash*, v. 2). At the end (v. 10), the link up with the wisdom tradition is unambiguously established by the citation of a cliché which is then immediately interpreted in terms of righteous, presumably Torah-true, deeds. All in all, a striking anticipation of the Aboth ideal. 25

Psalm 112 is closely connected with the preceding Ps 111, but also with the introduction to the entire book of Psalms, Ps 1.

1Praise the Lord.
    Blessed is the man who fears the Lord,
    who greatly delights in his commandments!
2His descendants will be mighty in the land;
    the generation of the upright will be blessed.
3Wealth and riches are in his house;

---

25 The suspicion that v. 10 is a late addition may be overcome by two considerations: (a) the acrostic structure includes this verse, (b) v. 10c forms an *inclusio* with v. 1a.

and his righteousness endures for ever.
4Light rises in the darkness for the upright;
   the Lord is gracious, merciful, and righteous.
5It is well with the man who deals generously and lends,
   who conducts his affairs with justice.
6For the righteous will never be moved;
   he will be remembered for ever.
7He is not afraid of evil things;
   his heart is firm, trusting in the Lord.
8His heart is steady, he will not be afraid,
   until he sees his desire on his adversaries.
9He has distributed freely, he has given to the poor;
   his righteousness endures for ever;
   his horn is exalted in honor.
10The wicked man sees it and is angry;
   he gnashes his teeth and melts away;
   the desire of the wicked man comes to nought.

With Ps 111 it has in common its acrostic structure, its introductory
Hallelu-Ya and its opening emphasis on fear of the Lord (cf. Ps
111:10a). With Ps 1 it shares an introductory makarism and its
structuring contrast between the righteous man and the wicked, though
the balance is not so even here, since the wicked man only comes at
the last verse. But most important for us, and this too it shares with
Ps 1, is the delight in the commandments (*be-mitzvotai ḥafetz meʾod*),
a first glimmer of the much later rabbinic Simḥat Torah, the festival
of rejoicing in the Torah.

Psalms 1
1Blessed is the man
   who walks not in the counsel of the wicked,
   nor stands in the way of sinners,
   nor sits in the seat of scoffers;
2but his delight is in the law of the Lord,
   and on his law he meditates day and night.
3He is like a tree
   planted by streams of water,
that yields its fruit in its season,
   and its leaf does not wither.
In all that he does, he prospers.
4The wicked are not so,
   but are like chaff which the wind drives away.
5Therefore the wicked will not stand in the judgment,
   nor sinners in the congregation of the righteous;
6For the Lord knows the way of the righteous,
   but the way of the wicked will perish.

Here we find an almost perfect diptych, contrasting not the wise and the foolish, but the righteous (defined only indirectly in vv. 1-3, and mentioned finally only in v. 5) and the wicked. The obvious emphasis of the psalm is ethical; wisdom is never mentioned. And yet the description of the righteous man in v. 2 has unmistakably late and sapiential, not to say proto-rabbinic, overtones as well as ancient roots. The Torah of the Lord is explicitly mentioned in both halves of the verse; in it the righteous man finds his delight (ḥeftzô) and it provides the subject of both his diurnal and nocturnal meditations (yehggeh). We have already met the theme of day and night study in Deuteronomy and Joshua, and will meet it again in Qumran. 26

Apart from these hints, there exist in the psalter outright Torah songs, songs in praise of Torah, which have never been exceeded in their esteem for it, namely, Ps 19:7-14 (HT vv. 8-15) and Ps 119. Ps 119 is far too long to cite in its entirety (176 verses), but part of Ps 19 may be quoted to give the flavor of both. It contributes a new sensuous metaphor, v. 10b, and, like 119, uses many terms to refer to the one central reality, Torah.

> 7The law of the Lord is perfect,
>   reviving the soul;
>   the testimony of the Lord is sure,
>   making wise the simple;
> 8the precepts of the Lord are right,
>   rejoicing the heart (meśammḥe leb);
>   the commandment of the Lord is pure,
>   enlightening the eyes;
> 9the fear of the Lord is clean, enduring for ever;
>   the ordinances of the Lord are true, and righteous altogether.
> 10More to be desired are they than gold,
>   even much fine gold;
>   sweeter also than honey
>   and drippings of the honeycomb.

In this Psalm many later rabbinic themes are distinctly adumbrated: simḥat Torah (rejoicing in the Torah, v. 8), the law as perfect (temimah, v. 7), and human moral perfection consisting in integral observance of Torah (v. 13, "blameless," ʾeitam), the importance of meditation (hegyôn), v. 14. We are on the threshold of another era.

---

26 The striking parallel to vv. 1-3 in Jer 17:7 f ("Blessed is the man who trusts in the Lord, whose trust is the Lord. He is like a tree planted by water, that sends out its roots by the stream, and does not fear when heat comes, for its leaves remain green, and is not anxious in the year of drought, for it does not cease to bear fruit.") raises

Hellenism and the Later Wisdom Books

This new era dawned as a result of the partial, gradual Hellenization of Israel. The decisive date in this regard is the conquest of Syria and Palestine by the Macedonian military genius, Alexander the Great, in 332 B.C., though the influence of Hellenism was making itself felt in the Levant even before this time, particularly in Phoenicia and Egypt. Jewish mercenary soldiers were perhaps the first to have contact with the powerful alien culture to any great degree, and these contacts multiplied when the Greeks replaced the Persians as the masters of the Eastern Mediterranean world. For a long time the interaction between the two cultures was generally peaceful. Only after a century of Hellenistic domination did a serious crisis arise, when the Seleucid king Antiochus IV and Epiphanes attempted a too hasty and forcible Hellenization of the Judean temple state. This forced program provoked the Maccabean revolt in 166 B.C. under Mattathias and at the same time led to a conscious rejection of many elements of Hellenism by the most zealous religious leaders of the Jews, especially a repudiation of the greatest cultural vehicle of the Greeks, the gymnasium (2 Macc 4:9-17). But by then much in traditional Israelite life had already changed. During the preceding years of peace Hellenistic culture had unobtrusively affected many aspects of the higher life of the Jewish state. 27

---

the following questions: Is there literary dependence of one upon the other? This is quite possible, despite some differences of vocabulary and in the shaping of the metaphor. For example, the makarism in each is worded differently: Ps 1: ʾasherei, Jer 17: baruch. This particular difference need not be decisive since it is not yet clear that the biblical language made any sharp distinction in these words when applied to men; cf. TDNT, s.v. eulogeo and makarios, and, for a New Testament example of non-differentiation, see Lk 1:42 and 45. Granting some dependence, which text is prior? It seems certain that the Jeremiah text is earlier; the makarism is more general, there is no mention of Torah study, the metaphor is more carefully worked out and even psychologized, and the verses are inserted into an ancient covenant framework of curses and blessings which comprises vv. 5-8. Ps 1:1-3 bears every sign of having reworked this simple combination of makarism and metaphor into a longer contrast, compressing the metaphor, and inserting v. 2., which has no parallel in Jeremiah, as a proto-rabbinic concretion.

27 It is entirely possible that some of the Psalms we have just considered were composed in Maccabean times but it seems impossible to date them precisely beyond any cavil, and on balance it has seemed best to treat them with other works of the Hebrew biblical canon, reserving for this section deuterocanonical works such as Sirach and the Wisdom of Solomon, which can be dated more securely.

For the period under consideration, from ca. 332 B.C. to about 63 B.C., the most reliable guides are Elias Bickerman, *From Ezra to the Last of the Maccabees* (New York: Schocken, 1962) and Martin Hengel, *Judaism and Hellenism*, 2 vols. (London: SCM, 1974).

The Greek influence on Judaism in the centuries up to the debacle of A.D. 66-73 may be summarized in the following points.

1. Hellenistic civilization represented the supreme spiritual challenge to the religion of Israel. It thereby provoked a heroic response, both spiritual and politico-military. This response, with that of the Romans, was unique in antiquity, and successfully preserved Judaism from simple absorption into Hellenistic civilization. The parties within Judaism which rose to the Greek challenge, first the Hasidim, later the Pharisees and Essenes, succeeded because they possessed the spiritual dynamism selectively to adapt elements from the treasure of Hellenism without being mastered by them. Judaism had to change itself from within to survive.

2. Perhaps the most important effect of Hellenism was to force the Jews into a program of universal popular education, at least on the elementary level. Hellenism did not create the synagogue with its annexed house of studies, but it probably led to the development of the synagogue in a particular direction, a direction it might not otherwise have taken. If the intellectually curious youth could not go to the gymnasium and the ephebeion, they had to go somewhere. The synagogue (bet ha-midrash, yeshivah) had to become the rival of the gymnasium. The Jews were led into the so-called Socratic error that virtue was knowledge, vice, ignorance in the peculiar form: Salvation for our people from the Greek threat will consist in the study of Torah. But before them many Greeks had elevated Hellenistic culture into the equivalent of a religion. [28]

3. Bickerman has suggested that the Pharisaic belief in the resurrection of the human body together with the related belief in an eschatological reckoning as a solution to the problem of evil derived from Hellenistic, more precisely Platonic, doctrines of the afterlife. Though he fails to distinguish sufficiently between the Greek expectation of the immortality of the soul, which presupposes a psychological dualism, and the Pharisaic hope in a resurrection of the body, i.e., the person, which presupposes a psychological monism biblical in origin, there can be no doubt that this Pharisaic doctrine marks a major break with Israel's past religious beliefs in this regard. That its emergence was at least encouraged by Hellenic views is also quite likely. Yet both its probable dependence on Hellenism and its charact-

---

[28] Cf. Bickerman, op. cit., pp. 160-165; Hengel, Judaism..., pp. 79, 81 f; H. I. Marrou, The History of Education in Antiquity (New York: Sheed and Ward, 1956), p. 100 f.

eristically bold independence (resurrection of the *body*) should be given equal weight. The doctrine of resurrection in fact is a perfect example of how Judaism was both deeply influenced by Hellenism and yet remained fundamentally true to her own deepest heritage. [29]

4. Another area in which the Pharisees certainly differed from the Sadducees was their acceptance of an oral Torah (*Torah shel be-ᶜal peh*) alongside the written Torah. Bickerman [30] suggests that this important difference derived from the Pharisees' borrowing the Greek concept of the "unwritten law" (*agraphos nomos*), but the differences between the Pharisaic and Greek understandings and applications of these concepts are so great as to make any dependence doubtful. The Greek unwritten law is related to the quest for a natural law or universal elementary ethics, whereas the oral Torah of the Pharisees was a precisely formulated collection of customary and sectarian regulations especially concerned with matters of ritual purity.

5. With Sirach, classically Hebrew in other respects, the personality of the individual wisdom teacher begins to emerge, this in striking contrast to Qohelet, who hides behind both a code name and the eponymous figure of Solomon. This emergent individualism, so characteristic of the Hellenistic age, continues in the traditions and anecdotes handed down about the individual Pharisaic and rabbinic teachers, though, to be sure, these traditions never develop into full blown biographies, except in the New Testament itself.

---

[29] Within Plato, note the following: (1) deep uncertainty about immortality at the end of the *Apology*; (2) strong affirmation of immortality in the *Phaedo*; (3) a last judgment depicted at the end of the *Gorgias*. Aristotle remains tentative, at least about *individual* immortality, in Book III of the *De anima*. For Old Testament beliefs, O. S. Rankin's presentation in chapters 5 to 8 of his *Israel's Wisdom Literature* (New York: Schocken, 1969) remains outstanding and sound, even after the challenge by M. Dahood in *Psalms* (The Anchor Bible; New York: Doubleday, 1970), vol. II, pp. 41-52, with respect esp. to Pss. 16, 17, 49, and 73. Rankin holds that the primary impulse behind a belief in resurrection was Iranian, not Greek, *op. cit.*, pp. 136-45. On later Judaism see two recent works: G. W. E. Nickelsburg, Jr., *Resurrection, Immortality, and Eternal Life in Intertestamental Judaism* (HTS, 26; Cambridge, Mass.: Harvard, 1972), and G. Stemberger, *Der Leib der Auferstehung* (An. Bib., 56; Rom: Biblical Institute, 1972). It may be noted that the relevant verse Acts 23:8 should probably be translated in the following way: "The Sadducees maintain that there is no resurrection, either in the sense of the survival of the body as an angel [the main Pharisaic and Christian view] or in the sense of the immortality of the soul [the Platonic view], but the Pharisees maintain them *both* (*amphotera*)." This is quite accurate, since some books accepted by the Pharisees, like Daniel (12:2), teach a resurrection, while others, of a more pronounced Hellenistic stripe, like the Wisdom of Solomon (3:4; 4:1; 15:3) and apparently 4 Maccabees (18:23) hold a doctrine of immortality attained immediately after death.

[30] *Op. cit.*, p. 163.

6. Connected with the preceding point, we note the development of an intimate master-disciple relationship at least partially based on Greek models (Rengstorf, TDNT, 4, 439-41). Among the rabbis there arises a dialectical form of instruction almost Socratic in character. Scribes enter the realm of public affairs as a group (1 Macc 7:12). [31]

7. The emerging sects or parties in Palestinian Judaism become assimiliated, at least in the mind of Josephus, to the prevailing Greek philosophical schools. Thus the Pharisees are sometimes compared with the Pythagoreans, most often with the Stoics, in which case the Essenes are associated with the Pythagoreans. The Sadduccees are in any case linked with the Epicureans, though not by Josephus himself. [32]

8. There is some affinity between the unhistorical allegorical interpretations of Greek literary classics, especially the Homeric epics, by Stoic philosophers and Alexandrian literary critics and the equally unhistorical though often more legally oriented rabbinic hermeneutics of the Bible. [33]

9. The most obvious and remarkable result of the confluence of Judaism and Hellenism is the creation of a large body of Jewish literature in Greek, both translations of Semitic originals and the composition of original works. This literature begins with the Septuagint, and proceeds through the letter of Aristeas, the Wisdom of Solomon, the novella of Joseph and Asenath and culminates in Philo, Josephus, and the New Testament. With the catastrophe of A.D. 70 this epoch in Jewish intellectual history comes to a close, surviving only in the emergent Christian movement which preserves the works of Philo who becomes the father of the Fathers. [34]

10. As the Jews became more and more successful in this cultural and especially religious competition with the Greco-Roman world, they were emboldened to undertake a considerable diaspora mission, primarily to retain the allegiance of their own young men, tempted as they were to full assimilation, but with the side effect of drawing many serious-minded pagans, especially those who admired the com-

---

[31] See Hengel, *Judaism...*, ch. 2, Excursus 1: The development of the Jewish school, pp. 78-83 and the literature there cited.

[32] Jos. *Vita* 12; B.J. 2:119-166; Ant. 13:171-173; 15:371; 18:11. Cf. Billerbeck, *Kommentar*, 4, 334-352 (excursus 14).

[33] D. Daube, HUCA 22 (1949): 239-64. S. Lieberman, *Hellenism in Jewish Palestine* (New York: JTSA, 1962), pp. 47-82, esp. 53 ff. Further literature in Hengel, *Judaism...*, II, p. 55, n. 180.

[34] Bousset-Gressmann, *Religion des Judentums*, fourth ed. (Tübingen: Mohr, 1966), pp. 16-47; Hengel, *Judaism...*, vol. I, pp. 88-102, 110-114.

paratively high standard of ethics in Jewish home life. The God-
fearers and proselytes whom we meet in the Acts of the Apostles and
the complementary reproach of Mt 23:15 attest to the effects of this
mission. The works of Philo indicate the remarkable extent to which
the particularistic election of a few small tribes had been transformed
into a universal message for all the religiously serious-minded men
of the ancient world. [35]

Now that we have surveyed some of the new elements in the era
200 B.C.-A.D. 90, we may consider some texts from this period
which bear more directly on our question, viz., was the high religious
value placed on *Torah* study which characterizes Pirqe Aboth and the
rabbinic literature as a whole present in the Julaism of an earlier
period, and if so, with what nuances?

The first work we will consider in this section is Ecclesiasticus, or
the Wisdom of Jesus the Son of Sirach (Ben Sira), the time of whose
composition may with confidence be set somewhere between 190 and
175 B.C. This large composite book represents the essence of the
teaching of a scribal school master in Jerusalem, active during the
reign of Seleucus IV Philopator. His reign was a time of Hellenistic
influence, but avoided the violence associated with the reign of his
successor Antiochus IV Epiphanes. Ben Sira is important as a transitional figure between the wisdom traditions of the Hebrew Bible and
the rabbinic circles which produced Aboth, because, as we have seen,
he makes explicit the link, or rather, the identification between wisdom
and Torah, thereby bringing wisdom's universality to an end, and
because he attempts to avert the threat to Israelite religious faith
represented by Job, and especially by Qohelet. For, as Hengel suggests, the radical fatalism and skepticism introduced by Qohelet,
if left unchecked, could and in some cases doubtless did lead to a
critique of Jewish religion in general, and to a total assimilation to
Greek culture, including its religious culture. [36]

We will take note of three texts: the introductory praise of wisdom,
ch. 1; the great praise of wisdom and Ben Sira's comment thereon,
ch. 24; the superiority of the scribe's vocation, 38:24-39:11. [37]

---

[35] B. J. Bamberger, *Proselytism in the Talmudic Period* (New York: Ktav, 1968),
with the literature cited in the new introduction, pp. xix-xxxi, to which add P.
Dalbert, *Die Theologie der hellenistisch-jüdischen Missionsliteratur* (Theologische
Forschung, 4; Hamburg: H. Reich, 1954).

[36] Hengel, *Judaism...*, I, p. 128.

[37] Unfortunately these passages are only extant in the Greek and later versions.
Due to confusion in the numbering of the verses, esp. between the manual edition of

The prologue strongly emphasizes the divine origin of wisdom when it asks (1:6): "To whom has wisdom's root been revealed? Who knows her subtleties?" The answer comes back (1:7 f): "There is but one, wise and truly awe-inspiring, seated upon his throne: It is *the Lord*; *he* created her, has seen her and taken note of her." Though this translation (NAB) makes the logical relation of the three verses clear, it obscures the directness of the statement *heis estin sophos*: one is wise. For Ben Sira then only God is truly wise (cf. Mt 23:8-10). V. 26 links wisdom with the commandments: "If you desire wisdom, keep the commandments, and the Lord will bestow her upon you." This link, which will be made more explicit in Sir 23, is not so directly made in Proverbs, but was to have a long future, and, surprisingly, to find its true home in the Johannine literature. [38]

In v. 27 wisdom is identified with culture (*paideia*) and its contents expressed in terms of fear of the Lord: "For fear of the Lord is wisdom and culture; loyal humility (*prautēs*) is his delight." [39]

Theologically the most impressive, and thus the most studied, passage of Ben Sira is the great address of Wisdom in favor of herself in ch. 24. The main section of this chapter (vv. 1-22) has the same general structure as the praises of Wisdom in Prov 1 and 8. Verses 3-6 are almost word for word taken from an Isis hymn, retouched in only one or two places. [40] But this classic address is then followed by an afterword by Ben Sira himself (vv. 23-34), asserting that wisdom is

---

Rahlfs and the newer critical edition of Ziegler, it is necessary to choose one system. We will follow Rahlfs. But, for comparative purposes, we have used the helpful quadrilingual edition of F. Vattioni, *Ecclesiastico* (Naples: Istituto Orientale di Napoli, 1968), which reprints Ziegler's text without the apparatus.

[38] References: Jn 1:49 f; 14:15, 21, 31; 15:10, 12; 1 Jn 2:3 f, 7 f; 3:22-24; 4:21; 5:2 f; 2 Jn 4-6. In this literature of course the commandments are reduced to love and belief, their goal is eternal life (Jn 12:50), and wisdom is not mentioned explicitly, though of course there is a sapiential "atmosphere." See F. M. Braun, "Saint Jean, la Sagesse et l'histoire," *Neotestamentica et patristica* (Cullmann Fs.), (Leiden: Brill, 1962), pp. 123-133.

[39] According to the major monograph by Josef Haspecker, *Gottesfurcht bei Jesus Sirach* (An. Bib., 30; Rome: Biblical Institute, 1967), the fear of God is the main theme of the book. This is challenged by G. von Rad, *Wisdom in Israel* (Nashville: Abingdon, 1972), p. 242. On the other hand, von Rad denies the common interpretation that in Ben Sira nomism (Torah) and wisdom have formed a firm alliance. For him "Torah plays only a negligible part in Sirach's thought" (p. 244), since what really interests him is primeval wisdom (pp. 245-7). But this is to miss Ben Sira's profoundly ethical orientation. Sounder here then is the fine study by Hengel, *Judaism...*, pp. 131-153; 157-162; 249. See now also the excellent mediating work by Johann Marböck, *Weisheit im Wandel* (BBB, 37; Bonn: Hanstein, 1971), esp. the excursus on law and wisdom in Ben Sira, pp. 81-96, and the literature cited there.

the Torah (vv. 23-29) and that Ben Sira is the "channel" of Wisdom (vv. 30-34). Only two parts of the complex whole concern us. Wisdom, personified as a woman, seeks a dwelling among the nations, but God sends her different orders:

> 8Then the Creator of all gave me his command,
>   and he who formed me chose the spot for my tent,
>   Saying, "In *Jacob* make your dwelling,
>   in *Israel* your inheritance."
> 9Before all ages, in the beginning, he created me,
>   and through all ages, I shall not cease to be.
> 10In the *holy tent* [the Temple] I ministered (*eleitourgēsa*) before him,
>   and in *Zion* I fixed my abode.
> 11Thus in the *chosen city* he has given me rest,
>   in *Jerusalem* is my domain.
> 12I have struck root among the glorious people,
>   in the portion of the Lord, his heritage (NAB).

In this rather mythic description, there is no doubt left that Wisdom is no longer homeless, disconsolately returning to heaven, or dwelling pantheistically everywhere, but has become incarnate concretely in Israel. Thus did Ben Sira boldly particularize, indeed, nationalize, the international belle, Wisdom. [41]

After Lady Wisdom has finished speaking Ben Sira comments:

> All this [sc., wisdom] is the book of the covenant of the Most High God, the law which Moses commanded us as an inheritance for the congregations (*synagōgais*) of Jacob (v. 23).

This verse has been seen as the extreme limit of Ben Sira's conservative reaction to the threat of assimilation to Hellenism. As we have seen, the basic idea, an association between Torah and Wisdom, is not new, but anticipated in Deuteronomy and Ezra. Perhaps Ben Sira's thought is more moderate. Note that in the Greek there is no main verb. NAB translates: "all this *is true of* the book of the covenant...." If that is legitimate, and, in view of Ben Sira's overall openness to new ideas from any source, it is likely so, then Marböck's nuanced comment is in order:

> Ben Sira, with his view of the Torah as the final concretizing of the presence of God active in creation and history (which is what wisdom comes down to), did not intend to pursue an anti-Hellenistic polemic;

---

[40] H. Conzelmann, "The Mother of Wisdom," in *The Future of our Religious Past* (Bultmann Fs.) (London: SCM, 1971), pp. 230-243.

[41] Cf. the analysis in Christ, *Jesus-Sophia*, pp. 33-38 .

rather, as a genuine wise man, he tried to present to his hearers, and indeed also with a view to the diaspora, positively, through the acceptance of new ideas, faith in the election of Israel, and this at a time when the world with its wisdom was fast changing. Perhaps one could formulate it thus: for Israel, wisdom, with all that can be understood thereby (24:23 *tauta panta*), is best, and most securely, conceivable in Torah; to the peoples of the world, Torah is Israel's wisdom. But both come from the Lord, are modes of his working and of his presence in the world. [42]

The point is this: the traditional interpretation holds that Ben Sira *identified* Torah and Wisdom. The newer view holds that he related them closely, but, given the range of interests of his work as a whole, he did not simply identify them. Even supposing that this is the correct view, it does not exclude that Ben Sira was understood, especially by the rabbis, in the first sense, so that for later Torah-true Judaism wisdom was at least theoretically, and to a large extent in practice, "reduced" to the dimensions of Torah. [43]

The most intriguing Sirach text for our interests is his elitist comparison of various craftsmen with the scribe, Sir 38:24-39:11:

> 24The wisdom of the scribe depends on the opportunity of leisure
> (*scholē*);
>   and he who has little business may become wise.
> 25How can he become wise who handles the plow,
>   and who glories in the shaft of a goad,
> who drives oxen and is occupied with their work,
>   and whose talk is about bulls?
> 26He sets his heart on plowing furrows,
>   and he is careful about fodder for the heifers.
> 27So too is every craftsman and master workman (*tektōn kai architektōn*)
>   who labors by night as well as by day;
> those who cut the signets of seals,
>   each is diligent in making a great variety;
> he sets his heart on painting a lifelike image,
>   and he is careful to finish his work.
> 28So too is the smith sitting by the anvil,
>   intent upon his handiwork in iron;
> the breath of the fire melts his flesh,
>   and he wastes away in the heat of the furnace;
> he inclines his ear to the sound of the hammer,

---

[42] Marböck, *Weisheit im Wandel*, p. 94 f.

[43] Note that Torah is not normally the object of a poem of a large pericope; 32:14-33:1-4 is the exception. More often Torah functions as a resumé of a wisdom poem (15:1; 24:33), as part of a comprehensive involvement with wisdom (19:20; 39:1-11) or as a part of the wise ordering of the universe (17:11-12).

and his eyes are on the pattern of the object.
He sets his heart on finishing his handiwork,
    and is careful to complete its decoration.
29So too is the potter sitting at his work
    and turning the wheel with his feet;
    he is always deeply concerned over his work,
        and all his output is by number,
30He moulds the clay with his arm
    and makes it pliable with his feet;
    he sets his heart to finish the glazing,
        and he is careful to clean the furnace.
31All these rely upon their hands,
    and each is skillful in his own work.
32Without them a city cannot be established,
    and men can neither sojourn nor live there.
33Yet they are not sought out for the council of the people,
    nor do they attain eminence in the public assembly.
    They do not sit in the judge's seat.
    nor do they understand the sentence of judgment;
    they cannot expound discipline or judgment,
        and they are not found among the rulers.
34But they keep stable the fabric of the world,
    and their prayer is in the practice of their trade.

Chapter 39

1On the other hand he who devotes himself to the fear of God
    and meditates on the law of the Most High
will seek out the wisdom of all the ancients,
    and will be concerned with the prophecies;
2he will preserve the discourse of notable men
    and will penetrate the subtleties of parables;
3he will seek out the hidden meanings of proverbs
    and be at home with the obscurities of parables.
4He will serve among great men
    and appear before rulers;
    he will travel through the lands of foreign nations,
    for he tests the good and the evil among men.
5He will set his heart to rise early
    to seek the Lord who made him,
    and will make supplication before the Most High;
    he will open his mouth in prayer
        and make supplication for his sins.
6If the great Lord is willing,
    he will be filled with the spirit of understanding;
    he will pour forth words of wisdom
        and give thanks to the Lord in prayer.
7He will direct his counsel and knowledge aright,

and mediate on his secrets.
8He will reveal instruction (*paideia*) in his teaching (*didaskalia*),
and will glory in the law of the Lord's covenant.
9Many will praise his understanding,
and it will never be blotted out;
his memory will not disappear,
and his name will live through all generations.
10Nations will declare his wisdom,
and the congregation will proclaim his praise;
11if he lives long, he will leave a name greater than a thousand,
and if he goes to rest, it is enough for him.

1. *The Text*

We have kept to the Greek text as translated by RSV, with two exceptions. We have accepted P. W. Skehan's emendation in 38-33: where the Greek reads *en parabolais*, he retrojects *mšlym* which the Greek translator erroneously vocalized *mašalîm* (proverbs), but which would better be read *môšelîm* (rulers). 44 Also, in 39:1 the parallelism is imperfect as the Greek text stands, since the first stich has no object. This can be supplied from the Syriac: fear of God. Then one is free to take *dianooumenou* verbally, in the sense of meditate, which I take to represent an original *hagah* (cf. 39:7).

2. *Structure*

The poem is a carefully composed diptych, the first half 38:24-34 describing four craftsmen, each with a similar refrain, and concluding with a summarizing evaluation (38:31-34). On the whole the description is respectful and admiring, the only touch of irony being the remark about the farmer's conversation (v. 25d). In this it marks a notable improvement over its Egyptian model. The two parts are linked together by a common focus: on what does a man direct his heart (*epidonai kardian*)? The second half 39:1-11 is harder to break down, but perhaps this outline will do: vv. 1-4, the range of the scribe's activities; vv. 5-8, his personal relationship to God (prayer life); vv. 9-11, the fame of the wise man in public life. 45

3. *Content*

The entire passage shows a remarkable affinity to two ancient Egyptian texts: The Satire on the Trades (otherwise known as the

---

44 "They shall not be found in Parables (Sir 38:33)," CBQ 23 (1961): 40.
45 For further details see Marböck, *Weisheit im Wandel*, pp. 118-120; Haspecker, *Gottesfurcht...*, pp. 179-181.

sayings of Duauf, or the Sayings of Khety), and In Praise of Learned
Scribes, but they differ in the intensity of malice towards the trades,
and in the exaggeration of enthusiasm for the scribal life. One might
think that the much older Egyptian texts represent an initial burst of
appreciation/deprecation following fairly soon upon the development
of a scribal profession, while Ben Sira benefits from a longer experience
during which time the scribes' enthusiasm for their vocation has been
tempered by reality. There is a later parallel in the Testament of Levi
XIII, on which more below. The introductory verse 38:24, with its
recognition of leisure (*scholē*) as the basis of culture, seems to reflect
at least a popular echo of Aristotle's statement to the same effect. [46]

   With the actual development of the rabbinic tradition in mind we
may consider the following passage from Marböck.

> In 39:11 ff the fear of God and the study of the Law are again the
> characteristics of the "sofer." The fear of God stands first as the basic
> attitude (cf. 39:5 on prayer). The law of the Most High (39:1) and
> the law of the covenant of the Lord (39:8) is however only a *part*
> of the wise man's investigation and meditation, which also includes the
> "wisdom of the ancients" and the sayings of the prophets; beyond this
> Ben Sira is also acquainted with the wisdom and proverbial tradition
> of foreign peoples (vv. 2 and 4). This basic range and openness
> beyond the law of Moses finds abundant confirmation in numerous
> texts where Ben Sira is concerned with general human proverbial
> wisdom.... His program is humanism in the best sense, a synthesis of
> openness to the world, knowledge and piety. We must finally give
> up speaking of a "nomistic wisdom" (Fichtner) in Ben Sira. Wisdom
> is also to this extent more comprehensive than the Torah, since it is
> the personal gift and presence of the Lord, bestowed according to his
> good pleasure (39:6; cf. 1:10; 1:26). [47]

This rings true enough, though there is a hint of prejudice that
"nomistic wisdom" could not be humanism in the best sense, whereas
the open-minded reader of the rabbinic literature as a whole is struck
by the wide range of its interests even as it strives to remain bound
to the sacred traditions of its people.

   Summing up the relationship between Ben Sira and the ideal of
Aboth, we may note first the difference in style: Ben Sira is often
poetic, the rabbis aphoristic, juridic, and anecdotal. The rabbis prefer
to ignore history, whereas it is one of the great achievements of Ben
Sira to have linked the wisdom tradition in Israel with the history

---

[46] Metaphysics, I, 1 and 2, 980a-982b.
[47] Marböck, *Weisheit im Wandel*, p. 89.

of his people (the Praise of the Fathers 44:1-50:24). Yet Ben Sira is crucial to our understanding of what came after him above all because, while stressing and praising wisdom, he set limits. Wisdom is not free, skeptical, irreverent speculation and theological criticism. This is rejected as arrogance (*ga'awa*) in ch. 10 (cf. Hengel, *Judaism...*, p. 150 f). The criticism of providence found in Job and Qohelet is excluded in ch. 15, and indeed by the retributive theology of the whole book (see the echo in James 1:13). Finally, the ideal of knowledge, which Ben Sira assumed could be attained only by the leisured scribe, was extended by the Pharisees to all men willing to combine a life of work with study and piety. In this respect their movement represents a petit bourgeois transformation of Ben Sira's aristocratic elitism, a transformation which was continued even more radically by Jesus' invitation to the *am ha-aretz*.

We need not delay long over the book entitled the Wisdom of Solomon, because, though, as we shall see, it contains exhortations to the study of Torah and is itself in its latter half (9:18-19:22) a midrash on Exodus, it did not have a directly traceable influence on the Palestinian schools. R. M. Grant says flatly, "it was not used by Palestinian or Hellenistic Jewish writers; its transmission was a matter only for Christian concern." [48]

This view is supported by the absence of direct quotations from the book in the Talmuds and midrashim. He goes on to show that its main function in early Christianity was its use by especially Second Century Alexandrine Fathers as a corrective to the extreme mythological wisdom speculation of some Gnostics, and as a basis, especially 7:25-26, for a philosophical Christology. He only admits a single case of clear literary dependence in the New Testament on Wisdom, viz., Heb. 1:3 on Wis. 7:25-26. This view requires qualification on two grounds: (1) "In Khirbet Mird a fragment ... of the Greek text of Wisdom has come to light," [49] indicating that the book was known in Palestine, though this find seems not to have any thing to do with the Essenes, but rather with a Christian library. (2) If, as seems to me correct, one detects a strong influence of Wisdom on Paul, especially Rom 1 and 9, in the form not of direct quotation but rather of condensation, then some basis for its influence on Jewish students trained in Palestine

---

[48] "The book of Wisdom at Alexandria," *After the New Testament* (Philadelphia: Fortress, 1967), pp. 70-82.

[49] Eissfeldt, *The Old Testament, an Introduction* (New York: Harper, 1965), p. 603; cf. p. 640.

and further north exists. [50] Granted that there is no distinctly dis-
cernable influence of the Wisdom of Solomon on the rabbinic Torah
ideal, its high evaluation of religious knowledge (one of its major
themes), its peculiar theological use of the concept of "seeing," and
the way in which malice and ignorance interact throughout but especially in the section on idolatry (cc. 13-15) combine to make it very
close to Aboth in general orientation. [51]

In 2:12 *nomos* and *paideia* are put in parallel verses; in 1:5 and 6
wisdom is termed the holy spirit of discipline (*paideia*). Thus wisdom
and culture are identified with law. In 6:4 the law is identified with
the will of God. The author's purpose is described in 6:9 and 10.

> To you, therefore, O princes, are my words addressed
>   that you may *learn wisdom* and that you may not sin.
> For those who keep the *holy precepts* hallowed shall be found only,
>   and those *learned* in them will have ready a response.

In 6:17-20 we find a marvelous sorites, an ascending chain of syllo-
gisms, or climax, a rhetorical figure common to classical and rabbinic
literature, in this case mixing biblical and Greek themes in an astonishing and perfectly characteristic combination: [52]

> For the first step toward discipline (*paideia*) is a very earnest desire
> for her;
>   then, care for discipline is love of her;
>   love means the keeping of her laws (cf. Jn 14:15);
> To observe her laws is the basis for incorruptibility;
>   and incorruptibility makes one close to God;
>   thus the desire for Wisdom leads up to a kingdom.

Change incorruptibility (*aphtharsia*) to *ha-ʿolam ha-ba* and, possibly,
basileia to *malkuth ha-shamayim* and the sentiment could not be more
rabbinic.

From the pseudepigrapha only two documents need be drawn into
our consideration, the letter of (Pseudo-) Aristeas and the Testaments
of the Twelve Patriarchs. The letter of Aristeas is an Alexandrian

---

[50] This is not a subject on which we can enter here in detail, but see the excursus
in Sanday-Headlam, *Romans* (ICC; Edinburgh: T & T Clark, 1902⁵), pp. 51 f; 267-9.
[51] See the study of leading themes in J. M. Reese, *Hellenistic Influence on the
Book of Wisdom and its Consequences* (An. Bib., 41; Rome: Biblical Institute, 1970),
esp. pp. 141 f. For a careful study of the wisdom theme, see B. L. Mack, *Logos und
Sophia* (SUNT, 10; Göttingen: Vandenhoeck & Ruprecht, 1973), pp. 63-107.
[52] See H. A. Fischel, "The uses of sorites (*climax, gradatio*) in the tannaitic
period," HUCA 44 (1973): 119-151, and J. Reider, *The Book of Wisdom* (New
York: Harper, 1957), p. 104 f.

Jewish document written in Greek, datable between 170 and 130 B.C. The two relevant sections occur, appropriately enough, at the beginning of a conversation of Aristeas and another courtier, Andreas, with the high priest Eleazar concerning the deep spiritual meaning of the Jewish food laws (sections 121-171), that is, a section which attempts to defend fidelity to Torah.

> I shall describe the work of translation in what follows. He (the high priest Eleazar) selected men of the finest character and the highest culture (*paideia*), such as one would expect from their noble parentage. They were men who had not only acquired proficiency in Jewish letters, but had studied those of the Greeks as well. They were specially qualified therefore for serving on embassies and they undertook this duty whenever it was necessary. They possessed a great facility for *homiliai* (assemblies, lectures, conversations) and the discussion of problems connected with the law (*tas eperōtēseis tas dia tou nomou = midrashē ha-Torah?*). They espoused the middle course—and this is always the best course to pursue. They abjured the rough and barbarous manner *(dianoia = method of reasoning?)*, but they were altogether above arrogance and never assumed an air of superiority over others, and were willing to discuss with, and listen to, others ... and to answer every question fittingly. They all observed these (rules), and only in these respects were they anxious to surpass one another. They were all of them worthy of their leader and of his virtue (sections 121, 122). 53

The exaggeration and striving to display the close affinity to Greek ethical theory (the golden mean) are obvious. Further, what is depicted is, from a Pharisaic point of view, a rather archaic aristocratic, i.e., priestly, learned tradition, closely connected with the Temple and its schools. In this respect it represents the same stage of development as Ben Sira. Learning is still the prerogative of the Temple's scribal staff. But on the other hand there can be no mistaking the author's intent to stress the importance for them of learning whether directed toward Torah or toward secular subjects, besides a tradition of corporate study and debate concerning the text of Torah, a tradition carried on in the rabbinic academies. This remains true even if we must reject the suggestion of Ralph Marcus that some of the virtues connected with learning in this passage are to be directly connected with the list of forty-eight virtues in Aboth 6:6. 54

---

53 Translation mine, but based upon that in Charles, *Apocrypha and Pseudepigrapha of the Old Testament* (Oxford: Clarendon, 1913), p. 106.
54 Ralph Marcus, *Law in the Apocrypha* (New York: Columbia U.P., 1927), p. 60 f.

The second work of this class to be considered is the Testament of the Twelve Patriarchs. This predominantly ethical work remains a subject of scholarly dispute, but we may now set aside with some confidence the view that it is entirely the composition of a Christian author since, in view of mounting evidence to the contrary, its main proponent, Dr. Marinus de Jonge, has now abandoned it. [55]

Rather, R. H. Charles' basic view that it is a Jewish work (likely of Essene provenance) which in its main Greek textual tradition has undergone some Christian interpolations is the view maintained by those authors who have dealt with the work in recent years. [56] The work is also difficult to date but we cannot go far wrong if we place it in somewhere between Charles' date of 109-107 B.C. and Rengstorf's "dass die Grundschift zu ihrer endgültigen Gestalt gekommen ist, als im Zeichen der Pax Romana die Verbindung zwischen dem Tempel und dem Land einerseits und der Diaspora andererseits sich mehr und mehr konsolidierte," that is, I take it, a short time after 63 B.C. [57]

The most extended text of relevance to us comes from the otherwise central and important Testament of Levi:

> [1]And now, my children, I command you:
>   Fear the Lord your God with your whole heart,
>   and walk in simplicity according to all His law.
> [2]And do ye also teach all your children letters,
>   That they may have understanding all their life,
>   Reading unceasingly the law of God.
> [3]For everyone that knoweth the law of the Lord shall be honoured,
>   And shall not be a stranger whithersoever he goeth.
> [4]Yea, many friends shall he gain more than his parents,
>   And many men shall desire to serve him,
>   And to hear the law from his mouth.
> [5]Work righteousness, therefore, my children, upon the earth,
>   That ye may find it in heaven.
> [6]And sow good things in your souls,

---

[55] So M. Delcor's report in *La littérature juive entre Tenach et Mischna*, ed. W. C. Van Unnik, (Journées bibliques de Louvain, 20; Leiden: Brill, 1974), p. 115.

[56] See Chr. Burchard-J. Jervell-J. Thomas, *Studien zu den Testamenten der Zwölf Patriarchen* (BZNW, 36: Berlin: de Gruyter, 1969); K. H. Rengstorf, "Herkunft und Sinn der Patriarchen-Reden in den Testamenten der Zwölf Patriarchen," in *La littérature juive entre Tenach et Mischna*, ed. W. C. Van Unnik, pp. 29-47; J. Becker, *Untersuchungen zur Entstehungsgeschichte der Testamente der Zwölf Patriarchen* (AGSU, 8; Leiden: Brill, 1970).

[57] R. H. Charles, *Apocrypha...*, p. 290; Rengstorf, "Herkunft und Sinn...," p. 47. Becker, *op. cit.*, p. 376, dates the first stratum a century earlier.

That ye may find them in your life.
But if ye sow evil things,
Ye shall reap every trouble and affliction.

7Get wisdom in the fear of God with diligence;
For though there be a leading into captivity,
And cities and lands be destroyed,
And gold and silver and every possession perish,
The wisdom of the wise no one can take away,
Save the blindness of ungodliness, and the callousness (that comes)
of sin.

8Then even among his enemies shall wisdom be a glory to him,
And in a strange country a fatherland,
And in the midst of foes shall prove a friend.

9Whosoever teaches noble things and does them,
Shall be enthroned with kings,
As was also Joseph my brother.

(Test. Levi, 13:1-9) 58

This text does not require extensive commentary. Its main purpose is clear enough: universal Torah-education and unceasing study are primary conditions for righteousness, wisdom and honor. It makes plain that in the Jewish circles from which it derives, whether Essene, or, as Becker thinks, Hellenistic Jewish (Egyptian?), a high evaluation of Torah study and learning was a basic religious characteristic. 59 Though it is thematically almost without parallel in the Testaments in their final Greek form, more concerned as they are with ethics and messianic expectation, this text does find a highly sapiential counterpart in the Cambridge Aramaic fragment of the Testament of Levi, vv. 83-95 (Charles, p. 366 f). 60

Turning now to the texts discovered in the caves above the wadi Qumran southeast of Jerusalem and associated with the Essene move-

---

58 Charles' translation, corrected to conform with Cambridge Library Ms Ff 1.24; cf. M. de Jonge, ed., *Testamenta XII Patriarcharum* (Leiden: Brill, 1964).

59 Becker, *op. cit.*, p. 373-377.

60 Though further texts from the apocrypha and pseudepigrapha will not be considered, since we cannot be exhaustive in this chapter, we will simply list references, as complete as we could make them, to every passage in Charles, vol. II, which in any way refers to study, learning, truth, wisdom, the Torah. I Macc. 7:12-13; Test. Reuben 4:1; 3:9; Test. Benj. 5:3; Jubilees 19:14; 11:16; 23:26; 45:16; 47:9; Life of Adam and Eve 27:3; Eth. Enoch 12:4; 25:2; 69:9-11; 82:3 (98:3); Sibylline Books V, 324-7; Slav. Enoch 36:1; Syr. Baruch 3:6; 57:2; 77-15-16; IV Macc: the whole book is in a sense relevant but esp. 1:1-35; 5:34-38; 18:11-19. Fourth Ezra 7:20; 8:29; 9:19, 31, 37, but esp. chapter 14:1-48, the seventh vision which contains the legend of Ezra and the holy Scriptures, with the Syriac addition of the *translatio Ezrae*. To these add Pseudo-Philo, *Liber antiquitatum Biblicarum*, 22.5.

ment, we will consider only two texts. The first is a noncanonical psalm known also in the Syriac which well expresses the prolongation of wisdom poetry in this community, a community which lasted until the Romans dispersed its members in 68-69 A.D.

11 Q Ps^a XVIII

1With a loud voice glorify God;
   in the congregation of the many (*qahal rabbîm*) proclaim his
   majesty.
2In the multitude of the upright (*berôv yasharim*) glorify his name
   and with the faithful recount his greatness.
3Bind your souls with the good ones
   and with the pure ones to glorify the Most High.
4Form an assembly to proclaim his salvation,
   and be not lax in making known his might
   and his majesty to all simple folk (*pôt³îm*).
5For to make known the glory of the Lord
   is Wisdom given,
6And for recounting his many deeds
   she is revealed to man:
7To make known to simple folk his might,
   and to explain to senseless folk his greatness,
8Those far from her gates,
   those who stray from her portals.
9For the Most High is the Lord of Jacob,
   and his majesty is over all his works.
10And a man who glorifies the Most High
   he accepts as one who brings a meal offering,
11as one who offers he-goats and bullocks,
  as one who fattens the altar with many burnt offerings,
  as a sweet-smelling fragrance from the hand of the righteous.
12From the gates of the righteous is heard her voice,
   and from the assembly of the pious her song.
13When they eat with satiety she is cited,
   and when they drink in the community together (*beheber yahdîw*),
14Their meditation (*sîhatam*, from *sîhah*, cf. Ps. 119:97) is on the Law
      of the Most High,
   their words on making known his might.
15How far from the wicked is her word,
   from all haughty men to know her.
16Behold the eyes of the Lord
   upon the good ones are compassionate,
17And upon those who glorify him he increases his mercy;
   from an evil time will he deliver (their) soul.
18Bless the Lord
   who redeems the humble from the hand of strangers

and delivers the pure from the hand of the wicked,
19Who establishes a horn out of Jacob
  and a judge of peoples out of Israel;
20He will spread his tent in Zion
  and abide for ever in Jerusalem. 61

This psalm is clearly of the wisdom type, with affinities to Sir 15:1-10. It remains uncertain whether it represents a piece of late wisdom poetry from the same time as Sirach, a time, that is, before the emergence of parties like the Essenes (so Polzin and Lührmann), or whether it derives from the Essene community itself, at least in its early formative stages (so Delcor, Philonenko, and, with caution, J. A. Sanders). 62

Of interest for our theme are the following points. Verse 4 speaks of forming an assembly to make known the salvation of the Lord, using the terms *ḥabar, yaḥad*, and *yadaᶜ*. Whether these are to be understood in the technical sense of the Pharisaic *ḥaburah* and the Essene *yaḥad* must remain doubtful but that they represent a stage on the way to such communities is likely enough. Note further the importance attached to educating the "simple folk" (*putaᵓîm*). Are these the forerunners of the *am ha-aretz* of Pharisaic literature and the *nēpioi* of the Gospels? In v. 5 f wisdom is personified as a woman, usual in wisdom literature but not in the psalms. In v. 10 f God accepts the praise of a righteous man as though it were rich sacrifices. This idea looks back to the prophetic critique of the cult (e.g., Hos 6:6) and forward to the rabbinic view that deeds of loving kindness and Torah study suffice to replace the Temple as a means of atonement for sin (ARNᴬ, ch. 4). Most important of all are vv. 13 f which speak of Torah-talk at table in community as well as meditation (*śîḥah*) on

61 Translation from J. A. Sanders, *The Psalms Scroll of Qumran Cave 11 (11 QPsa)*, Discoveries in the Judean Desert of Jordan, IV (Oxford: Clarendon, 1965), pp. 64-5. The text is otherwise known as Syriac Psalm II and 11 Q Psa 154. Cf. the editio minor, J. A. Sanders, *The Dead Sea Psalms Scroll* (Ithaca: Cornell, 1967), and the earlier literature there cited, p. 152, to which now add D. Lührmann, "Ein Weisheitspsalm aus Qumran," ZAW 80 (1968) 87-98, and F. Christ, *Jesus-Sophia*, pp. 39-42. Further, J. Strugnell, "Notes on the text and transmission of the apocryphal Psalms 151, 154 (= Syr II) and 155 (= Syr III)," HTR 59 (1966): 257-281; R. Polzin, "Notes on the dating of the nonmassoretic psalms of 11 Q Psa," HTR 60 (1967): 468-76. For an excellent recent reconstruction of the history of the sect, see J. Murphy-O'Connor, "The Essenes and their history," RB 81 (1974): 215-244.
62 M. Delcor, "Cinq nouveaux psaumes esséniens?" RQ 1 (1958): 85-102; *idem*, "Zum Psalter von Qumran," BZ 10 (1966): 15-29; M. Philonenko, "L'origine essénienne des cinq psaumes syriaques de David," *Semitica* 9 (1958): 35-48; Sanders, *The Psalms Scroll*, p. 70.

Torah). This immediately awakens echoes of Aboth 3:2, 6 and Mt 18:20, as well as Old Testament meditation texts already cited in this chapter, usually employing the verb *hagah*. The same idea is present in unmistakably Essene texts (1 Q S 10:16; 1 Q H 6:11; 9:7; 11:5).

Of primary significance for illustrating the centrality of Torah study in the prerabbinic period in at least one Palestinian Jewish movement is the section of the Qumran community rule which makes specific provision for keeping up this study at all times (1 Q S 6:6-8). The fuller context of this crucial passage is well entitled by Dupont-Sommer "The common life," embracing 6:1b-8a. [63]

באלה

יתהלכו בכול מגוריהם כול הנמצא איש את רעהו וישמעו הקטן לגדול למלאכה
ולממון ויחד יואכלו

ויחד יברכו ויחד יועצו ובכול מקום אשר יהיה שם עשרה אנשים מעצת החיד אל ימש
מאתם איש

כוהן ואיש כתכונו ישבו לפניו וכן ישאלו לעצתם לכול דבר והיה כיא יערוכו השולחן
לאכול או התירוש

לשתות הכוהן ישלח ידו לרשונה להברך בראשית הלחם או התירוש לשתות הכוהן
ישלח ידו לרשונה

להברך בראשית הלחם והתירוש ואל ימש במקום אשר יהיו שם העשרה איש דורש
בתורה יומם ולילה

תמיד על יפות איש לרעהו והרבים ישקודו ביחד את שלישית כול לילות השנה לקרוא
בספר ולדרוש משפט

ולברך ביחד

Translation:

In these [precepts] (2) should they walk in all their dwellings, every man who finds himself with his fellow. And the little shall listen to the great with respect to work and money. And in community shall they eat, (3) and in community shall they pray (*yebarekû*), and in community shall they take counsel. And in every place where there are ten men of the council of the community there shall not lack among them a man who is a (4) priest. And they shall, each according to his rank, sit before him and thus shall they be questioned for their counsel on every matter. And it shall be, when they set the table to eat or (5) to drink the new wine, the priest will put forth his hand first to say the blessing over the first fruits of the bread or the new wine [dittography]. (6) And there shall not lack in the place where there will be the ten a man who searches (studies) in the Torah day and

---

[63] Millar Burrows, ed., *The Dead Sea Scrolls of St. Mark's Monastery*, vol. II (New Haven: American Schools of Oriental Research, 1951), plate VI. See also E. Lohse, *Die Texte aus Qumran* (Darmstadt: Wissenschaftliche Buchgesellschaft, 1964), pp. 20-23.

night, (7) continually, on beautiful things, every man with his fellow. But the Many (the Notables) shall keep vigil in community a third of all the nights of the year, to read in the book, and to study legislation (8) and to pray in community.

Notes on the Text and Translation

The text is generally well preserved and clear. The ms. is marred in lines 5 and 6 by dittography (see 4 Q S d), and at least one spelling error, *ḥḥyd* for *ḥyḥd* in line 3. A more serious problem concerns the *ᶜl ypwt* of line 7. Is this to be taken literally, as we have done in our extremely literal translation, as "on beautiful things," whether in the sense of a euphemism for Torah, or, in Gaster's rather free translation, "for the harmonious adjustment of their human relations"? Or should we read, with Brownlee, *ᶜl pywt* = orally? Or should we accept what is by now the commonly accepted emendation *ḥlypwt* = alterations, that is, by turns? Leaney leaves a gap. No matter what solution is preferred, a word must be supplied in order for the text to be perfectly coherent. The third proposal (alterations, turns) makes the best sense. If we supplied, after *tamid, yqḥw* or the like, we could read: "they shall take turns, every man with his fellow." Cf. 1 Kg 5:28 MT.

For convenience in commentary, a second, smoother translation will now be given, this time numbered by sentence or verse. A comment on each will follow.

Translation:

1In these precepts should they walk in all their dwellings, every man who finds himself with his fellow.

2And the little shall listen to the great with respect to work and to money.

3And in community shall they eat, and in community shall they pray, and in community shall they take counsel.

4And in every place where there are ten men of the council of the community there shall not lack among them a man who is a priest.

5And they shall, each according to his rank, sit before him and thus shall they be questioned for their counsel on every matter.

6And it shall be, when they set the table to eat or to drink the new wine, the priest will put forth his hand first to say the blessing over the first fruits of the bread or the new wine.

7And there shall not lack in the place where there will be the Ten a man who studies in the Torah day and night, continually.

8They shall take turns, every man with his fellow.

9And the Notables shall keep vigil in community a third of all the nights of the year, to read in the book, and to study legislation and to pray in community.

Literary Analysis

This passage is in a sense the heart of the rule since it comes after the description of the aim of the community and of the conditions and rites of admission and is followed by a lengthy penal code to punish members when they fall from the ideal norm. What the ideal norm involves is given in our brief but crucial text. This is the life— when it is properly lived. After an introductory pair of verses (the first is virtually a title), we are given an *inclusio* in verses 3 and 9, in which the common element is the phrase "in community," but in which there is also noticeable an escalation of emphasis on the intellectual side of the life. The rule undoubtedly underwent revisions, especially in the way of expansions and glosses. Here verses 5 and 6 are probably later commentary on 4. Originally verse 7 probably followed directly on 4, since they begin in almost the same way. In verse 7 this repetition is doubtless resumptive. 5 and 6 explicate some of the results of a priestly presence among the members of the community.

Commentary

1. The term *dwellings* implies either (1) more than one Essene community following this rule, or (2) more than one migration of a single community. Though Essenes were to be found elsewhere than Qumran, we know of no other location where they attempted to live a full community life. That the community migrated at least once, originally from Babylonia, is the opinion of a growing majority of interpreters (e.g., Stegemann, Murphy-O'Connor). The frequent repetition of the phrase "every man with his fellow" seems not to imply some kind of pairing off, as with the Pharisaic *ḥaberim*, but is just an idiom for community relations. A frequently occurring grammatical feature of our text is beginning a sentence with a plural verb, following it with a compound subject in the singular. This is to be put down as *constructio ad sensum*.

2. The word for rank, *tikkun*, is peculiar to Qumran in Hebrew literature (Brownlee). The members of the community were to subject themselves voluntarily to those of higher rank. This usage has some parallels in the New Testament, e.g., subjection to the higher powers

Rm 13:1, 5; of wife to husband, Col 3:18, Eph 5:21; of slave to master, Titus 2:9; but becomes closer in 1 Clement and Ignatius where Christians are to be subject to their bishop. In the case of the Qumran community subjection in matters of money was a necessary consequence of their decision to hold all goods in common. Compare the case of Ananias and Sapphira, Acts 4:32-5:11. See further, G. Delling in TDNT, 8, 44-46.

3. The emphasis on community, and indeed on an ordered community (*tikkun*, v. 2), could not be plainer. What is striking is how for the men of Qumran there is no tension, but rather the closest harmony, between piety and intense application to study. We may even speak of an intellectualization of piety. Were these consultations in the nature of scholastic disputations, i.e., rabbinic *pilpul*, or were they more pragmatic? See comment on v. 5 below. For a similar pattern of thought, see 1 Cor 10:31.

4. The importance of the ten provides a parallel (or is it an anticipation) to the rabbinic custom of a *minyan* or a quorum of ten men for public prayer. Cf. CD 13:1 f, 1 Q Sa 2:22; M. Sanh 1:3, 6; M. Meg 4:4; Ab 3:6. On groups of ten among the Essenes, cf. Jos. B. J. 2:146. The Qumran movement, unlike the Pharisaic, was decidedly sacerdotal. Were there in fact always enough priests for every group of ten, or was this prescription an often unrealizable ideal?

5. The precise nature of the interrogation remains unclear. Was it an examination of the member's conduct and morals, a kind of chapter of faults (cf. the penal code 8:20-9:7)? Or was it a matter of sounding out the rank and file on their attitude toward future policy of the community? Or was it a kind of school examination on the member's mastery of Torah? The second possibility seems best in the context but it is impossible to be sure. Complete freedom of speech was not highly valued at Qumran, but only speech within a certain formal framework. [63a]

6. The emphasis lies on doing things in the right order, observing precedence where prescribed. Meals in common are an important element in the rhythm of life at Qumran, as in later intentional communities. Among the Pharisees, the emphasis was rather on ritual purity than on community, though the latter concern is also present. Other mentions of meals at Qumran: CD 13:2 f; 1 Q Sa 2:17-21;

[63a] On school questions and answers as a literary form in the wisdom literature, see G. von Rad, *Wisdom in Israel*, pp. 18-21.

Jos. B. J. 2:131. The meals at Qumran are only in a loose sense cultic; that is, there is prayer at them. [64]

7. With respect to this crucial verse there is one main uncertainty of interpretation. Is the "man who searches in the Torah day and night" a single officer or is study of Torah a duty for all, a study which they fulfill by taking turns at it throughout the day and night, in addition to joining together in the evening for common study? The former view, favored by O. Betz and B. Gerhardsson, in effect supposes that the text read *"doresh ha-Torah"* (the Torah researcher), whereas in fact, it reads *"doresh be-Torah"* (one who researches in the Torah), that is, it does not sound like the title of an officer but rather like the statement of a task. That some were better at this task than others is not in question (*pace* Betz). [65] At Qumran all shared in the common task of study. Each was to be a *doresh be-Torah*, as is the ideal of Aboth. The phrase "day and night," derived from Josh 1:8 and Ps 1:2, is here explicitly interpreted by *tamîd*, continuously. We have met its Greek equivalent, *adialeiptōs*, in T. Levi 13:2. Cf. the New Testament ideal of persevering in prayer without ceasing, 1 Thess 5:17, and, combined with a service of the Word, Acts 6:4. Cf. CD 6:7; 7:18; Jos. B. J. 2:136. [66]

8. The idea of studying in shifts throughout the day and night as an attempt to live out with radical seriousness Ps 1:2 and Josh 1:8 gives eloquent expression to the high idealism of the men of Qumran and is almost without precedent, though all night vigils of prayer are common enough in the later desert monasticism of the Christians. I. Sonne offers one parallel in rabbinic literature (Eccl. R. 9:9), but

---

[64] On meals at Qumran, see K. G. Kuhn, "The Lord's Supper and the communal meal at Qumran," in *The Scrolls and the New Testament*, ed. K. Stendahl, pp. 65-93; E. F. Sutcliffe, "Sacred meals at Qumran," *Heythrop Journal* 1 (1960): 48 ff; M. Delcor, "Repas cultuels esséniens et thérapeutes, Thiases, et Haburoth," RQ 6 (1967): 401-25; for a good comparison of Essene, Pharisaic and Christian meals, see J. Neusner, *Rabbinic Traditions about the Pharisees*, v. III (Leiden: Brill, 1971), pp. 297-300.

[65] Betz rejects the emendation *haliphoth* ("they took turns") for largely unconvincing reasons, e.g., the passage deals with love of neighbor, not piety toward God, when in fact the context speaks three times of prayer. Betz's strongest argument is that accepting the emendation entails reading as one word what in the manuscript are plainly two words. He does not explain how he would read it. Gerhardsson would like to accept the emendation but has not reconciled his interpretation with it.

[66] Otto Betz, *Offenbarung und Schriftforschung in der Qumransekte* (WUNT, 6; Tübingen: Mohr, 1960), pp. 19-21; Gerhardsson, *Memory and Manuscript*, pp. 235-39. For the opposite view, A. R. C. Leaney, *The Rule of Qumran and its Meaning* (Philadelphia: Westminster, 1966), pp. 184-5.

this looks back to a defunct past. The *tamîd* of our text is perhaps to be taken, with Sonne, as an implied polemic against laxer views of the obligation to study Torah day and night such as the one preserved in the Midrash on Psalms: morning and evening prayer suffice as a minimum fulfillment. [67]

9. The word *rabbîm*, the subject of the sentence, is usually translated "the many," but J. Carmignac has argued cautiously and persuasively that in some contexts at Qumran it is highly possible that it has a qualitative, and not merely a quantitative reference; thus, "the notables," or "the dignitaries." It seems that the word refers to a class in the community that consisted of those who were neither priests nor novices nor those on penance, but what we might call "full members in good standing" or "professed members." The word is not to be understood in the sense of the later Jamnian rabbis, though this usage may have been a stage in the development of that office and title. [68]

Another problem arises with the phrase "a third of all the nights of the year." This can be understood in two ways: (a) the community kept all night study vigils 120 days of the year; (b) the community held a study session more or less every night of the year for about three hours (one third of the night), that is, a regular evening study period after the day's physical labor was done. Since the former sense seems so impractical, it seems best to take it in the latter.

This evening study session is distinct from the perpetual round of study mentioned in the preceding two verses. The *waw* is to be taken as adversative. The idea of having a set time for study is reminiscent of Ab 1:15.

Summing up, it is obvious that the idea of Torah study as a religious good was present in an extreme form in the Qumran community, with its all-night study vigil or its regular evening study periods, its examinations and its combination of study with prayer. That the Pharisees and indeed all Jews of the first century held this practice as a religious value at least in principle even if not always in practice seems a safe inference. What is peculiar about the Essenes is the extreme measures they took to guarantee that the ideal was realized.

---

[67] I. Sonne, "Remarks on 'Manual of Discipline,' Col. VI, 6-7," VT 7 (1957): 405-408. *Midrash on Psalms*, ed. William Braude, Yale Judaica Series, v. 13 (New Haven: Yale, 1959), I, 17, p. 23. Other, less proximate, examples in Gerhardsson, *Memory and Manuscript*, pp. 235-239. Cf. further the humorous case in Acts 20:7-12.

[68] J. Carmignac, "HRBYM: les 'Nombreux' ou les 'Notables'?," *Revue de Qumran* 7 (1971): 575-586.

A.-M. Denis describes their community as "une école d'exégèse" and its literary fecundity bears this description out. [69]

Since Philo pertains rather to Diaspora than to Palestinian Judaism and our concern is with the background of the Aboth ideal, we will not investigate him thoroughly but only consider a single text. It should however be pointed out that though Alexandrian by birth and education, Philo was aware of Palestinian exegetical traditions and was, it seems, from a family only recently migrated from Palestine to Egypt, [70] so that his writings do possess an at least indirect bearing on conditions in Palestine.

Philo, in his life of Moses, attempted to present the religion of his people both to themselves and to their cultivated neighbors in the most attractive light. To this end he presented the national hero Moses as almost a divine man, the fulfillment of the Greek ideal of the philosopher king (*De vita Mosis*, II, 2). In Philo's Moses four offices were combined, king, lawgiver, high priest and prophet (*De vita Mosis*, II, 3). This combination re-emerged later as the *triplex munus Christi*. While commenting on the passage in Num 15:32-36 about stoning a man for sabbath violation, Philo first describes the ancient ideal as he learned it, then adds a note on contemporary practice.

> It was customary on every day when opportunity offered, and pre-eminently on the seventh day, to pursue the study of wisdom with the ruler expounding and instructing the people what they should say and do, while they received edification and betterment in moral principles and conduct. Even now this practice is retained, and the Jews every seventh day occupy themselves with the philosophy of their fathers, dedicating that time to the acquiring of knowledge and the study of the truths of nature [or: "of theology"]. For what are our places of prayer throughout the cities but schools of prudence and courage and temperance and justice and also of piety, holiness and every virtue by which duties to God and men are discerned and rightly performed?
>
> (*De vita Mosis*, II, 215f)

The transformation of synagogue practices and Torah study into Hellenic categories of philosophy and *kalokagathia* is here obvious.

---

[69] Obviously much more could be said about Qumran in this connection, but much has already been done and need not be repeated here. Cf. W. D. Davies, " 'Knowledge' in the Dead Sea Scrolls and Matthew 11:25-30," *Christian Origins and Judaism* (Philadelphia: Westminster, 1962), pp. 119-144; J. Murphy-O'Connor, "Truth: Paul and Qumran," *Paul and Qumran* (London: Chapman, 1968), pp. 179-230; A. M. Denis, *Les thèmes de connaissance dans le Document de Damas* (Studia hellenistica, 15; Louvain: Publications universitaires, 1967).

[70] So J. Daniélou, *Philon d'Alexandrie* (Paris: Fayard, 1956), pp. 12-20.

The study of Torah (*darashat ha-Torah*) becomes the contemplation of the truths of nature (*theoria tōn peri physin*). This is possible for Philo because he thinks of the laws revealed to Moses as the literary embodiment of the law of nature for man. [71] The synagogue becomes a school for the acquiring of the four cardinal virtues, traditional in Greek thought from an undatable antiquity, supplemented by others more obviously religious in character. This is obviously slanting the truth, but it does accurately reflect that even before Jamnia the synagogue was a school; the *beth ha-tefillah* was a *beth-ha midrash* even then. [72]

Philo elsewhere explains the emperor Gaius' hostility to Jews on the ground that they alone opposed him on religious principle "trained as they were ... even from the cradle, by parents and tutors and instructors and by the far higher authority of the sacred laws and also the unwritten customs, to acknowledge one God" (*De legatione ad Gaium*, 115; cf. 2 Tim 3:15; Lk 2:56-52). Here the oral Torah also emerges as an object of study.

In general Philo is a thorough-going intellectual who believes in Torah as the true and highest *paideia*; this divine *paideia* or culture brings salvation (*De Plantatione*, 144). Since Philo is not known to have been a member of any particular Palestinian Jewish sect, we may take him as a representative of "Catholic" Judaism, though, of course, a representative *sui generis*. [73]

As our final witness to the ideal of Torah study as a central religious value for the Jews in the pre-Jamnian period we must consider Josephus. Two of his works are especially relevant to our concern— his apology *Contra Apionem* and the *Antiquities of the Jews*. The *Antiquities* were completed by A.D. 93-94, when he was an old man, upwards of 63. The *Contra Apionem* seems to have been completed later, possibly in the early part of the second century. [74] These works have an apologetic bias, presenting Judaism in as favorable a light as possible to the educated Greco-Roman world, and answering that

---

[71] See H. Koester, "Nomos physeōs: the concept of natural law in Greek thought." in *Religions in Antiquity*, ed. J. Neusner (Suppl. to *Numen*, 14; Leiden: Brill, 1968), pp. 521-541.

[72] The four cardinal virtues first emerge in Greek thought clearly in Plato (*Symposium*, 196; *Res publica*, IV, 427-432) and enter the biblical world explicitly in Wisdom 8:7.

[73] On Philo and *paideia* see G. Bertram, TDNT, V, 612-616, and the tractate *De congressu quaerendae eruditionis gratia*.

[74] See H. St. J. Thackeray's introduction to the Loeb edition of his works (Cambridge, Mass.: Harvard, 1966), pp. xii-xiii.

world's critics of his ancestral faith. This accounts for the transfer of categories from Hellenism, e.g., speaking of the major Judean parties or sects as though they were philosophical schools analogous to Greek schools, emphasizing, as did Philo, the role of Torah in teaching the four cardinal virtues. There is undoubtedly an element of idealization in Josephus' picture, but on the other hand, we should not assume that in this particular instance Josephus would have notably altered the picture he gave in his earlier work, the *Jewish War*, for political reasons, since Jewish zeal for Torah was a well-known phenomenon long before A.D. 94. [75]

Since Josephus repeats himself on several relevant topics, we will group his texts together when they treat of common themes. The education of children and the observance of laws.

> Above all we pride ourselves on the education of our children (*paido-trophian*), and regard as the most essential task in life the observance of our laws and of the pious practice, based thereupon, which we have inherited. *Contra Apionem*, I, 60.
> The Law does not allow the birth of our children to be made occasions for festivity and an excuse for drinking to excess. It enjoins sobriety in their upbringing from the very first. It orders that they shall be taught to read, and shall learn both the laws and the deeds of their forefathers, in order that they may imitate the latter, and, being grounded in the former, may neither transgress nor have any excuse for being ignorant of them. *Contra Apionem*, 2:204.
> (Paraphrasing Deut. 11:19). Let your children also begin by learning the laws, most beautiful of lessons and a source of felicity. *Antiquities*, 4:211.

This point is clear enough and requires no comment. The follow two major passages, one explicitly apologetic (*C. Apionem*, 2:170-78), the other (*Ant.*, 4:209-11) summarizing Deut 31:9-12.

---

[75] Morton Smith and Jacob Neusner have claimed that in his later works Josephus has changed his portrait of the Pharisees substantially, heightening their political significance, and in effect making the claim that the country was ungovernable without them. He did this, they claim, because he wished to persuade the Roman authorities that now, in the post-70 situation, when the other parties had disappeared, they had to come to terms with the heirs of the Pharisaic party, the Jamnian rabbis. See Neusner, "Josephus' Pharisees," *Ex orbe religionum*, studia Geo. Widengren... oblata, vol. 1 (Suppl. to *Numen*, 21; Leiden: Brill, 1972), pp. 224-244. Though there may be some truth in this view, it does not bear directly on our point since in both his early and his late portraits of the Pharisees, Josephus stresses their mastery of the laws. Doubtless this gave them a certain political significance throughout their existence, though this significance may well have varied in importance from one time to another.

He [Moses] did not make of religion a department of virtue, but the
various virtues—I mean, justice, temperance, fortitude, and mutual
harmony in all things between the members of the community—
departments of religion. Religion governs all our actions and occupations and speech; none of these things did our lawgiver leave un-
examined or indeterminate.

All schemes of education and moral training fall into two categories;
instruction is imparted in the one case by precept, in the other, by
practical exercising of the character. All other legislators, differing in
their opinions, selected the particular method which each preferred
and neglected the other. Thus the Lacedaemonians and Cretans employed practical, not verbal, training; whereas the Athenians and
nearly all the rest of the Greeks made laws enjoining what actions
might or might not be performed, but neglected to familiarize the
people with them by putting them into practice.

Our legislator, on the other hand, took great care to combine both
systems. He did not leave practical training in morals inarticulate;
nor did he permit the word of the law to remain inoperative. Starting
from the very beginning with the food of which we partake from
infancy and the private life of the home, he left nothing, however
insignificant, to the discretion and caprice of the individual. What
meats a man should abstain from, and what he may enjoy; with what
persons he should associate; what period should be devoted respectively
to strenuous labour and to rest—for all this our leader made the Law
the standard and rule, that we might live under it as under a father
and master, and be guilty of no sin through wilfulness or ignorance.
For ignorance he left no pretext. He appointed the Law to be the most
excellent and necessary form of instruction, ordaining, not that it should
be heard once for all or twice or on several occasions, but that every
week men should desert their other occupations and assemble to listen
to the Law and to obtain a thorough and accurate knowledge of it,
a practice which all other legislators seem to have neglected.

Indeed, most men, so far from living in accordance with their own
laws, hardly know what they are. Only when they have done wrong
do they learn from others that they have transgressed the law. Even
those of them who hold the highest and most important offices admit
their ignorance; for they employ professional legal experts as assessors
and leave them in charge of the administration of affairs. But, should
anyone of our nation be questioned about the laws, he would repeat
them all more readily than his own name. The result, then, of our
thorough grounding in the laws from the first dawn of intelligence
is that we have them, as it were, engraven on our souls. A transgression
is a rarity; evasion of punishments an impossibility.

(*Contra Apionem*, 2:170-78)

The mention of the four cardinal virtues links this passage up with
the section of Philo's *Life of Moses* which we have already considered

and suggests that this point was a commonplace of Hellenistic Jewish religious propaganda, not without a basis in fact. Then the original point is made that Mosaic legislation is superior to the various Greek polities because it combines, as they do not, practical and theoretical training. Ignorance is excluded as an excuse on account of the provision for regular sabbath study. All are expected to memorize the law.

> When the multitude hath assembled in the holy city for the sacrifices, every seven years at the season of the feast of tabernacles, let the high priest, standing upon a raised platform from which he may be heard, recite the laws to the whole assembly; and let neither woman nor child be excluded from this audience, nay nor yet the slaves. For it is good that these laws should be so graven on their hearts and stored in the memory that they can never be effaced. Thus will they be kept from sin, being unable to plead ignorance of what the laws enact; while the laws will speak with great authority to sinners, in that they forewarn them what they will have to suffer and will have so graven on their hearts through the hearing that which they command, that they will forever carry within their breasts the principles of the code: which if they disdain they are guilty, and will have brought their penalty upon themselves. Let your children also begin by learning the laws, most beautiful of lessons and a source of felicity.
>
> (*Antiquities*, 4:209-11)

Over against Deuteronomy 31:9-13, Josephus omits the mention of the *gerim* (resident aliens, in rabbinic literature Gentile proselytes) as present at the reading of the law, but adds on his own the slaves. Once again we note that the law is to be memorized, that ignorance is no excuse, that children are to begin their education in Torah early.

Finally a text on the peculiarity of the Jewish view of wisdom will be appropriate:

> Our people do not favor those persons who have mastered the speech of many nations, or who adorn their style with smoothness of diction, because they consider that not only is such skill common to ordinary freeman but that even slaves who so choose may acquire it. But they give credit for wisdom to those alone who have an exact knowledge of the law and who are capable of interpreting the power of the Holy Scriptures.
>
> (*Antiquities*, 20:264)

With Josephus our account of the background of the rabbinic ideal of Torah study as a high religious value, as a form of worship, is complete. It is clear that in this respect the authors of the Mishnah tractate Aboth were not inventing a wholly new understanding of their ancestral religion. The ideal existed in Israel (a) before the Pharisees, and especially before the Jamnian rabbis, though not the peculiar extension of the purity laws to the laity; (b) in all branches of Jewry save perhaps the Sadducees, though not enough information has come down about them for us to be sure.

We may safely assume that this ideal was a given part of Jesus' religious presuppositions, no matter how obscure these may be in other respects, that is, even if he did not have direct knowledge of the men who produced Aboth.

CHAPTER THREE

THE SYNOPTIC GOSPELS AND THE RABBINIC IDEAL OF TORAH-STUDY AS A FORM OF WORSHIP

In our earlier chapter on Aboth many connections between its sayings and New Testament passages have already been pointed out, but no overall statement was made about the awareness or the attitude of either Jesus or the early church or the Synoptic evangelists to the kind of religious ideal which emerges. It is now time to confront Aboth directly from the viewpoint of the New Testament. For the sake of brevity we will limit ourselves to a consideration of the Synoptics.

Since the Gospels do not directly discuss either the existence or the spirit of early Christian schools, nor the attitude of the Jesus or the early Church toward the theology of Aboth, our investigation meets with several difficulties. We must conduct it for the most part by asking texts which directly aim at something else what indirect light they might shed on our question. Also, as is well known, it is not always easy to sort out accurately the redactional layers within the Gospel tradition as it has come down to us. But we must in any case try to distinguish between the thought of the evangelist, the concern of the early Christian communities, and the teaching of Jesus himself. Finally, since the greatest affinities with Aboth are to be found in the Gospel according to Matthew, our attention will be drawn in a special way to his redactional theology.

1. *School-related Language in the Synoptics*

Though the New Testament never mentions schools and hardly ever Scripture study, it does contain an abundance of language derived from school activities. For example, all four canonical Gospels present Jesus as, at least on the lowest level of appreciation by his contemporaries, a teacher (*didaskalos*), or, as is more familiar to us from older English Bibles, a master. So too his followers are commonly designated disciples, that is literally, learners. Thus the most elementary social description of Jesus' relationship to his followers and their to him is derived from the language of the schoolroom, or at least, from the learners' circle. The question then naturally arises: granted that the pattern of this relationship between Jesus and his disciples does not immediately derive from the model of Greek philosophical schools, does it have affinities with the contemporary pattern of relationship between teacher (denominated variously *ḥakam, moreh, melamed, rabbi, rabban, rab* with varying shades of meaning and varying chronologies of importance) and disciple (*talmid-ḥakam*) which prevailed in Pharisaic Judaism, the group from which the majority of Jesus' religious interlocutors as depicted in the Gospels stem?

While everyone would be willing to admit such affinities in a general way, many authors [1] are at pains rather to emphasize the differences between the learning relationships which obtained among Pharisees and those characteristic of Jesus and his circle. This emphasis has two motives. The first is Christological. If Jesus is indeed the incarnate word of God, how dare we reduce him to the level of a Pharisaic teacher, even if we suppose (what no one denies) that he was a religious genius? Would not this be to flatten out the mystery, to lose the pearl of great price? The second motive must regrettably be described as theologically anti-Semitic in character. (Note the qualification: theologically.) If the heart of the Gospel is understood to be freedom from the law, and Judaism is understood to consist of fidelity to the law, then Judaism becomes the incarnation of everything wrong in religion. The corallary follows naturally that Jesus must be kept as distant as possible from any taint of affinity with his fellow Jews. The one noteworthy exception, Rudolf Bultmann, rather proves the rule. In his work *Jesus and the Word* [2] he directly characterizes Jesus as a rabbi, at least in a loose sense. In his later *Theology of the New Testament* [3] he draws the, for him, necessary anti-Semitic consequence: the teaching of Jesus is irrelevant for the theology of the New Testament, precisely *because* it is so rabbinic. It is precisely in order to refute Bultmann that Rengstorf and Hengel feel obliged to dig as deep a chasm as possible between Jesus and the Pharisaic-rabbinic Jews.

But this is an impossible impasse to which previous research has brought us. We must break out of it, and that, by attacking the two above-mentioned motives. Research into the life of Jesus must be freed

---

[1] K. H. Rengstorf, s.v. *didaskalos*, TDNT, ed. G. Kittel (Grand Rapids: Eerdmans, 1964), vol. II, pp. 148-165; *idem*, s.v. *mathētēs, ibid.*, Vol. IV, pp. 415-461; Martin Hengel, *Nachfolge und Charisma* (BZNW, 34; Berlin: Töpelmann, 1968).

[2] (London: Collins-Fontana, 1958; first German edition, 1926), pp. 48-51.

[3] (New York: Scribner's, 1951), p. 3.

from Lutheran prejudices, based as they are on Pauline, or, as I rather
think, pseudo-Pauline, prejudices, prejudices whatever their origin,
of an anti-Semitic tendency. This proposal hardly requires justification,
but if reasons are sought, apart from a quest for the historical truth
itself, we may suggest (a) that first century Judaism, even Pharisaism,
was too complex a value system to be so easily reduced to fidelity to
the law, and our analysis of Aboth has, we trust, shown the enormous
range of virtualities within an ideal of fidelity to Torah, (b) that
neither the message of the New Testament as a whole, nor that of
Paul in particular can be reduced to or adequately characterized as
freedom from, or rejection of, the law. [4]

With respect to christology, the issues are more delicate. Research
into Jesus' self-understanding eludes a consensus, and even the "assured
results" of a period of research appear to be erected on shaky pillars
and can easily be overturned. For example, the results of a recent
overview of New Testament christology with respect to the self-consciousness of Jesus [5] amount to this: "Jesus understood his mission in
terms of eschatological prophecy and was confident of its vindication
by the Son of Man at the end." This may be saying too little. Can Jesus'
understanding of his life in terms of the suffering servant of Isaiah
40-55 ,of the Son of God in an absolute sense (Mt 11:27 par Lk 10:22;
Mk 13:22, amounting to a Marcan-Q overlap of idiom), and even of
the Son of Man of Daniel 7 be so confidently set aside? For our
purposes this may remain an open question, except perhaps for Mt
11:27 par. The important point is that it not be thought of as a closed
question. On the other hand, research should avoid the extreme which
operates on the principle: whatever is not clearly christological is
unimportant. [6] Rather, the goal must remain an accurate understanding
of Jesus in his historical context.

Having set aside some main theoretical obstacles to a fair consideration of the evidence, we may now turn to a closer look at the
synoptic data.

---

[4] As pointers to a larger body of literature, all of which tends to support this
point, see C. H. Dodd, Gospel and Law (New York: Columbia University Press,
1951); W. D. Davies, Paul and Rabbinic Judaism (London: SPCK, 1948): idem,
Setting of the Sermon on the Mount (Cambridge: U.P., 1964); J. Jeremias, The
Proclamation of Jesus (New York: Scribner's, 1970; J. Dupont, Les Béatitudes,
3 volumes (Études bibliques; Paris: Gabalda, 1965-73).

[5] R. H. Fuller, The Foundations of New Testament Christology (London: Collins-
Fontana, 1969, first ed. 1965), pp. 102-41, esp. p. 130.

[6] Cf. O. Cullmann, The Christology of the New Testament (Philadelphia: Westminster, 1963), pp. 5 f.

a. *Master and disciple* (*teacher and learner, didaskalos and mathētēs*)
   in the Synoptics

For the sake of objectivity a statistical word survey is a good place
to begin. [7] The word *didaskalos* appears in the New Testament with
the following distribution:

	Mt	Mk	Lk	Jn	Acts	Paul	Total NT
didaskalos	12	12	17	8	1	7	59

It appears in the vocative in the Gospels thus:

6	10	12	3

It refers directly to Jesus thus:

10	12	14	7

It will be evident at once that while the incidence is high in all the
Synoptics, the word is especially preferred by Luke.

Cognate words occur in the following statistical patterns:

	Mt	Mk	Lk	Jn	Acts	Paul	Total NT
didaskein	14	17	17	9	16	15	95
didache	3	5	1	3	4	6	30
didaskalia	1	1				19	21
didaktos			1			2	3
didaktikos						2	2

The situation with respect to *mathētēs* and cognates is simpler.

	Mt	Mk	Lk	Jn	Acts	Paul	Total NT
mathētēs	73	46	37	78	28		262

This distribution leads with remarkable clarity to the conclusion that
the term disciple was used to refer to followers of Jesus in the earliest
period predominantly in the Jesus tradition which arose on Palestinian
soil. As soon as the gospel spread to other lands, other terms were
found more suitable. Paul, for example, prefers to speak of slaves
(*douloi*) of Jesus Christ, or simply of "those in Christ." Though the
term disciple fairly quickly comes back into vogue in the Apostolic
Fathers and receives an even greater development among the Alexandrine theologians, as a term for Christians, [8] it may be concluded with

---

[7] Simple word frequencies derive from R. Morgenthaler, *Statistik des neutestamentlichen Wortschatzes* (Zurich: Gotthelf, 1958). Other statistics are my own.

[8] *Mathētēs* occurs 14 times in the Apostolic Fathers, *mathēteuō* four times. See
E. J. Goodspeed, *Index Patristicus* (Leipzig: Hinrich, 1907), s.v. On this and on
the development in Justin and the other apologists, as well as in Irenaeus and
Clement of Alexandria, a development which may be described as a "doctrinification"
of the Good News, see F. Normann, *Christos Didaskalos* (Münster: Aschendorff,
1967), pp. 78-179. This reduction of the Gospel to a doctrine took place in the

some assurance that its original background was Palestinian. This means that its Semitic correlate is *talmid* and that the term is to be understood primarily in connection with Pharisaic-rabbinic institutions, whatever similarities and differences may be noted. The term is especially frequent in Matthew and John. The Talmud itself speaks of *talmidim* of Jesus (b. Sanh. 43a).

The cognate *matheteuein* (to make disciples) occurs three times in Matthew, once in Acts, and is a word not attested in Greek before the New Testament. That the linguistic creativity of the early Church was exercised in precisely this area is striking in itself. 9 Finally, in Acts 9:36 we find the unusual word *mathētria* which refers to a woman disciple. 10

The nuances of the application of these terms within the synoptic Gospels have been the object of a number of recent studies. 11 There is no need to repeat these investigations. It will suffice to summarize their chief relevant results before going on to examine two passages whose significance for our theme has not yet perhaps been sufficiently brought out.

After surveying the relevant Marcan texts (1:17; 2:14; 10:21, 28 f., 32; 8:31-33, 38, besides Mt 8:19-22 par) which have a high claim

---

course of the struggle both against inner-Christian heretics and against pagan and Jewish opponents of Christianity, but also, as P. Nautin points out in his review of Normann in RHR 175 (1969) 85 f, because of the particular social structure which the Christian communities assumed at the end of the first century and which is seen clearly in Ignatius of Antioch.

9 G. Strecker, *Der Weg der Gerechtigkeit* (FRLANT, 82; Göttingen: Vandenhoeck & Ruprecht, 1966), p. 1952, makes the point that *mathēteuein* not only means "to make disciples," but also has overtones of meaning "to instruct," and "to accept into the school."

10 F. Normann, *op. cit.*, p. 52, regards this word *mathētria* as a Lucan invention, and takes it as an expression of Luke's universalism, his concern for women, and his distance from the mentality of rabbinic schools where such a concept was barely conceivable.

11 Erich Fascher, "Jesus der Lehrer," ThLZ 79 (1954): 325-42; Eduard Schweizer, *Lordship and Discipleship* (SBT, 28; London: SCM, 1960), especially pp. 11-21, 77-92; G. Barth in Bornkamm-Barth-Held, *Tradition and Interpretation in Matthew* (Philadelphia: Westminster, 1963), pp. 105-124; G. Strecker, *op. cit.*, pp. 191-206; Friedrich Normann, *op. cit.*, pp. 1-65; Sean Freyne, *The Twelve: Disciples and Apostles* (London: Sheed & Ward, 1968); R. P. Meye, *Jesus and the Twelve* (Grand Rapids: Eerdmann, 1968). On the theme of following see further, besides the work of Hengel, *Nachfolge und Charisma*, mentioned above, Anselm Schulz, *Nachfolgen und Nachahmen* (SANT, 10; Munich: Kösel, 1962), and, esp. on imitation (*mimēsis*) as the Pauline equivalent, H. D. Betz, *Nachfolge und Nachahmung Jesu Christi im N.T.* (B.H.T., 37; Tübingen: Mohr, 1967). Most recently, Mark Sheridan, "Disciples and Discipleship in Matthew and Luke," *Biblical Theology Bulletin* 3 (1973): 235-255.

to reflect the original *Sitz-im-Leben Jesu*, E. Schweizer comes to the
following conclusions.

1. Jesus has called men to follow him; this allegiance to his person
   he regards as a decisive, indeed as *the* decisive act.
2. His calling is the beginning of something new, changing all things.
   It takes place in sovereign liberty and can at once assume the
   character of an act of divine grace.
3. Following Jesus means togetherness with Jesus and service to him.
4. It entails giving up all other ties, to boat and tax-office, to father
   and mother, in short, to one's own life, to oneself.
5. As Jesus' own way, by divine necessity, leads to rejection, suffering
   and death, and only so to glory, so also the way of those who
   follow him. [12]

Was Jesus, as teacher, radically different from contemporary Jewish
teachers? Certain differences may be noted at once: there is his
astonishing independence over against the Pharisaic oral tradition
(Mk 7:1-23; but note the more cautious presentation of this material
in Mt 15:1-20; this presentation, in the light of Acts 10:1-29, probably
reflects the original historical situation more accurately); he often
teaches out of doors, under the open sky, and to large crowds of
ordinary, and even nonobservant, Jews (this may in fact not be a
difference from rabbinic practice: note the frequent references in
rabbinic literature to the "Vineyard of Jamnia" and M. Men. 10:9); [13]
he works miracles readily and as though by personal power, unlike
his Galilean contemporaries Honi (Onias) the Circle-Drawer and
Hanina ben-Dosa, both renowned for effecting miracles, but by ardent
prayer, not by a commanding word or touch; [14] the content of his
teaching passes over easily from ethical instruction to apocalyptic
warning. It remains more uncertain how to interpret the "authority"
with which he spoke, and which aroused the astonishment of his
listeners (Mk 1:22 and 27).

Opinion varies widely partly because, as we have said, the Christological problem can arise here. Some representative views: (1) Cull-

---

[12] *Lordship and Discipleship*, p. 20.

[13] See A. Büchler, "Learning and Teaching in the Open Air in Palestine," JQR
n.s. 4 (1913): pp. 485-491; S. Krauss, "Outdoor Teaching in Talmudic Times," JJS 1
(1948-49): pp. 82-84.

[14] See the stories in b. Taᶜanit 19b-26a (Sonc., pp. 94-135): P. Fiebig, *Rabbinische
Wundergeschichten des neutestamentlichen Zeitalters*, (Kl. T. 78, Bonn, 1911); *idem,
Jüdische Wundergeschichten des neutestamentlichen Zeitalters* (Tübingen: Mohr, 1911);
A. Schlatter, *Das Wunder in der Synagoge* (BFCT, 16, 5, Gutersloh: Mohn, 1912);
G. Vermes, JJS 22 (1973): 25-48.

mann, [15] Bultmann, [16] and Bornkamm [17] deny the titles *didaskalos/ rabbi* any Christological weight in themselves. Cullmann admits a use of *didaskalos* as opposed to *rabbi*, but this he treats as merely a variant of the "prophet like Moses" title. Bultmann speculates that Jesus was even rabbinically ordained after a regular course of studies. Bornkamm calls attention to a bold, new freedom in Jesus' teaching but denies any final break with Judaism. (2) Daube believes that Jesus taught as a rabbi; he understands Jesus' authority (Mk 1:22-27) as *reshut*, the authority to lay down doctrines and decisions that are of binding force. [18] The shock of the crowds (Mk 1:27) may have been due to this: Jesus had not received proper ordination (*semicha*), and yet presumed to act as a rabbi. A decision on this view is bedeviled by the fact that we do not know how tightly rabbinic training and orders were controlled in the first century. Before A.D. 70 teachers had a freer hand in developing the law than later. In any case Jesus was not a mere legal expert (cf. Mt 7:29). (3) For Dodd, Jesus' authority was originally *ke-shalet*: "he taught them like a sovereign" (Mk 1:22), in any case not simply "like one authorized to teach." Jesus as teacher is also a prophet, and yet more than a prophet, because the message is realized in him. Thus the teaching activity contains the germ of Christology. [19] (4) Finally, for Rengstorf, Jesus associates himself directly with God through his teaching, he is the new Moses, the absolute *didaskalos*. [20] As such, he alone has the right to be called *didaskalos* for Christians. According to Rengstorf, the strict rule of Mt 23:8 was observed in earliest Christianity, and the later abridgement of this rule was a declension from primeval purity. But violations of the rule begin with Paul and Acts, and the rule itself is evidently a product of the Matthean redaction, so that Rengstorf's exegetical contortions to maintain his view are quite unconvincing.

For our purposes there is no need to decide on the intrinsic Christological weight of the title *didaskalos* as applied to Jesus. We merely observe that (a) when, whether on other grounds or not, Jesus is

---

[15] *Op. cit.*, p. 6 n. 1, p. 13.

[16] *Op. cit.*, pp. 48-51.

[17] Gunther Bornkamm, *Jesus of Nazareth* (New York: Harper, 1961), pp. 96-100.

[18] David Daube, "*exousia* in Mk 1:22 and 27," JTS 39 (1938): 45-59.

[19] C. H. Dodd, "Jesus as Teacher and Prophet," *Mysterium Christi*, ed. G. K. A. Bell and A. Deissmann (London: Longmans, 1930), pp. 53-66.

[20] TDNT, II, pp. 156 f. For a cautious critique of Jesus as new Moses, see W. D. Davies, *Setting of the Sermon on the Mount* (Cambridge: U.P., 1964), p. 108, and on Jesus as teacher, prophet and rabbi, *ibid.*, pp. 418-425.

believed to be the Christ, the fact that he was a teacher cannot be passed over but remains as a significant aspect of his total person and work; (b) it does not automatically follow that if one rejects a Christological weight to the title, Jesus would cease to be for many the absolute *didaskalos*, i.e., it is possible to choose a human teacher, e.g., Socrates or Plato, as an ultimate guide to life.

The preceding observations attempted to deal with the earliest stratum of the material, mainly Marcan, insofar as it could shed light on the situation at the time of Jesus. We may now consider some of the redactional nuances as they emerge in the individual gospels.

Contrasting Mark and Matthew we notice two main differences. First, for Mark the disciples (*hoi māthētai*) are primarily the tight circle of the twelve. Jesus is primarily *their* master and they address him as such. In Matthew, by contrast, the rabbi of twelve talmidim has become the teacher of the entire community of Christians. That is, the disciples include not only the original twelve but also all those who heard him gladly then as well as all those who follow him in the post-Easter church. [21] On the other hand, the disciples do not address him any longer as master but as lord (*kyrie*). Only polite outsiders now address Jesus as master. Over against Mark then, Matthew has achieved an escalation of Christology. [22]

The second difference is this. Mark is obliged by his theme of the messianic secret, however, that is to be explained, to emphasize the incomprehension of the disciples with respect to Jesus. Their hearts are hardened (Mk 6:52; 8:17 f) and they are even guilty of unbelief (*apistia*) (6:6; cf. 9:24). In Matthew by contrast this incomprehension is transformed into understanding (*synienai*, nine times in Matthew out of a total of twenty-six times in the New Testament) and this trait becomes one of the chief characteristics of Jesus' followers. In this they differ from the obdurate multitude. This understanding is not a

---

[21] F. Normann, *op. cit.*, p. 41. Strecker, *op. cit.*, p. 192 f has the situation exactly reversed. "The assertion that this concept [*hoi mathētai*] contained an historicizing tendency and was reserved for the Twelve stands the matter on its head," G. Bornkamm, "The Risen Lord and the Earthly Jesus," in *The Future of our Religious Past* (Bultmann Fs.), ed. J. M. Robinson (London: SCM, 1971), p. 218 n. 50. On the title *kyrios* in Matthew see now J. D. Kingsbury, "The title 'kyrios' in Matthew's Gospel," JBL 94 (1975): 246-255.

[22] In Mk Jesus is addressed as *didaskalos* by his own disciples four times: 4:38; 5:35; 10:35; 13:1; he calls himself *didaskalos* once: 14:14. In Mt Jesus is never called *didaskalos* by his own disciples, but note 10:24 f; 23:8 (on both of which see further below); and finally 26:18, derived from Mk 14:14.

purely intellectual matter because its opposite is not stupidity but obduracy. Positively, it consists in the opening of the understanding to revelation. Thus, like faith, it is a gift, though the sensitivity of the intellect is not excluded. The consequence of this understanding is "bearing fruit" (Mt 13:23). [23]

This transformation of the image of the disciples has often been described as an idealization in contrast with the rather unflattering picture in Mark. But with the greater awareness of the theological motives behind Mark's picture it is reasonable to suppose that Matthew's presentation reflects some historic truth suppressed by Mark, though, given Matthew's concern for the church and its ministers, he also had theological motives for his presentation. [24]

Other redactional contributions of Matthew include his emphasis on the disciples' faith as trust in Jesus. This occurs because the intellectual element in faith has been shifted to the *synienai* theme. The willing element thus becomes paramount. Faith comes to be understood as obedience and fidelity to the covenant (in this case, the promise of Jesus), and is therefore also closer to the Old Testament *he²emin*. A curious aspect of faith in Matthew's gospel is that it presupposes understanding on the part of the disciples. Weakness of faith in the disciples is characterized as "little faith" (*oligopistia*, a Matthean word [once]; *oligopistos*: Mt four times, Lk once), a defective, disobedient faith. [25]

Disciples in Matthew are also characterized as little ones (*mikroi*; Mt 18 and 5:3-6), that is, by the qualities of humility, weakness and helplessness before God which typify the *anawim* of the Old Testament. *Praus* (meek) is a peculiarly Matthean word and signifies the one who waits empty-handed before God. [26] The disciples are sent out to preach and, in Matthew, their preaching as well as their authority are assimilated to the message and authority of Jesus and indeed of God himself (cp. 10:1 with 9:35 and 4:23-25; 10:7 with 4:17; contrast 9:8 with Lk 2:1-12; note further Mt 10:40 on which more below, 16:19 and 18:18). The range of their mission is the same as Jesus' (cp. 10:5 to 15:24), only to the lost sheep of the house of Israel ,until after the resurrection, when a new epoch begins (28:19).

---

[23] Barth, in Bornkamm-Barth-Held, *op. cit.*, pp. 105-112.

[24] Strecker, *op. cit.*, pp. 193 f, still speaks of idealization. Barth, *op. cit.*, prefers to speak of a toning down, a passing over, a twisting round of the unbelief and sin of the disciples.

[25] Barth, in Bornkamm-Barth-Held, *op. cit.*, pp. 112-121.

[26] *Ibid.*, pp. 121-24.

In their task, Strecker suggests, the ministry of the word is made more important than that of healing which is subordinated to it (10:5-8), though this is not quite certain. [27]

Turning to Luke's redactional characteristics, we note the statement that Luke keeps the scholastic framework of Jesus' relationship to his followers, because it is an ineradicable part of the tradition about Jesus, but he is not attracted to it nor does he emphasize it. [28] While this general statement contains some truth, the facts are not quite so simple. For, as we have seen, Luke employs *didaskalos* more often than either Matthew or Mark (12/12/17). On the other hand, the frequency of *mathētēs* falls behind that in Matthew and even that in brief Mark (73/46/37). He consistently replaces rabbi with his peculiar word *epistatēs*. He emphasizes Jesus as the compassionate doer, the healer, as over against the teacher (cf. Lk 22:51 with Mt 26:52-54). He extends the term disciple to *all* followers of Jesus, even (in Acts) to those who never met him, thereby giving expression to the universalism characteristic of his gospel. [29]

b. *Scribe (grammateus)*

Here we may simply observe a peculiarity of Matthew's gospel. While all the synoptists use this term, consecrated by its use in the later books of the Old Testament, to describe the educated opponents of Jesus, Matthew twice uses it to describe some followers of Jesus (13:52; 23:34). It becomes, along with prophets, wise men, and apostles, one of the terms to describe leaders in the church. Thus Matthew presupposes a role for men of some learning in the church. Their task is defined in 13:52 as interpreting the Christ-event in terms of the Old Testament revelation and correspondingly interpreting the Old Testament in the light of the Christ-event. The best example of their work is the gospel of Matthew itself. Indeed, this passage (13:52) might almost be taken as a little self-portrait of the author of the Gospel. [30]

Before leaving this section two texts must be examined. The first is Mt 23:8-10: "But you are not to be called rabbi, for you have one teacher (*ho didaskalos*), and you are all brethren. And call no man

---

27 Strecker, *op. cit.*, pp. 194-6.
28 Normann, *op. cit.*, pp. 45 f, 55.
29 *Ibid.*, pp. 45-54.
30 See further Joseph Hoh, "Der christliche *grammateus* (Mt 13:52)," B.Z. 17 (1926): 256-269. On rabbi, see Chapter 1 above on Aboth 1:6.

your father on earth, for you have one Father, who is in heaven. Neither be called masters (*kathēgētai*), for you have one master (*kathēgētēs*), the Christ." (These are the only two instances of the word *kathēgētēs* in the New Testament.) These verses are unattested outside of Matthew, and at least the phrase "heavenly father" in v. 9 is characteristic of the Matthean redaction. There can be little doubt that these verses represent a late construction, motivated partly by antirabbinic polemic (vv. 2-7), partly by a concern for the exalted and unique dignity of Jesus as the Christ (v. 10), and partly by an ethical concern for humility as an abiding characteristic of all disciples (vv. 11 and 12). They were probably never rigidly enforced. Compare for instance the nervous compromise in James (3:1); "Let not many of you become teachers, my brethren, for you know that we who teach shall be judged with greater strictness." That Paul, who was from an earlier time, knew no such rule as we find in Mt 23:8-10 is plain from 1 Cor 12:28 f: "God has appointed in the church first apostles, second prophets, third teachers (*didaskalous*)...." Why then the strange impractical rule in Matthew? Perhaps partly because Matthew, unlike the other biblical authors, takes Jesus' activity as teacher with Christological seriousness as part of his messianic or rather Mosaic dignity. However that may be, he had another motive sufficiently strong to account for his redactional activity. This may be described, in the sense to be explained, as an antignostic motive.

This motive can now, since the discovery of the Gospel of Thomas, be seen at work more clearly in the second of the texts we must consider: Mt 10:24 f par. Lk 6:40 (cf. Jn 13:16).

Mt 10:24 f	Lk 6:40
(24) A disciple is not above his teacher, nor a servant (*doulos*) above his master (*kyrios*); (25) it is enough for the disciple to be like his teacher, and the servant like his master. If they have called the master of the house Beelzehub, how much more will they malign those of his household.	A disciple is not above his teacher, but every one when he is fully taught will be like his teacher.

In order to understand the tradition-history of these verses, i.e., how the more elaborate Matthean form developed out of the simpler, theologically more problematic Lucan form, it will help to consider logion 13 from the Gospel of Thomas, whose complete text was discovered in Coptic translation at Nag Hammadi in Egypt in 1945.

Jesus said to his disciples (*mathētēs*): Make me a comparison; tell me what I am like. Simon Peter said to him: you are like a righteous (*dikaios*) angel (*aggelos*). Matthew said to him: You are like a man who is a wise philosopher (*philosophos*). Thomas said to him: Master, my mouth will not at all (*holos*) be capable of saying what you are like. Jesus said: I am not your master, because (*epei*) you drank (and) became drunken from the bubbling spring (*pēgē*) which I have measured out. And he took him (and) went aside (*anachorein*) (and) spoke three words to him. Now (*de*) when Thomas came (back) to his companions, they asked him: What did Jesus say to you? Thomas said to them: If I tell you one of the words that he said to me, you will take up stones (and) cast (them) at me, and a fire will come forth from the stones (and) will burn you up. [31]

Apart from their value for the elucidation of Mt 23:8-10, these (canonical) gospel texts are important because they provide the only explicit comment on the master-disciple relationship in early, possibly authentic, material. We may reconstruct the tradition history thus. The Lucan form is more original. It contains no mention of the slave-to-lord relationship, but it does say that everyone when he is fully taught, or perfected (*katērtismenos*), will be like his teacher. Though these last words may be understood in ways compatible with what became Christian orthodoxy, by themselves, in their extreme brevity, they may be understood in a way which may fairly be characterized as gnostic. This interpretation would run something like this: the kingdom which Jesus brought is actually a message about the self of the disciple. The kingdom is his divine self if he would only recognize it. Once he does, he has no more need of the master who has enlightened him. He himself becomes divine and self-sufficient. In this scheme any sense of the finality of Jesus Christ or of our abiding dependence upon him in the sense of Mt 23:8-10 disappears.

This may be the sense of logion 13 of the Gospel of Thomas, when Jesus replies to Thomas: "I am not your master, because you drank and became drunken from the bubbling spring which I have measured out." It is even possible that the secret words then spoken by Jesus to Thomas, which must have been highly offensive to orthodox opinion, made explicit precisely this point. [32]

---

[31] Coptic text in A. Guillaumont, H.-Ch. Puech, G. Quispel, W. Till and Yassah Abd al Masih, *The Gospel according to Thomas* (New York: Harper, 1959), pp. 8-10; English translation from K. Aland, *Synopsis quattuor evangeliorum* (Stuttgart: Württembergische Bibelanstalt, 1964), p. 519.

[32] Other explanations of the three secret words in R. M. Grant, *The Secret Sayings of Jesus* (New York: Doubleday, 1960), pp. 131-4. For the view presented

It is not our intention to suggest that Matthew's version of the gospel saying is intended as a direct refutation of the Gospel of Thomas. The logion from the Gospel of Thomas is relevant only as a (possibly) late literary precipitate of a danger present from the beginning. In any case Matthew clearly seems to be exercising his redactional prerogative to parry precisely this kind of interpretation. [33]

He achieves his end in two stages. (a) He adds the slave-master contrast. That this is an addition may be indicated by the resulting grammatical awkwardness in v. 25b, where *doulos* should properly be in the dative if it is to be really parallel to *tō mathētē* (Lagrange, *Mt., in loco*). The addition shows that Matthew is unwilling that Jesus be considered merely a teacher. By shifting the relationship to that of slave and lord he transforms it into a post-Easter context and, perhaps unwittingly, employs the same terminology as Paul. (b) He suppresses the dangerous second half of the Lucan verse altogether and replaces it with a quite new construction (v. 25c), which has as its point the familiar theme that the follower can expect to share the sufferings and opprobrium of the leader. [34]

In summary then, it is clear that the most certain features of the relationship of Jesus to his followers was that it took the form of master to disciples, a form for which there was ample precedent in the Jewish parties of Palestine at that time, especially among the Pharisees and Essenes. Jesus more than fulfilled the injunction of the men of the Great Synagogue: "Raise up many disciples" (Aboth 1:1). His followers heeded, in their fashion, the counsel of Joshua ben Perahyah: "Provide thyself with a teacher and get thee a fellow [-disciple]" (Aboth 1:6). To this extent at least Jesus and his followers shared the values of the wise men of Israel of their day. This feature of the Gospel tradition is least ambiguous in the earliest strata. It recedes

---

above see E. Haenchen, *Die Botschaft des Thomasevangeliums* (Berlin: Töpelmann, 1961), pp. 39-49.

[33] For a statement of how Paul, the Pastorals, John and Luke-Acts met the challenge of Hellenistic religious culture in its gnostic-theosophist form, see Hans von Campenhausen, "Faith and Culture in the New Testament," in *Tradition and Life in the Church* (Philadelphia: Fortress, 1968), pp. 19-41.

[34] The form of this novum is that of the rabbinic argument *a fortiori* (*a maiori ad minus, qal va-homer*). The word for members of the household (*oikiakos*) is peculiar to Mt's gospel (twice) and unattested in pre-Christian Greek. That Jesus was in fact accused of being aided by Beelzebul is attested both in Mk (3:22) and Q (Mt 12:24 and 27; Lk 11:15 and 18). Verse 25a has a close parallel in b. Ber 58b (bar.). Bultmann, HST, thinks of a proverb inserted into the Gospel but this can not be shown for v. 24 which must therefore be ascribed to Jesus (so Grundmann, *Mt, in loco*).

gradually under the pressure from advancing Christology, though it never disappears entirely from the Gospels.

Given this basic terminological and sociological similarity, the room for differences remains considerable. What is unlikely however is that Jesus' attitude to the religious intellectual culture of his people and his day be one of simple rejection. Nor it is likely that this would be his people's attitude to him. [35]

2. Jesus' Relation to the Pharisees and to the am ha-aretz

In this section we will first frame an overall hypothesis and then measure it against several important gospel texts. These texts all have some claim to derive from a stage of the tradition prior to the final redaction, but whether they exactly reflect the teaching of Jesus himself remains a subject of earnest dispute. Their interpretation also remains disputed, but it is not necessary for us to exhaust their meaning, but only to notice the support they lend to our overall hypothesis.

This hypothesis may be stated as follows: Jesus did not simply reject the religious values of the Pharisees of his day, values which later came to literary expression in the tractate Aboth, and which may be summarized as taking the Torah with radical seriousness. On the contrary, he shared their deep love of Torah and their concern to take it with radical seriousness as the word of God addressed to men. As far as party affiliations go, there seems little doubt that he felt closer to the Pharisees than to any other group in contemporary Judaism, precisely because they were more in earnest about doing the will of God than any of the other groups, with the possible exception of the Essenes. [36] His positive attitude was more likely also reciprocated by

---

[35] On the virtualities within this relationship see the profound essay by Joachim Wach, "Master and Disciple: Two Religio-sociological Studies," JR 42 (1962): 1-21.

[36] The Essenes are never mentioned in the gospels, though their influence may be represented therein to some extent by the figure of John the Baptist. The Pharisees are the most frequently mentioned of the sects (21/12/27/19), followed by the Sadducees (7/1/1/0), plainly a Matthean concern. The Herodians are only mentioned in Mt and Mk (1/2), Mk 3:6 and 12:13; Mt 22:16, the question of tribute to Caesar), the Zealots only by Luke (6:15, Simon). Matthew's relatively frequent mention of the Sadducees is taken by Kilpatrick to mean that Matthew used the name "Sadducees" as a collective label for all non-Pharisaic Jews (cp. 16:6 with Mk 8:15), without knowing much about them (G. D. Kilpatrick, *The Origins of the Gospel according to St. Matthew* (Oxford: Clarendon, 1964), p. 120. R. Hummel, *Die Auseinandersetzung zwischen Kirche und Judentum im Matthäusevangelium* (Munich: Kaiser, 1963), pp. 18-20, holds that Mt regarded the doctrinal differences between the two parties as unessential. Thi can be seen in 22:34 f where Pharisees come to the rescue of the Sadducees who have just been bested in verbal combat. Also Mt joins them

some Pharisees, as the rather tantalizingly brief verse Lk 13:31 may suggest.

On the other hand, Jesus did not accept the Pharisaic view without qualifications. (1) He opposed their halachic interpretation of the law on many points as what may most accurately be described as a trivialization or atomization of the law, and that precisely at the points where the Pharisaic movement seems to have made its firmest and even constitutive stand, the question of tithing (Mt 23:23 f. = Lk 11:42 = Q), and the question of "wings" (cleanness of hands) (Mk 7:1-23; Mt 15:1-20). [37] (2) He opposed the breakup of religious Judaism into small, tightly organized sects since this development had the practical effect of abandoning and excluding large numbers of the people, especially the Galilean peasantry and/or what were called the *am ha-aretz*. This exclusion was made necessary in part by the greater and greater refinement of halachic jurisprudence. The refinement made people more and more dependent upon the learned scribes and also put pressure on them to become lifelong students of the law if they wished to be fully righteous (*tammim*) before God. Jesus was not opposed to study of Torah as a high religious value, if his familiarity with it and his readiness to expound it in the synagogue are any indication (Lk 4:16-22; Mk 6:2; Mt 13:54; Mt 4:23; 9:35; Mk 1:39; Lk 4:55), but he was unwilling to make proficiency in it a condition or measurement of salvation (cp. Mt 16:12 with M. Kid. 1:10).

It seems evident that he considered that the Pharisees were developing the Torah in a false, impractical and unrealistic direction which would in fact prove disastrous for the nation. To avert this disaster he may at least have begun the development of a new halacha with respect to matters like Sabbath observance (an area where the rabbis admitted that their halacha had weak scriptural foundation, M. Hag. 1:8). This was the more possible in that often he was building on tendencies which already existed within observant Jewry (cf. the mitigation of the extremes of sabbath observance, 1 Macc 2:37 f, by Hillel, Tos. Erubin 4:7 (Zuckermandel, p. 142); Tos. Shab. 15:17 (Z., p. 134); Mek. Ex. 31:13 (Lauterbach, III, p. 203). The same intent may be observed in his deliberate eating with "sinners" (Mk 2:14-17;

---

under one article (3:7; 16:1, 6, 11, 12, 12), a usage which must have offended Pharisees, who regarded Sadducees as heretics. See further Sjef Van Tilborg, *The Jewish Leaders in Matthew* (Leiden: Brill, 1972), pp. 1-3.

[37] See J. Neusner, "The Fellowship (*haburah*) in the Second Jewish Commonwealth," HTR 53 (1960): 125-142.

Mt 11:19), his teaching of neutrality toward the imperial state (Mk 12:13-17 par), his concentration on the second table of the ten commandments (in the six antitheses of the Sermon on the Mount, Mt 5:21-48, which have the overall effect of both radicalizing or sharpening the ethical commandments and also bringing them down to the level of everyday life, e.g., not just murder but anger, not just adultery but lustful intent) and on the double commandment of love and on the Golden Rule (Mk 12:28-34 par; Mt 7:12 = Lk 6:31), a tendency then overall to elevate the ethical over the ceremonial and the ritual precepts without however ever abolishing these latter. In addition there is in Jesus' ministry an emphasis on the charismatic (the many healings and exorcisms), the prophetic and the sapiential, all forms of Israel's earlier religious life which remained either dormant or peripheral in the Pharisaism of his day. [38]

With respect to the *am ha-aretz* or religious lower class of Palestinian Jewry, our hypothesis would run: Jesus was sensitive to their needs, he judged that the Pharisees could never meet them, and he directed his mission to them in a special way (Mt 15:25; 11:25 par; Mk 2:17 par; 6:34 par). Little wonder then that many of them received him as a messenger of God sent directly to them (Mk 1:45; 1:22; 12:37). [39]

---

[38] Cp. R. Bultmann, "We can say the following concerning Jesus' activity: Characteristic for him are exorcisms, the breech of the Sabbath commandment, the abandonment of ritual purifications, polemic against Jewish legalism, fellowship with outcasts such as publicans and harlots, sympathy for women and children; it can also be seen that Jesus was not an ascetic like John the Baptist, but gladly ate and drank a glass of wine. Perhaps we may add that he called disciples and assembled about himself a small company of followers—men and women," "The Primitive Christian Kerygma and the Historical Jesus," trans. and published in C. E. Braaten and Roy A. Harrisville, eds., *The Historical Jesus and the Kerygmatic Christ* (Nashville: Abingdon, 1964), pp. 15-42.

The picture provided by Bultmann differs from ours primarily in the use of the words like "breech" and "abandonment." The difference stems from a somewhat different view of Jesus' attitude toward the Torah, a notoriously delicate issue. It is hoped that what follows will provide some justification for our view. On meals with "sinners" see J. R. Donahue, "Tax collectors and sinners," CBQ 33 (1971): 39-61, and the literature there cited.

[39] Whether those of Jesus' followers whose former occupations are known to us should be described as members of the Galilean peasantry is not clear. Perhaps it would be more accurate in the case of the fishermen and tax collectors to speak of members of the "industrial" and bureaucratic (lower) middle class. B. Reicke, *The New Testament Era* (Philadelphia: Fortress, 1968), pp. 102 f., speaks of the Galilean fishing industry as a major enterprise, which exported its products even to foreign countries. As to their educational level there are two texts in the New Testament which offer some information: John 7:49 (cf. 7:15): "But this crowd, who do not know the law, are accursed"; Acts 4:13: "Now when they saw the boldness of Peter and John, and perceived that they were uneducated, common men (*agram-*

Summing up, then, we may say that Jesus' relation to the Pharisaic ideal of Torah study as a form of worship was dialectical. On the one hand he affirmed the abiding religious value of the Torah and the study which it demands, as well as of the ethically oriented proverbial wisdom traditional in Israel and of which he was a master. On the other hand, he was opposed to the social division, exclusivity, and at least unintentional arrogance which accompanied it, even in its best representatives (Ab 2:6), as well as to its misplaced emphasis on ritual purity as a paramount value, because this led almost inevitably to a trivialization and flattening out of the Torah. One could indeed conclude with the insight that it was precisely because of his great love and respect for Torah, or rather, for the great and sacred realities to which it gave access, which led to his break with and attack upon the Pharisaic way. [40]

---

matoi ... kai idiōtai), they wondered; and they recognized that they had been with Jesus." The text from John refers to a whole crowd, whose cultural level might be quite varied. The accusation that they knew not the law may mean no more than that they disagreed with the Pharisaic interpretation of it and were hence ritually unclean ("accursed") from a Pharisaic point of view. A. Souter, *Lexicon to the Greek New Testament* (Oxford: Clarendon, 1943), s.vv., explains them: "(a) *agrammatos*, unlettered, illiterate, uneducated, perhaps with the narrower idea, unacquainted with Rabbinic teaching; (b) *idiōtēs*, an amateur an unprofessional man, a layman." All that is certain is that they had not received a formal course of rabbinic higher education. Otherwise, their religious culture should probably not be underestimated.

It has been suggested, e.g., by S. S. Cohon, "The place of Jesus in the religious life of his day," JBL 48 (1929): 82-108, that Jesus himself was an *am ha-aretz*. Though this is an initially attractive hypothesis, on balance it seems better to avoid it. After all, what can it mean? Only that Jesus was not a dedicated member of one of the existing religious parties? Then it does not tell us much. That he was ignorant of Torah or of Pharisaic customary law and interpretation of Torah? This is not borne out by our information. In view of the fact that we know so little of Jesus' family background and social class and education during his years of adolescence and early manhood, it is better to remain silent on this point, except to assert both for Jesus and for his inner circle of followers that they were literate, and had some biblical culture. See the stronger assertions of D. Flusser, *Jesus* (New York: Herder & Herder, 1969), pp. 18-20; 44-64, who makes the interesting point that in talmudic circles joiners (*naggar*) (= carpenters?) were regarded as particularly learned (p. 20), based on j. Yeb 9b; j. Kid, 66a; b. AZ 50b.

[40] Our view as here stated does not differ materially from that of John Bowker, *Jesus and the Pharisees* (Cambridge: U.P., 1973), pp. 38-52, who however adds a discussion of how this comparatively nuanced disagreement with the Pharisees could have led, as one among several factors, to his death. Geza Vermes, in conversation, has described the disagreement between Jesus and the Pharisees not as a Yes-No, but as a Yes, But, something finally more unbearable than a total rejection. As Albert Einstein has well said: "Richtig streiten kann man nur mit seinen Brudern und nahen Freunden; die andern sind einem zu fremd." For a comparison of fellowship among early Christians, Pharisaic associations, and Qumran sectaries, see the fine pages of J. Neusner, *The Rabbinic Traditions...*, vol. 3, pp. 297-300.

This then is the hypothesis, not startling in itself, though somewhat singular in urging the commonality between Jesus and the Pharisees of love of Torah and its study as an important religious value. It remains to test this hypothesis by the examination of relevant gospel texts. Our hypothesis is supported not only by certain programmatic passages which we will examine in detail (Mt 5:17-20; 11:25-30; 10:40-42 and their Lucan parallels), but also by the conflict or controversy stories (*Streitgespräche*) in the gospels, e.g., Mt 9:1-8; 9:9-13; 12:1-8; 12:9-14; 15:1-20; 19:1-9 and their Marcan parallels. It would be valuable to examine all these passages as a preparation and support for our interpretation of the first texts mentioned, but this work has already been done for the redactional level and there is no need to do it over again. [41] But the contribution which the conflict stories make may be illustrated by one example, Mk 7:1-23 par Mt 15:1-20, and a case made for the great historical plausibility of the Matthean version as over against the Marcan, when one presses the text for information with respect to the earliest stratum (something Hummel does not do).

Mk 7:1-23 par Mt 15:1-20

A careful comparison of these two passages makes clear that Matthew has systematically, even subtly, rewritten and rearranged his Marcan *Vorlage*. He has done this with the intent of showing that Jesus remained faithful to Torah, although he broke with the Pharisaic oral traditions of how it was to be applied and supplemented. Two things hold our attention: (1) How did Matthew achieve his end? (2) With what historical right did he effect his editorial revision?

1. Without going into an exhaustive analysis of the pericope we may note the following major points. First, the division or structuring of the material has been delicately altered. The pericope in Mark has as its overall theme Jewish ritual traditions and their abrogation. Though a sharp contrast is drawn between the word of God in Torah and the tradition of the elders (five times as opposed to three times in Matthew), in fact no pains are taken to distinguish ritual practices based on Torah from those which are not, nor biblical vices from others. Thus the most logical and natural division of the pericope is into three parts corresponding to three different ritual practices: Mk 7:1-8 hand-

---

[41] R. Hummel, *op. cit.*, pp. 34-56; English summary in J. Rohde, *Rediscovering the Teaching of the Evangelists* (Philadelphia: Westminster, 1968), pp. 102 f (inadequate); Latin summary by M. Zerwick, in *Verbum Domini* 41 (1963): 217-222.

washing; vv. 9-13 Corban; vv. 14-23 the belief in *kashrut* or defilement from unclean foods. Matthew has broken this clear structure by the suppression of two Marcan clauses (*ou dynatai auton koinōsai*, Mk 7:18, and the crucial gloss in Mk 7:19b) and by one addition, Mt 15:20b, which brings back the subject of handwashing (Mark's first point) at the very end, giving the impression that handwashing is the main subject of the whole pericope. Matthew knew what he was doing. He concentrated attention on Jesus' rejection of Pharisaic customs (handwashing and Corban oaths) but suppressed any suggestion that Jesus broke any biblical precepts (kosher food laws). Thus his pericope is most naturally divided not according to subject matter, but according to the different audiences addressed: Mt 15:1-9 scribes; vv. 10 and 11 the crowd; vv. 12-20 the disciples. This same grouping is present in Mark (vv. 1-13; 14 and 15; 17-23), but is not dominant there. Second, for Mark the crucial logion comes in v. 15: "There is nothing outside a man which by going into him can defile him; but the things which come out of a man are what defile him." This logion is then commented on in vv. 18-20. This radical logion is rather warily repeated in Mathew's v. 11 with some apparently insignificant changes, and then followed in Mt 15:12-14 by two verses probably from Q which have the effect of heightening the anti-Pharisaic point, while v. 17 goes on, as we have noted, to weaken Mark's antibiblical ritual point (*kashrut*). Matthew formulates the logion in v. 20, restricting it to the matter of handwashing and expressing it as a new *halacha*. Third, the catalogue of thirteen vices listed in Mark 7:21 f which includes both biblical and general Hellenistic items is shortened by Matthew to seven vices, all derived from the ten commandments. Matthew presents Jesus as Torah-true throughout, breaking only with the Pharisaic halacha and formulating a new halacha for his followers.

2. Did Matthew have any historical grounds for his redaction of Mark? Is not this redaction simply a tendentious rewriting in the interests of the Jewish-Christian church? Probably not. The text of Mark, traditionally thought to have been written in Gentile territory, under the influence of leaders of the Gentile mission, betrays signs of having conflated the situation at the time of Jesus with the situation at the time and place of writing. We can see this especially in the interpretative gloss or inner-biblical exegesis at v. 19b, and in the inclusion of vices listed elsewhere in the New Testament only in Paul (e.g., *aphrosynē*). Matthew, by means of his deft alterations, may

have introduced a scholastic precision into the narrative foreign both to Mark and to Jesus, but he has nevertheless very likely retained or restored a more accurate overall picture of the original situation. That is, the probability is great that Jesus never formally and explicitly rejected the Torah, even with respect to ritual matters. Otherwise the early Christian opposition to Paul, who abrogated these ritual prescriptions, especially circumcision, for his Gentile converts, would be unintelligible (see Gal 2 and 3, Acts 15). With respect to kosher food laws, which are the principal point of difference here between Mark and Matthew, if Jesus had been so clearly opposed to them, there would have been no need for a special revelation to Peter on the point, in the case of the Gentile convert Cornelius and his family (Acts 10). Further, when accusations are brought against Jesus in Luke 23:2-5, though it is said that he is "perverting our nation" and that he "stirs up the people" by his teaching, the charge is never explicitly made that he taught violation of Torah as a principle.

We conclude then that in this crucial and typical conflict story, Matthew accurately portrays Jesus' attitude both to Torah (positive) and to Pharisaic halacha (negative), while Mark betrays a later stage of Hellenization or Paulinization. [42]

Mt 5:17-20 par Lk 16:16-17

In dealing with verses so controverted by interpreters, it seems important to approach the determination of the meaning by as objective a method as possible. Thus, with respect to the urgent question of authenticity we shall adopt a procedure which may perhaps be overly critical. Some authors accept the substantial authenticity of all four verses, or at least the first three. [43] Others assume that v. 17 goes back to Jesus, that vv. 18-19 probably go back to a Jewish-Christian

---

[42] Cf. Hummel's treatment, *op. cit.*, pp. 46-9, which differs from the above in that it argues that for Matthew even the scribal tradition has some authority in principal.

[43] W. D. Davies, "Matthew 5:17, 18," *Christian Origins and Judaism* (Philadelphia: Westminster, 1962), pp. 31-66; R. Banks, "Matthew's Understanding of the Law: Authenticity and Interpretation in Mt 5:17-20," JBL (1974): 226-242. This article contains an excellent documentation of the monographic literature on these verses and exempts us from repeating a full documentation here. To it add the article by A. Descamps cited in the next note and the recent works: A. Sand, *Das Gesetz und die Propheten* (Biblische Untersuchungen, 11; Regensburg: Pustet, 1974) and E. Schweizer, *Matthäus und seine Gemeinde* (Stuttgarter Bibelstudien, 71; Stuttgart: KBW, 1974), pp. 78-85, both of which arrived too late to be of use here.

community, while v. 20 most likely proceeds from the Matthean redaction. [44] Others will consider the whole as inauthentic. [45]

How can we break out of this impasse? The only unquestionable *evidence* we have that any of these verses existed prior to the writing of Matthew's gospel is the presence in Luke 16:16-17 of a parallel to Mt 5:18; on the most commonly accepted hypothesis some such saying must have been present in the earlier sayings source called Q. We propose then to begin from this bedrock and proceed from there. Of course, in principle, the whole pericope could be authentic. Alternatively, we cannot be absolutely certain that even v. 18 goes back to Jesus, however it is interpreted. What we can say is that we have evidence of it belonging to an earlier stratum of the gospel material, and that, in this sense, its claims to authenticity are higher than those of the rest of the passage. [46]

Literary Analysis

1. *Lk 16:16-17.* The interpretation of these verses is difficult. V. 16a lacks a verb. Which should be supplied?: (a) reigned, prevailed, were in force (implying that now they no longer are); or (b) taught, revealed God's will. We are aided here by the parallel Mt 11:12-13 where the verb *eprophēteusan* (prophesied) is supplied, resolving the dilemma in the sense of option (b). Thus there is no necessary suggestion that they are now abrogated, only that a new era of revelation has begun. V. 17 teaches the eternity or at least the perdurance of the Torah during the existence of the present world, as does the Matthean parallel. The question remains: in what sense does it teach this? In the sense of bitter irony against the unbending conservatism of the

---

[44] A. Descamps, "Essai d'interprétation de Mt 5:17-48. 'Formgeschichte' ou 'Redaktionsgeschichte,' ?" *Studia evangelica*, vol. 1, ed. K. Aland et al. (TU, 73; Berlin: Akademie, 1959), pp. 156-173.

[45] E.g., R. Bultmann, HST, p. 138; G. Barth, in Bornkamm-Barth-Held, *op. cit.*, pp. 64-73, after some hesitations; G. Harder, "Jesus und das Gesetz (Mt 5:17-20)," in *Antijudaismus im Neuen Testament*, ed. W. P. Eckert et al. (Munich: Kaiser, 1967), pp. 105-119, esp. pp. 106-8.

[46] On the other hand, from the point of view of the criterion of dissimilarity, even v. 18 would not stand well since it simply affirms a commonplace of Israel, the imperishability of Torah. Already in the deuterocanonical-apocryphal books: Wis 18:4; Bar 4:1; Jub 6:14; Tob 1:6; 4 Ezra 9:37; Apoc. Bar 48:47; 77:15; also Philo, *Vita Mos.* 2:14 f; Jos. *c. Ap.* 2:277; j. Sanh 2:20 (= SB I, p. 244). On the criterion, see N. Perrin, *Rediscovering the Teaching of Jesus* (New York: Harper, 1967). pp. 39-43. This difficulty can be overcome by reference to the congruence of this verse with Jesus' teaching and behavior elsewhere.

scribes, as T. W. Manson thought? [47] Or in the sense of a plain acceptance of Torah as a stable background against which Jesus' teaching ministry took place? This dilemma is unnecessary once it is realized that on Manson's interpretation of the *keraia* (tittle, hornlet, crownlet), (derived from SB I, 248 f) scribal elaboration is being attacked, not the Torah itself, since the *keraia* is not part of the actual lettering of Torah but only decorative ornamentation. This interpretation only suits the Lucan form. Once the *iota* is added, the Torah itself comes into question. It seems fair to conclude that Lk 16:17 has as its background presupposition a common acceptance of the abiding validity of Torah as a basis for discussion of its true interpretation and that this, which remains only implicit in the Lucan form, is made very explicit in the Matthean form. Jesus did not come to abrogate Torah but, at least, to interpret it.

The truth of this last sentence depends on the intention of Jesus in such passages as the next verse (Lk 16:18), where divorce is ruled out, as well as of those antitheses in Mt 5:21-48 which can be understood as abrogations rather than as interpretations (vv. 31 f, 38 f, 43). On these cases two things should be noted. (a) In none of these cases is the law made easier. Rather the tendency is away from laxity to a new rigor. "Abrogation" does not well express this fact. (b) The closest Old Testament parallel to Jesus' explanation of his position on divorce (Mt 19:8) is Samuel's concession to the Israelites of a king (1 Sam 8-12). Samuel calls their asking for a king wickedness and sin (1 Sam 12:7, 19, 20) yet concedes to their weakness. So too, says Jesus, did Moses concede to your weakness. But as the kings have gone, so should divorce. The time for concessions is over, for the reign of perfect justice is at hand. Further, the sectaries of Qumran seem to have excluded divorce or at least second marriages (CD 4:19- 5:6; see Dupont-Sommer, *Essene Writings,* p. 129, n. 1), yet they are not described as antinomians who abrogated the law, but as rigorists who adhered to it strictly.

2. *Mt 5:18.* This verse shares with Lk 16:17 a common element: the permanence of the law is compared to (Lk) or connected with (Mt) the permanence of the natural universe. Matthew however provides the logion with a solemn introduction ("for amen I say to you") and rounds it off with a variant of the first clause which gives the effect of surrounding the central statement with an artistic frame-

---

[47] *Sayings of Jesus* (London: SCM, 1937), pp. 134 f.

work, an *inclusio*. (The same technique may be seen at work in Mt 11:25-30 where the centerpiece is v. 27 and everything else is grouped around this. This is called in classical studies ring-composition). 48 Matthew also adds the *iota hen* as a doubling of the *mia keraia*, and so makes a literary parallel to "heaven and earth." He further strengthens the parity of thought and of value judgment by repeating the verb *parerchomai* in the second clause rather than retaining the Lucan *piptō* which damages the parallelism.

The form of words in Matthew could be understood as implying a temporal limit to the law; Luke rather implies a relative difficulty in the law (or its Pharisaic interpretation) changing, but not its absolute impossibility. (Cf. the parallel comparisons of the rich man's relative difficulty entering heaven Mk 10:25 parr.) Its meaning is that (a) the whole of the Old Testament has religious value for the followers of Jesus and would continue to be preserved, prayed, studied, and preached in the movement he began. (Thus was Marcion checked in advance.) (b) The prescriptions of the law still bind the immediate (Jewish-Palestinian) followers of Jesus. This is certainly true for the ethical prescriptions (cf. the antitheses), but also for the ritual (cf. Mt 23:23) though in a subordinate way. That Paul found this teaching unworkable with respect to the ritual law, especially circumcision, must not affect our judgment on these verses. Neither Jesus nor Matthew should be Paulinized.

3. *Mt 5:19.* Is this verse a product of the Matthean redaction or does it derive from the Jewish-Christian debate with the Hellenists? If the former, as we are inclined to think, then it is so not because of a characteristically Matthean vocabulary, but because of its contents. Yet since both the great and the least mentioned in it remain in the kingdom, the situation it has in mind differs from that in v. 20 where the feebly righteous are excluded from the kingdom. Yet v. 20 is almost certainly Matthean on the grounds of both content and vocabulary. So, if both are Matthean, they must aim at different groups. V. 19 may reflect a grudging, reluctant acceptance by Matthew's church of the Pauline missionary policy of waiving the requirement to be circumcised. If so, then perhaps the *elachistos* is to be identified with Paul, and the *megas* with James. The verse would recognize Paul as a fellow Christian but as a Christian of a sort one doesn't like. If James be the *megas*, then it is hard to see why Matthew should teach in 16:16-18 that Peter is the rock, since in the Gospel of Thomas, logion 12, James is the great one to whom the disciples must go. So, while the verse may

be redactional, we should not rule out the possibility that it is a fragment of Jewish-Christian polemic.

The pairing of doing and teaching, in that order, suggests a horror
of hypocrisy characteristic of this gospel, and since it supposes that
the addressee is or could be a teacher, the verse is most likely aimed
at community leaders rather than at the community as a whole. The
"loosing" denounced in this verse is later granted by Jesus to Peter
and to the disciples (16:19; 18:18) as one of their ruling powers,
so it is not ruled out altogether, though it is possible that the sense
shifts. [49] With respect to the "least commandments" we note that like
Aboth the verse presupposes that all the commandments bind in
conscience (cf. Mt 23:23), but, unlike Aboth (2:1; 3:18; 4:2), it
admits some commandments are less important.

4. *Mt 5:20*. It is perhaps fair to say that for Matthew the essence
of the Gospel, the kernel of what Jesus brought to men is a better
righteousness, a higher righteousness, a more abundant righteousness,
and this righteousness is conceived of in an ethical sense. Matthew's
piety is a moral piety. Note that the verse does not say that it is a
harder or an easier righteousness than that of the scribes and Pharisees.
It is both. It is easier (cf. Mt 11:30) to learn than the Mishnah, less
cumbersome in practical detail, (e.g., sabbath observance). But it is
harder to live and to do because it is so radical and inward (5:21-48).

5. *Mt 5:17*. Returning now to the first verse of the pericope, we
assume that at least in its present form it is Matthean and should be
interpreted as such. The introductory clause *"mē nomisēte hoti..."*
indicates that the verse is intended to correct a misunderstanding which
might have been present in the minds of both devout traditional Jews
and of libertine Christians, viz., that Jesus came as a great negative
force to destroy the faith of the fathers. The sentence is so constructed
that its weight falls on the last, climactic word: to fulfill (*plērosai*).
It would be hard to imagine a more effective counterpresentation of
the intention and effect of Jesus, accentuating as it does the aspect of
positive fulfillment. [50]

---

[48] C. H. Lohr, "Oral techniques in the gospel of Matthew," CBQ 23 (1961):
403-435.

[49] On binding and loosing, see J. Jeremias, s.v. *kleis*, TDNT, 3, 744-753.

[50] In reality, the overall effect of the early Christian movement, including both
Jesus and Paul, John and the *auctor ad Hebraeos*, on the preceding Israelite heritage
was threefold: fulfillment, replacement, and prefigurement, but Matthew was correct
to state clearly and emphatically one true aspect, and, from a certain point of view,
the most important. See P. Grelot, *Sens chrétien de l'Ancien Testament* (Tournai:
Desclée, 1962), pp. 16-27.

The right understanding of the verse turns on the interpretation given *plērosai*. The main options are: (a) to set out the true meaning of the law, to express its full significance (= Hebrew *mlʾ*); (b) to validate, establish, confirm the law by setting it on a better basis (= Heb. *qwm*); (c) to realize actively, to complete fully the law in the sense that as the prophecies which point toward Jesus are realized by him, so too the law is realized by him. This last view is that of R. Banks who rules out the sense *qwm* on the basis that the Septuagint never translates *qwm* but only *mlʾ* by *plēroō*, and who tries to interpret the word in the same sense as Matthew's formulaic use of it in introducing reflexion citations. These arguments overlook two facts. If, as Dalman supposes, the term here is based on a technical rabbinic sense of *qwm*, the fact that the Septuagint never translates it by *plēroō* is quite irrelevant since the Hebrew Bible does not contain this later technical usage. Moreover, in the introductory formula to Old Testament citations, the verb is always in the passive voice (*plērothē*) whereas here (as in 3:15 and 23:32) it is in the active. It seems best to see *qwm* behind *plēroō*, and *bṭl* behind *katalyō*, and to understand the former in the sense of (b) above, viz., to establish the law by putting it on a better (exegetical) footing. That the term in Matthew could have a more comprehensive meaning than in rabbinic terminology should by no means be excluded. But this remains its background. This terminology no doubt also lies behind the parallel Pauline passage Rm 3:31, as well as Rm 13:9 and 10. [51]

Matthew's emphasis on fulfillment, on continuity with the past, implies, besides a hostility to libertinism, also a sense of security in the possession of the *novum* brought by Jesus which might be characteristic of a member of the third generation of Christians which is free from any defensive need to denigrate the past antecedents of the Master. Rather these are now prized with a nostalgic look backwards. But beyond their redactional significance, the words fairly represent a true and neglected side of Jesus' ministry. On Jesus' part there was no *"gran rifiuto"* of Israel's main religious institutions but only a penetrating critique and the showing of a better way.

Conclusions for Thesis

Aboth emphasizes the abiding religious value of the study of Torah. Mt 5:18, which, as we have argued, has of these verses the best claim

---

[51] See Banks, *art. cit.*, pp. 229-232, for a list of authorities supporting each view. Our view coincides substantially with that of G. Barth, in Bornkamm-Barth-Held, *op. cit.*, pp. 67-69.

to authenticity, states that Torah will abide in the new era. Mt 5:19 builds on this. It implies that the preceding verse is not a neutral, value-free statement, but rather that whoever "does" Torah and teaches it is blessed. We could see therein an implicit shift away from the apparently scandalous conclusion of the debate at Tarfon's house in Lydda (b. Kid 40): study comes before teaching, though in fact this conclusion need not be taken as a disagreement if it could be expanded into a three-part program: study first, then doing, finally teaching. Mt 5:20 stresses a zeal for righteousness superior to that of the Pharisees, and implicitly also a greater zeal for Torah rightly interpreted. Mt 5:17 states the overall orientation of the pericope and indeed of the entire gospel: Jesus' ministry is not destructive but constructive. So then both Matthew and the community which may have produced some of the material (vv. 17, 19) which he incorporates here share the basic viewpoint of Aboth and provide a biblical basis for welcoming this viewpoint in its essentials into the Christian church. The attitude of Jesus himself as probably expressed in 5:18 = Lk 16:17 remains, from the point of view of the most rigorous criticism, uncertain, though the interpretation we have given, in which he affirms the abiding validity of Torah as positive spiritual fact, seems to account best for his conduct when treating of individual details of the law. It is clear then that our thesis rests secure on the level of the Matthean redaction though not absolutely so on the level of the historical Jesus.

Mt 11:25-30 par Lk 10:21-22

Selected Specialized Bibliography

Arranged Chronologically

Strauss, F. D. "Jesu Weheruf über Jerusalem und die *sophia tou theou*. Matthäus 23, 34-39, Luk, 11, 49-51; 13, 34 f. Ein Beitrag zur johanneischen Frage," ZWT 6 (1863): 84 ff.

Harnack, Adolf. *The Sayings of Jesus*. New York: Putnam, 1908. Pp. 272-310.

Norden, Eduard. *Agnostos Theos*. 1912. Stuttgart: Teubner, 1956. Pp. 277-308.

Bousset, W. *Kyrios Christos*. 1913. Nashville: Abingdon, 1970. Pp. 83-89. Cf. thereto C. Colpe, *Die religionsgeschichtliche Schule*. FRLANT, 78; Göttingen: Vandenhoeck & Ruprecht, 1961. Pp. 26-30.

Weiss, J. "Das Logion Mt 11:25-30," *Heinrici Festschrift*. 1914 (non vidi). Cf. also Weiss' article in *Die Schriften des Neuen Testaments*, 1, pp. 320-25.

Meyer, Eduard. *Ursprung und Anfänge des Christentums*, vol. 1. 1921. Darmstadt: Wissenschaftliche Buchgesellschaft, 1962. Pp. 280-91.

Dibelius, M. *From Tradition to Gospel*. 1919. New York: Scribners, 1934. Pp. 279-83.

Bultmann, R. *History of the Synoptic Tradition*. 1921. New York: Harper, 1963. Pp. 159 f.

Arvedson, T. *Das Mysterium Christi*. Uppsala: Lundequist, 1937.

Davies, W. D. " 'Knowledge' in the Dead Sea Scrolls and Matthew 11:25-30,"

Christian Origins and Judaism. Philadelphia: Westminster, 1962, pp. 119-44 = HTR 46 (1953): 113-39.

Cerfaux, L. "Les sources scriptuaires de Mt 11:25-30," ETL 30 (1954): 740-46; 31 (1955): 331-42.

Feuillet, A. "Jésus et la Sagesse divine d'après les évangiles synoptiques," RB 62 (1955): 161-96.

Mertens, H. *L'hymne de jubilation chez les Synoptiques.* Gembloux: Duculot, 1957 (non vidi).

Hunter, A. M. "Crux criticorum—Matt. xi, 25-30—a re-appraisal," NTS 8 (1961-2): 241-49.

Robinson, J. M. "Die Hodajot-Formel in Gebet und Hymnus des Frühchristentums," *Apophoreta* (Fs. Haenchen). BZNW, 30; Berlin: Töpelmann, 1964, pp. 194-235.

Betz, H. D. "The logion of the easy yoke and of rest (Mt 11:28-30)," JBL 86 (1967): 10-24.

Jeremias, J. *The Prayers of Jesus.* SBT, n.s., 6; London: SCM, 1967. Pp. 48-52. *New Testament Theology.* New York: Scribners, 1971. Pp. 56-61.

Légasse, S. *Jésus et l'enfant.* Études bibliques. Paris: Gabalda, 1969. Pp. 121-85.

Suggs, M. J. *Wisdom, Christology and Law in Matthew's Gospel.* Cambridge, Mass.: Harvard Univ. Press, 1970.

Christ, Felix. *Jesus Sophia.* ATANT, 57. Zurich: Zwingli, 1970.

Commentaries on Matthew

Wellhausen, Allen, M'Neile, Plummer, Loisy (Les évangelies synoptiques), Lagrange, Montefiore (*Synoptic Gospels*) Billerbeck, Schlatter, Schniewind, T. H. Robinson, Lohmeyer, Schmid, Benoit, Gaechter, Bonnard, Grundmann, Hill, Boismard (*Commentaire sur le Synopse*).

In this section reference will be made to these works by the name of the author only, or by author and page number.

Introductory Questions: History of Interpretation and pris de position

1. *Did Mt 11:25-30 form a unity in Q?* It is commonly admitted that vv. 25-27 of our pericope derive from Q since they are also found in Lk 10:21-22. Thus, whether they are authentic words of Jesus or not (on which see below), at least they are earlier than the final editing of the gospels. Since however vv. 28-30, though closely related both in content and in structure to the preceding verses, are not found outside Matthew, there is some doubt whether they formed part of the original unit. That vv. 28-30 were also in Q, and are therefore pre-Matthean, was held by Norden, J. Weiss (with reservations), Eduard Meyer, M. Dibelius, and T. Arvedson. Bousset remained uncertain. So does F. Christ (p. 100), but he treats it as pre-Matthean on the basis of the shorter form found in the Gospel of Thomas (GT, 90). The presence of these verses in Q has been denied by Bultmann, Klostermann, Kümmel, Dinckler, Strecker, J. M. Robinson, and H. D. Betz, on the basis of their absence from Lk. Norden confessed himself unable to account for a deliberate omission of them by Luke. Though certainty

in the matter cannot be attained, we are inclined to think they were present in Q for three reasons: (a) they form a unity of structure with vv. 25-27 (on this see below); (b) except for the word *praus* their vocabulary is not peculiarly Matthean; (c) Luke would have omitted them on the ground that they were expressed in terms too rabbinic to be either readily intelligible or attractive to the Gentile readers at whom he aimed his gospel.

2. *Do the verses represent authentic words of Jesus?* The question of authenticity, especially of the Christologically crucial v. 27, has been so bitterly contested that H. D. Betz with good reason speaks of the problem as "bound up with a whole episode of scholarly research" (p. 10). The authenticity of the whole pericope has been most plainly defended by Hunter. Harnack and Jeremias defend the authenticity of v. 27 but only after rewriting it (Harnack) or reinterpreting it (Jeremias). Bultmann, Bousset and many others leave open the possibility of vv. 25 f being authentic but reject the rest, though most authors assume that even vv. 28-30 may be pre-Matthean, even if from a tradition other than Q. On the other hand, those who argue for the unity of the whole pericope (e.g., Norden and Dibelius) feel that they must deny its authenticity altogether, mainly on the grounds that since v. 27 is expressed in the language of a "Hellenistic revealer" it could not have been spoken by Jesus. It is only with hesitation that one disagrees with a viewpoint which has become so predominant, but we believe that the question of the authenticity of vv. 25-27 should at least be kept open. The reasons against the authenticity of v. 27 reduce themselves to two: (a) the language and sentiment are Hellenistic; (b) Jesus could not have had such an exalted self-consciousness. Now as W. D. Davies has shown, the kind of language in v. 27 has ample companionship in the religious language of Qumran, and Betz too realizes that by this time Oriental and Greek styles of religious expression have mingled and interpenetrated so that a simple decision one way or the other on the basis of conceptual background can no longer be so confidently made. With respect of Jesus' Christological self-consciousness (for the absolute use of Father and Son see below), we must take Harnack's point seriously: "The transition from the designations of Teacher and Prophet to that of the future Messiah demands, both in the self-consciousness of Jesus and also in outward expression, *some middle term*, and it is difficult to see why tradition must be supposed to be in error when it presents us here with the designation 'the Son' " (p. 300, italics added). Though the point is

not strictly relevant to our concern, we believe that under the circumstances of feeble arguments on either side this question should remain open. With respect to vv. 28-30, R. Otto (*Reich Gottes und Menschensohn* [Munich: Kaiser, 1934], p. 137 f) holds that they are the most typical and genuine of all Jesus' words. Mertens (pp. 19-50) devotes half his book to the proof of their authenticity. F. Christ concludes (p. 117) that they are probably authentic but that this is unprovable.

3. *Religio-historical background.* This is a domain where unclarity and a loose use of terms reign. Norden described the background as the "mystical-theosophical literature of the Orient." Bousset and Davies locate the text against the background of the wisdom literature of the Old Testament and, in the case of Davies, of Qumran. Norden and Betz both see this, but Betz goes on to link it up with the protognosticism of the Nag Hammadi GT, and thus lends support to Dibelius' view expressed in 1919. Bultmann, Arvedson and others see in the text a combination of elements of different kinds: v. 27 Hellenism, vv. 28-30 Old Testament wisdom. Cerfaux, Feuillet, Boismard see vv. 25-27 as apocalyptic (Dan 2 and 7), vv. 28-30 as sapiential (Prov 9:5; Sir 24:19; 51:23-27; 6:19-28). We should keep in mind two things: (a) at this period the categories of Old Testament literary genres were breaking down as new forms were emerging (cp. the Thanksgiving Hymns of Qumran with the Old Testament Psalms); (b) the entire passage, with the possible exception of v. 27, is most readily intelligible, as our exegesis will indicate, in terms of Jesus' ongoing polemical struggle with the Pharisees in favor of the *am haaretz.* Thus the primary background is first-century Palestine. Of course, Matthew and Q share this background. This situation is the heir both of wisdom, prophetic and apocalyptic traditions form the Old Testament and the intertestamental literature. The main sources of the verses, insofar as there are any, are in fact Sirach and Jeremiah. That the Gnostics found the passage to their liking says nothing about its origins and original intent.

4. *Literary form.* Various terms have been used to describe the literary character of the pericope: hymn, revelation discourse (Norden), enthronement liturgy (Arvedson), baptismal liturgy (M. Rist, JR 15 [1935] 73), eucharistic liturgy (J. M. Robinson, pp. 221-26), Jesus' thanksgiving after a confession of faith (Hunter). This list moves from literary forms to life-settings. It seems to us best to speak of a revelation discourse since the term *apokalyptō* figures in the first two strophes and "yoke" is a figure for Torah here.

Analysis and Exegesis

1. *Structure.* The pattern discerned by Norden still makes the most sense, at least on the latest redactional level:

I 25 f   = thanksgiving for revelation,
II 27   = statement of its contents,
III 28-30 = invitation and appeal to accept the revelation.

Norden discerned the same pattern in Sir 51; 24; Odes of Sol 33; Corp. Herm. 1:24 ff; Rm 11:25 ff; Rm 2:17 ff; Mt 23:4 ff and Jn 8. Arvedson restated this view in a rather anachronistic form. The best arguments against an *original* unity of the three parts have been brought forward by Robinson (p. 227, n. 63): (a) Sir 51 is not a unity since vv. 13-30 are an acrostic, which has now been found separately preserved (i.e., apart from vv. 1-12) in 11 Q Ps; (b) Mt 11:28-30 lead a separate existence in GT 90. But these arguments are far from conclusive. Despite the Qumran discovery, there can be no doubt that Sirach 51 formed a unity before the first century A.D. and so could have influenced the pattern of Mt 11:25-30. Logion 90 of GT could be a late Gnostic abbreviation of the original form of vv. 28-30 preserved in Matthew. Thus an original three-part structure remains possible, indeed, in view of the reasons for the unity of the pericope in Q mentioned above, perhaps even probable. Certainly on the redactional level the juxtaposition of elements is not accidental but deliberate in view of the congruence of the material.

2. *Exegesis.* V. 25. For our purposes only the following need be noted. The sharp, indeed paradoxical, contrast between the wise and understanding (*sophōn kai synetōn*) and the "babes" (*nēpiois*) is striking because in these precise terms it does not occur elsewhere in the Gospels and runs counter to Matthew's redactional emphasis on *synienai* as a primary characteristic of the disciples. It is readily intelligible as an expression of Jesus' polemic against the exponents of the refined but ultimately self-defeating halacha of the Pharisees and in favor of the *am ha-aretz* who stand behind the *nēpioi*. The "babes" are not infants but this religiously disenfranchised class to whom Jesus felt especially drawn and whom he identified with the *anawim-aniyyim* of the Psalms and Jeremiah. The babes are also the heavy-laden of v. 28, people born down by the overdeveloped halacha of the chief religious party of the day. The struggle between the two outlooks is broken through by a divine revelation which, for Jesus and his followers, resolves the dispute as no human judicial decision

could. Which halacha is from Sinai, that is, from the Father?—that is the question being resolved here. The *tauta-auta* in v. 25 doubtless includes, interpreting the entire pericope as a unity, both Jesus' absolute relation to the Father (v. 27) as the guarantee of his revelation, as well as his message of the near approach of the kingdom and of the new ethic which is proper to it (his yoke, vv. 29 and 30).

3. V. 26. Talk of the Father's gracious will (*eudokia*), as of the Son's willing (*boulētai*, v. 27), derives from the prophetic-apocalyptic language of election and predestination, a doctrinal heritage which in the New Testament is more commonly associated with Paul (especially Rm 9-11) and John, but also is present in the Synoptics. [52]

4. V. 27. *Panta* has the same sense in the context of the pericope as a unity as *tauta-auta* of v. 25. *Paredothē* has here the technical sense of *massorah-paradosis*, tradition, as a human background against which it develops a major theological point. Jesus, the text is saying, is the direct recipient of divine revelation; indeed he is the unique and definitive fountainhead of divine revelation. This is the force of the *oudeis*, which, if pressed to an extreme, would not only exclude any use of the Old Testament, but also any truth value in the great world religions, or any inspiration to Paul and the other New Testament authors. If the verse is studied in isolation such drastic conclusions cannot be excluded in principle. But, interpreted as part of the pericope, the sense is easier. The Pharisees claimed that their Torah tradition, that is, their oral Torah, including mishnah and midrash, halacha and haggadah, began at Sinai when Moses received it all in a revelation from God. This is the claim of the first mishnah of Aboth. [53] A counterclaim in direct reference to this is being made here. The Old Testament is not being discarded, but the claim is made that only in and through the revelation made to Jesus is the earlier revelation rightly understood. (The problem of world religions is of course not directly envisaged at all.) Nor is any further revelation excluded, provided that it be revealed through the Son.

Positively, what is being asserted is (a) that Christianity has a tradition whose fountainhead is Jesus himself. Indeed, in the sense

---

[52] See K. Stendahl, "The Called and the Chosen," in A. Fridrichsen et al., *The Root of the Vine* (New York: Philosophical Library, 1953), pp. 63-80.

[53] At this point we may with profit cite the words of B. Gerhardsson (*Memory and Manuscript*, p. 258): "All historical probability is in favor of Jesus' disciples, and the whole of early Christianity, having accorded the sayings of the one whom they believed to be the Messiah at least the same degree of respect as the pupils of a Rabbi accorded the words of their master!"

of Mt 10:40 (of which more in a moment), it may be fair to say that Christianity *is* a tradition, of which both the content (*traditum*) and the first tradent are Jesus himself. (b) Christianity is a revealed *gnōsis* or better still an *epignōsis* (Mt as against the simpler Lucan version), that is, a form of divinely given knowing whose object is the Father himself as revealed in the Son. [54] (Of course this knowing does not exclude loving, as the next verses suggest. It is a matter of emphasizing an important aspect of a total process-experience.) Cf. Jn 17:3: "This is eternal life, that they know thee the only true God, and Jesus Christ whom thou hast sent." This is the authentic Christian gnosis of which Clement of Alexandria wrote (*Stromateis*, II, 19, 20; IV, 21-23), a source of embarrassment to some perhaps, but of the essence of the gospel.

With respect to the absolute use of the terms Father and Son, we note that this Johannine-sounding idiom (e.g., Jn 10:15) is found on the lips of Jesus in the Synoptic tradition at only two places, here and in Mk 13:32, where it is a matter of the Son himself not knowing the day nor the hour. Since Mt 11:27 is commonly regarded as a Q saying, what this amounts to is a Marcan-Q overlap *of idiom*, a doubly attested saying. And as F. C. Burkitt has taught us:

> Where Q and Mark appear to report the same saying, we have the nearest approach that we can hope to get to the common tradition of the earliest Christian society about our Lord's words. What we glean in this way will indicate the general impression His teaching made upon His disciples. [55]

In his treatment of the divine sonship of Jesus, Geza Vermes comes to this negative conclusion: "Thus, on the basis of his surviving teaching, it turns out that it is impossible to prove, and unwise to suppose, that Jesus defined himself as the *son of God*." [56] It is our

---

[54] With respect to *epignōsis/epiginōskō*, Norden (p. 280, n. 1) is followed by many others in saying that it in no way differs in meaning from *gnōsis/ginōskō*. But we prefer to follow M. K. Sullivan "Epignosis in the epistles of St. Paul," *Studiorum Paulinorum Congressus* (An. Bib., 17-18; Rome: PBI, 1963), vol. 2, pp. 405-416. She discerns in some uses a religious overtone that the knowledge in question in many instances of *epignosis* is revealed knowledge.

[55] Burkitt, *The Gospel History and Its Transmission* (2nd ed; Edinburgh: Clark, 1907), p. 147; cf. pp. 167 f.

[56] *Jesus the Jew* (New York: Macmillan, 1973), pp. 200 f. R. H. Fuller, on the basis of this Mark-Q overlap, has suggested orally that we should speak of Jesus' filial consciousness, rather than of his messianic consciousness.

conclusion that these words would be more true if they were exactly inverted.

5. Vv. 28-30. This carefully constructed section is remarkable in many respects. One is struck first by the structure: again there is a ring composition, with the introductory and concluding clauses corresponding to one another thematically, grouped as they are round the centerpiece, "Learn from me." It is striking too that every theme is repeated at least twice except that central statement: the fourfold invitation-command, the description of the audience, the promised rest, the yoke, the description of Wisdom, the description of the yoke—a constant twinning. Only the invitation to learn stands out in its singleness. With respect to form we note further the shift of persons throughout vv. 25-30: beginning with direct address to the Father, it passes to third person indicative in v. 27, and then returns to invite the heavy laden in the imperative. On a higher level, the literary form is that of a wisdom teacher (Sir 51:23 f, 26 f; 6:38) sending out an invitation to potential students, but also of Lady Wisdom herself descended from heaven, who invites men to dine of her delights (Sir 24:25 [19]). This identification of Jesus with the hypostatized Sophia is especially stressed by Suggs and F. Christ and is supported by the singular piling up of rather feminine attributes, for example, the meekness and comfort-giving gentleness. One is reminded of the Jungian concept of animus-anima, the presence of feminine traits in a man and of masculine traits in a woman, both necessary for balancing off of the whole person.

With respect to the more precise identification of those who labor and are heavy laden, there are two possibilities, not necessarily mutually exclusive. The first is that, as we have suggested, they are identical with the *nēpioi* v. 25, that is, with the *am ha-aretz* (= *anawim*) who are burdened with the pain of exclusion from full religious communion in Israel through the rigid policy of the Pharisees. The second is that here, shifting slightly from v. 25, the invitation is extended not precisely to the *am ha-aretz* but rather directly to the members of the Pharisaic sect, who labor and are heavy laden due to the heavy yoke of the Pharisaic halacha. G. Barth favors the first solution, but the second intrigues because it carries the thought a step further, carrying the war so to speak into the enemy's camp. In any case, the anti-Pharisaic edge is present throughout.

The theme of rest is also peculiar. From ancient inscriptions it is clear that rest (*anapausis, requies*) was a common euphemism for death. On the other hand, recently the effort has been made to see in the word a Gnostic sense, for example, *synousia* with *gnosis*. [57] But here the background is plainly the Old Testament. This is rendered certain by the direct citation from the Hebrew of Jer 6:16 in v. 29 (the LXX diverges). This rest is the result of following along the right paths, of knowing that you are living in accord with God's will; in a word, of justice before the Lord, and with justice the peace and contentment which flow from it.

For our purposes two themes are decisive: the yoke and the invitation to learn. The metaphor of the yoke has several applications in rabbinic idiom (cf. SB *in loco*) of which the two chief are: to take upon oneself the yoke of *heaven* which means to say the Shema^c, and to take upon oneself the yoke of *Torah*, that is, the study, interpretation and living of *Torah* (Ab 3:5). Thus when Jesus invites the laboring to his yoke, he is in effect inviting them to study Torah, to accept his interpretation of it, that is, his halacha, and to live it. He is not setting up a second or even a new Torah against the old, but inviting men to approach the one and only Torah, once given by God on Sinai, through him and his teaching.

The invitation in the form of a command to learn says in effect that Jesus' way is not only a *halacha* but a *mathēsis*, a *didaskalia*, a life-long learning from Jesus. Is the *hoti* which follows explicative (so H. D. Betz) or justificatory? Probably the latter, though the two are related. On the one hand one learns from Jesus *to be* gentle and lowly of heart, but that does not exhaust what one learns. On the other hand, one *should* learn from Jesus *because* he is gentle and humble of heart, in contrast to the at least unintentional arrogance (Ab 2:6) of the Pharisaic and other sectarian teachers in Israel. The term *praus* is a Matthean feature and links the passage up with the spirit of the Beatitudes (Mt 5:3-11) (so Betz). So then one learns both from Jesus' person and from his teaching. The two are inseparable when the issue is how to live.

Is his yoke really easier? It is easier to learn than the mishnah. But it is not easier to do (cf. Mt 5:20). What is striking is that there is any yoke at all. In some distortions of Paul's teaching one receives the impression that what Jesus did was to *remove* all burdens, especially the yoke of the law. What W. D. Davies has called the quintessence of the Matthean understanding of the gospel (Mt 11:28-30) is not only

---

[57] See, besides Kittel, TDNT, Ph. Vielhauer, "Anapausis," in *Apophoreta* (Haenchen Fs.) (BZNW, 30; Berlin: Töpelmann, 1964), 281-299.

that but probably also closer to the original situation and to the realities of life.

Concluding our consideration of these verses we note that there is in them a kind of dialogue with the ideals of Aboth. They hold in common the value of Torah-study, taking upon oneself its yoke, of knowing the will of God through revelation. They differ on the source of the right interpretation of Torah: Jesus the Son or the view that the interpretation came from Sinai to the Pharisees, and on the character of the recipients: the ritually pure who refrain from contact with people who might defile them, or the meek, the humble, the child-like. [58]

Mt 10:40-42

These verses are of interest to us because they indicate to some extent the early Christian equivalent of the principle of rabbinic succession such as it is illustrated in Aboth. For the question of authenticity the literary situation is not without interest. This situation is rather complex. What is clear is that all four evangelists know the principal logion (Mt 10:40) in some form, suggesting that it is an old, widely diffused saying, perhaps stemming from Jesus himself. The three Synoptics also offer another saying (Mt 18:5; Mk 9:37; Lk 9:48) with the same pattern "whoever receives x receives me...," only in this case the x is the child instead of the disciple. It is possible, as Bultmann thinks, that the disciple-form is a back-formation from the original child or *paidion*-form, but this is not certain since in the Marcan and Lucan forms of the *paidion* saying the theme of apostolic mission is present. If Grundmann (*Mt*, p. 301) is correct in supposing that Mt 10:40-42 is from Q, one might even speak (in a loose sense) of a Marcan-Q overlap. Boismard (*Comm. Syn.*, p. 264 f) is more cautious: "probably from a collection of logia known to Mt."

The commentaries are remarkably thin on these verses but the most recent ones at least recognize the rabbinic legal background behind v. 40. But, as Billerbeck (I, 589-90) points out, there are really two backgrounds. The first is the value of hospitality to students and

---

[58] What is certain is that Eduard Meyer's interpretation (p. 289 f) of the verses as a rejection of all intellectual culture is not supported by the text. This view has been well characterized by Betz (p. 15) as a "glorification of irrationalism" popular in the Weimar culture of the twenties. We may add that Meyer's misinterpretation is one which continues to recur in some Christian circles and is usually due to a lack of awareness of the Jewish background and context of the gospel sayings.

teachers of Torah (cf. Ab 1:4, and connect Ab 1:5 on hospitality to the needy with Mt 10:42). The second is the institution of the *shaliach* or agent with powers of attorney (attorney at law), concerning whom the basic principle is in M. Ber 5:5: *"miphnē šeššlûḥô šellʾadam kemôtô*: a man's agent is like to himself."* (See further b. Kid 41b.) It seems evident that this principle has directly influenced the formulation of v. 40. The verse in effect states that the disciples sent forth by Jesus are fully empowered to act in his name with respect to what concerns the kingdom of God and that those who receive them and their message receive Jesus himself and thereby also God himself. Thus the verse takes a mundane principle of synagogue administrative legislation and transforms it into a statement of the most elevated ecclesiology and Christology. The Christian missionary, because of the greatness of his task, enjoys a high dignity, even though, or perhaps precisely because, he does not teach in his own name and in his own right (Mt 23:8-10) (cf. Schlatter, *Mt in loco*).

The text further implies a Christian apostolic office built on the model of the synagogue *shaliach*, though not identical with it and not limited by it. Though it is not to our purpose to enter into the extensive debate on the nature of this apostolic office, [59] we accept as given its close relation to the Jewish *shaliach* institution. It differs first in that its task is not the conduct of business, whether financial or matrimonial or administrative or rubrical, but the preaching of a message of repentance and salvation. Moreover, the task of the *shaliach* usually is completed in a relatively brief span of time, whereas the mission of the Christian apostle in principle does not end till the parousia. This is especially so in the Matthean recension of the account of the sending out of the apostles, where there is no mention of their return. [60] And though the Jewish *shaliach* may not appoint another *shaliach* in his stead who enjoys the same powers as he himself received, it is also clear that he may appoint an agent in his own name and certainly so after the death of the original sender or commissioner.

---

[59] Cf. the article by K. H. Rengstorf, TDNT, I, pp. 398-447 and the earlier literature there (p. 407) cited. To it add Dom Gregory Dix's essay in K. E. Kirk, *The Apostolic Ministry* (London: Hodder and Stoughton, 1946); M. Hengel, "Die Ursprünge der Christlichen Mission," NTS 18 (1971): 15-38, esp. p. 32 and n. 56; T. W. Manson, *The Church's Ministry* (London: Hodder and Stoughton, 1948); W. Schmithals, *The Office of Apostle in the Early Church* (Nashville: Abingdon, 1969); G. Klein, *Die zwölf Apostel* (Göttingen: Vandenhoeck & Ruprecht, 1961).

[60] Cf. Schlatter, *Mt, in loco*, and F. W. Beare, JBL 89 (1970): 1-13.

And so it happened that the early Christians (especially Irenaeus) did not speak of new apostles (though in some churches, especially Pauline ones, they did speak of others as apostles in the broad sense of missionaries), but rather of successors of the apostles. Thus there early came to be a principle of succession in the Christian movement, a succession in teaching and in handing down the tradition (among other tasks). This succession is identical neither with the rabbinic use of *shelichim* nor with the succession of teachers listed in Aboth, which is not based on the *shaliach* principle, but it is comparable with them.

Conclusion

It should by now be clear in what respect Jesus and the earliest Christian communities and the evangelist Matthew agreed and disagreed with the Pharisaic-rabbinic ideal of Torah study as a paramount religious value as this ideal is expressed in Aboth. The main points may be briefly summarized.

Jesus shared with his contemporaries a conviction as to the abiding value and normative character of Torah. His ethical seriousness is not less but more intense than theirs, and theirs was very intense. For him too the relationship between master and disciple was habitual and central. But he differed from them in his rejection of the Pharisaic development of Torah, its oral tradition, which, on account of its fatal arrogance (entailed in its complexity), excluded too many sons of Abraham, and from among these excluded sons he called forth his disciples.

The chief difference between the *earliest Christians* and the rabbinic movement in the area of study was the centrality of one teacher for the Christians, one whom they recognized, at least after the resurrection, as not only their teacher sent from God, but as the Anointed one and their Lord. This is in contrast with the multiplicity of rabbis none of whom was worshipped as Lord or even as Messiah. The early Christians had at least several gifted teachers and authors and even a genius or two in their midst, but these were not paradigmatic to the same extent or in the same way as Jesus.

Finally, on the redactional level of *Matthew's* gospel, we see the hint of the emergence of the Christian scribe (13:52; 23:34-36), a master of the Old Testament in all its textual pluriformity, illustrated in the use of the Old Testament in the gospel itself. This gospel has indeed been spoken of as the product of an early Christian school, a school in the sense of a center of higher biblical learning, with a fairly extensive library. [61]

Further, one can see in Matthew's arrangement of his gospel a systematic effort to parallel the achievement of the rabbis after the fall of Jerusalem in 70 A.D., the codifying of Pharisaic oral tradition in a series of authoritative texts and decisions (e.g., the canon list of the Hebrew Old Testament). This codification process, traditionally associated with Johanan ben Zakkai and his academy at Jamnia, was matched by Matthew's efforts to recast the teaching of Jesus into an orderly body of doctrine which would even provide the start for a new interpretation of Torah and thus also for a new *halacha*.

---

[61] K. Stendahl, *The School of St. Matthew* (Philadelphia: Fortress, 1968); R. H. Gundry, *The Use of the Old Testament in St. Matthew's Gospel* (Leiden: Brill, 1967).

CHAPTER FOUR

CONCLUSION

It is our hope that the present study of Aboth and related texts as well as of its Old Testament sources and of its correspondences in the Synoptic gospels may have the effect of bringing out the large measure of their mutual agreement and compatibility, as well as making more precise the areas in which they differ.

Christians, we feel, must learn to appreciate more consciously these positive affinities between the message of Jesus (and of Matthew) and that of the sages recorded in Aboth, and must begin to appropriate those values of Aboth which have not been explicitly a part of Christian teaching hitherto.

We have also tried to determine and to delimit more precisely the respect in which Jesus (and Matthew) broke with the Pharisaic way to God. His disagreement centers, we suggested, on two issues. First, he rejected an arrogance of learning (fully compatible with personal humility, to be sure) which led, in effect, to the exclusion of many from full participation in the sacral life of the community. Second, he set aside an interpretative method, which, however noble its intentions, had the overall effect of trivializing the observance of Torah. As a result of our delimitation of Jesus' argument with the Pharisees, we hope to have laid a basis for Christian relations with Judaism which will free them from some of their past excesses, not to say horrors, a basis which recognizes the presence of deep disagreements and yet emphasizes the common veneration of Torah and its study as the indispensable preliminary to an ethic developed and lived in the context of faith.

For it is our conviction that Aboth contains treasures which, like the spoils of Egypt to which the Fathers compared the philosophical wisdom of the Greeks, should be appropriated by the people of God, and without which they are much the poorer.

BIBLIOGRAPHY

I. PRIMARY SOURCES

This section is alphabetized by title of work whereas the remainder of the bibliography is alphabetized by author or editor.

Apocrypha and Pseudepigrapha of the Old Testament. Edited by R. H. Charles. 2 vols. Oxford: Clarendon, 1913.
The Apostolic Fathers. Ed. by Kirsopp Lake. Loeb Classical Library. 2 vols. Cambridge, Mass.: Harvard, 1952.
The Babylonian Talmud. Edited and translated by Isidore Epstein. 18 vols. London: Soncino, 1935.
Der Babylonische Talmud. Edited and translated by Lazarus Goldschmidt. 9 volumes. The Hague: Nijhoff, 1933-35.
Biblia Hebraica. Edited by Rudolf Kittel. 13th edition. Stuttgart: Württembergische Bibelanstalt, 1962.
Corpus inscriptionum judaicarum. Edited by Jean Baptiste Frey. 2 vols. Rome: Biblical Institute, 1936.
Corpus hermeticum. Edited by A. D. Nock and translated by A.-J. Festugière. 4 vols. 2nd edition. Collection Guillaume Budé. Paris: Les Belles Lettres, 1938-1954.
The Dead Sea Scrolls in English. Translated by Geza Vermeš. Harmondsworth: Penguin, 1962.
The Dead Sea Scrolls of St. Mark's Monastery. Edited by Millar Burrows. 2 vols. New Haven: ASOR, 1951.
The Essene Writings from Qumran. Edited by André Dupont-Sommer and translated by Geza Vermeš. New York: Meridian, 1962.
The Fathers according to Rabbi Nathan. Edited and translated by Judah Goldin. Yale Judaica Series, 10. New Haven: Yale, 1955.
Josephus. *Works.* Edited and translated by H. St. J. Thackeray and others. 9 vols. Loeb Classical Library. Cambridge: Harvard, 1926-1965.
Mekilta de Rabbi Ishmael. Edited and translated by J. Z. Lauterbach. 3 vols. Philadelphia: Jewish Publication Society, 1933.
Midrash on Psalms. Edited and translated by William Braude. 2 vols. Yale Judaica Series, 13. New Haven: Yale, 1959.
Midrash rabbah. Translated by H. Freedman and Maurice Simon. 13 vol. in 10. London: Soncino, 1939.
Mischna. Edited by Willem Surenhusius. 6 vols., fol. Amsterdam, 1698-1703.
Mishnah. Edited and translated by Herbert Danby. Oxford: University Press, 1933.
Novum Testamentum Graece. Edited by Eberhard Nestle and Kurt Aland. 25th edition. Stuttgart: Württembergische Bibelanstalt, 1963.
Padres Apologistas Griegos. Edited and translated by Daniel Ruiz Bueno. Madrid: Biblioteca de Autores Cristianos, 1954.
Philo. *Works.* Edited and translated by F. H. Colson and others. 10 vols. Loeb Classical Library. Cambridge, Mass.: Harvard, 1929-1962.
Pirke de Rabbi Eleazar. Edited and translated by Gerald Friedlander. New York: Hermon, 1971.
The Psalms Scroll of Qumran Cave 11 (11 Q Ps^a.). Edited by J. A. Sanders. Discoveries in the Judean Desert of Jordan, 4. Oxford: Clarendon, 1965.
Seder R. Amram Gaon, Part I. Edited by D. Hedegard. Lund: Lindstedts, 1951.

Septuaginta, id est Vetus Testamentum Graece juxta LXX Interpretes. Edited by A. Rahlfs. 7th edition. 2 vols. Stuttgart: Württembergische Bibelanstalt, 1962.

Shishah Sidre Mishnah. Edited by Chanoch Albeck. 6 vols. Jerusalem-Tel Aviv: Bialik Institute-Dvir, 1953-1959.

Siddur. The Authorized Daily Prayer Book. Edited and translated by J. H. Hertz. New York: Bloch, 1948.

Sifre ad Deuteronomium. Edited by Louis Finkelstein. Berlin: Jüdischer Kulturbund, 1939.

Synopsis quattuor evangeliorum. Edited by Kurt Aland. Stuttgart: Württembergische Bibelanstalt, 1964.

Le Talmud de Jerusalem. Edited and translated by Moise Schwab, 1871-1890. 7 vols. Repr. Paris: Maisonneuve, 1960.

Testamenta XII Patriarcharum. Edited by Marinus de Jonge. Leiden: Brill, 1964.

Die Texte aus Qumran. Edited and translated by Eduard Lohse. Darmstadt: Wissenschaftliche Buchgesellschaft, 1964.

Tosefta. Edited by M. S. Zuckermandel. Repr. Jerusalem: Wahrmann, 1970.

II. DICTIONARIES AND ENCYCLOPEDIAS

Bauer, Walter, *A Greek-English Lexicon of the New Testament and Other Early Christian Literature.* Translated and adapted by W. F. Arndt and F. W. Gingrich. Chicago: University of Chicago, 1957.

Blass, F., and Debrunner, A. *A Greek Grammar of the New Testament and Other Early Christian Literature.* Translated and revised by R. W. Funk. Chicago: University of Chicago, 1961.

Brown, Francis; Driver, S. R.; and Briggs, C. A. *A Hebrew and English Lexicon of the Old Testament.* Oxford: Clarendon, 1907, 1962.

Buttrick, G.A. *The Interpreter's Dictionary of the Bible.* 4 vols. New York: Abingdon, 1962.

Encyclopedia Judaica. 16 vols. Jerusalem-New York: Keter and Macmillan, 1972.

Jastrow, Marcus. *A Dictionary of the Targumim, the Talmud Babli and Yerushalmi, and the Midrashic Literature.* 2 vols. New York: Pardes, 1903, 1950.

Joüon, Paul. *Grammaire de l'hébreu biblique.* Rome: Biblical Institute, 1923, 1965.

Kittel, Gerhard, ed. *Theological Dictionary of the New Testament.* 9 vols. Grand Rapids: Eerdmans, 1964-1973.

Lisowsky, Gerhard. *Konkordanz zum hebräischen alten Testament.* Stuttgart: Württembergische Bibelanstalt, 1958.

Mandelkern, Solomon. *Veteris Testamenti Concordantiae.* 9th ed. Jerusalem-Tel Aviv: Schocken, 1971.

Morgenthaler, Robert. *Statistik des neutestamentlichen Wortschatzes.* Zurich: Gotthelf, 1958.

Moulton, W. F., and Geden, A. S. *A Concordance to the Greek Testament.* Edinburgh: T. & T. Clark, 1970.

Segal, M. H. *A Grammar of Mishnaic Hebrew.* Oxford: Clarendon, 1927, 1958.

Singer, Isidore, ed. *The Jewish Encyclopedia.* 12 vols. New York: Funk & Wagnalls, 1907.

III. SECONDARY LITERATURE

Albeck, Chanoch. "Aus der neuesten Mischnaliterature," *MGWJ* 73 (1929): 4-25; 155-157.

——. *Einführung in die Mischna. Studia Judaica,* 6. Berlin: de Gruyter, 1971.

Albright, W. F. "Canaanite-Phoenician Sources of Hebrew Wisdom," *VT Supplement,* 3 (1955): 1-15.

Allen, Willoughby C. *A Commentary on the Gospel according to Saint Matthew.* Edinburgh: T. & T. Clark, 1907, 1912.

BIBLIOGRAPHY 199

Allon, G. "The Application of the Laws on Ritual Purity," *Researches in the History of Israel*. Tel Aviv: 1957; I, 148-177.
——. "Concerning the History of Juridical Authorities in Palestine during the Talmudic Period," *Zion* 12 (1947): 101-135, 193.
Alt, Albrecht. "Die Weisheit Salomos," *Kleine Schriften*. Munich: Beck, 1959.
Arvedson, Thomas. *Das Mysterium Christi*. Uppsala: Lundequist, 1937.
Avigad, Nahman. *Beth She^carim*. Volume III. Jerusalem: Israel Exploration Society with the assistance of Mosad Bialik, 1971.
——. "The Necropolis of Beth Sche^carim," *Archaeological Discoveries in the Holy Land*. Archaeological Institute of America. New York: Crowell, 1967.
Bacher, W. *Die Agada der Tannaiten*. Strasburg: K. Trübner, 1884. 2nd ed., 1903.
——. "Zwei alte Abothkommentare," *MGWJ* 49 (1905): 641-666.
Baeck, Leo. *The Pharisees and Other Essays*. New York: Schocken, 1947.
Baltzer, Klaus. *The Covenant Formulary*. Philadelphia: Fortress, 1971.
Bamberger, B. J. *Proselytism in the Talmudic Period*. New York: Ktav, 1968 (1st ed., 1939).
Banks, R. "Matthew's Understanding of the Law: Authenticity and Interpretation in Matthew 5:17-20," *JBL* 93 (1974): 226-242.
Becker, J. *Untersuchungen zur Entstehungsgeschichte der Testamente der Zwölf Patriarchen*. AGSU, 8. Leiden: Brill, 1970.
Benoit, Pierre. *L'évangile selon St. Matthieu*. Paris: Cerf, 1961.
——. "Rabbi Aqiba ben Joseph, sage et héros du Judaïsme," *RB* 54 (1947): 54-89. Reprinted in *Exégèse et théologie* II. Paris: Cerf, 1961, 340-379.
——, and Boismard, M. E. *Synopse des quatre évangiles en français*, Vol. II, *Commentaire*. Paris: Cerf, 1972.
Bertram, Georg. "Der Begriff der Erziehung in der griechischen Bibel," *Imago Dei*. Gustav Krüger Festschrift, ed. H. Bornkamm. Giessen: Töpelmann, 1932. Pp. 33-51.
Betz, Hans Dieter. "The logion of the easy yoke and of rest (Matthew 11:28-30)," *JBL* 86 (1967): 1024.
——. *Nachfolge und Nachamung Jesu Christi im Neuen Testament*. BHT, 37. Tübingen: Mohr, 1967.
Betz, Otto. *Offenbarung und Schriftforschung in der Qumransekte*. WUNT, 6. Tübingen: Mohr, 1960.
Bickermann, Élie. "La chaine de la tradition pharisienne." *RB* 59 (1952): 44-54.
——. "The maxim of Antigonus of Socho." *HTR* 44 (1951): 153-165.
Black, Matthew. *An Aramaic Approach to the Gospels and Acts*. Third edition. Oxford: Clarendon, 1967.
Blank, S. M. "The Dissident Laity in Early Judaism." *HUCA* 19 (1945-46): 1-42.
Blau, L. "Origine et histoire de la lecture du Schema." *REJ* 31 (1895): 181-205.
Bokser, B. Z. *Pharisaic Judaism in Transition*. New York: Bloch, 1935. Reprinted Arno Press, 1973.
Bonnard, Pierre, *L'évangile selon St. Matthieu*. Neuchatel: Delachaux & Niestlé, 1970.
——. *La sagesse en personne annoncée et venue: Jésus Christ*. Paris: Cerf, 1966.
Bonsirven, J. *Le Judaïsme palestinien au temps de Jésus-Christ*. 2 vols. Paris: Beauchesne, 1934.
——. *Palestinian Judaism in the Time of Jesus Christ*. New York: Holt, 1964.
——. *Textes Rabbiniques des deux premiers siècles chrétiens*. Rome: P.B.I., 1955.
Bornkamm, Gunther. *Jesus of Nazareth*. New York: Harper, 1960.
——. *Studien zu Antike und Urchristentum*. Munich: Kaiser, 1959.
——; Barth, G.; and Held, H. J. *Tradition & Interpretation in Matthew*. Philadelphia: Westminster, 1963.

———. "The Risen Lord and the Earthly Jesus: Matthew 28:16-20." *The Future of Our Religious Past*. Bultmann Festschrift. London: SCM, 1971, pp. 203-229.

Boström, Gustav. *Proverbiastudien: die Weisheit und das fremde Weib in Spr. 1-9*. Lund: Gleerup, 1935.

Bousset, W. *Jüdisch-christlicher Schulbetrieb in Alexandria und Rom*. FRLANT, n. 23. Göttingen: Vandenhoeck & Ruprecht, 1915.

———. *Kyrios Christos*. 1913. Nashville: Abingdon, 1970.

———, and Gressmann, H. *Die Religion des Judentums im späthellenistischen Zeitalter*. 4th ed. Tübingen: Mohr, 1966.

Bouyer, Louis. "Gnosis: le sens orthodoxe de l'expression jusqu'aux Pères alexandrins." *JTS*, n.s., 4 (1953): 188-203.

———. *The Spirituality of the New Testament and the Fathers*. New York: Desclee, 1963.

Bowker, J. *Jesus and the Pharisees*. Cambridge: University Press, 1973.

———. *The Targums and Rabbinic Literature*. Cambridge: University Press, 1969.

Braaten, C. E., and Harrisville, Roy A., eds. *The Historical Jesus and the Kerygmatic Christ*. Nashville: Abingdon, 1964.

Brandt, W. *Jüdische Reinheitslehre und ihre Beschreibung in den Evangelien*. BZAW 19. Giessen: Töpelmann, 1910.

Braun, F. M. "St. Jean, la sagesse et l'histoire." *Neotestamentica et patristica*. Cullmann Fs. Supplement to *Numen*, 6. Leiden: Brill, 1962, pp. 123-133.

Braun, Herbert, *Spätjüdisch-häretischer und frühchristlicher Radikalismus*. Tübingen: Mohr, 1957.

Brown, R. E. *The Gospel according to John*. 2 vols. Anchor Bible. New York: Doubleday, 1966.

———. "Jesus and Elisha," *Perspective* 12 (1971): 85-104.

Brownlee, W. H. *The Dead Sea Manual of Discipline*. New Haven: BASOR, 1951. Supplementary Studies, nos. 10-12.

Bruce, F. F. *New Testament History*. London: Nelson, 1969.

Büchler, A. *Der Galiläische Am Ha-Ares des zweiten Jahrhunderts*. Vienna: A. Hölder, 1906.

———. "Learning and Teaching in the Open Air in Palestine." *JQR*, n.s., 4 (1913): 485-491.

———. "The Levitical Impurity of the Gentile in Palestine before the Year 70." *JQR*, n.s., 17 (1926-27): 1-81.

———. *The Political & the Social Leaders of the Jewish Community of Sepphoris in the 2nd and 3rd Centuries*. Jews' College Publications, No. 1. London: Jews' College, n.d.

Bultmann, Rudolf. *History of the Synoptic Tradition*. 1921. New York: Harper, 1963.

———. *Jesus and the Word*. London: Fontana, 1958.

Bunim, I. M. *Ethics from Sinai*. New York: Feldheim, 1964 .

Burchard, Chr.; Jervell, J.; and Thomas J. *Studien zu den Testamenten der zwölf Patriarchen*. BZNW 36. Berlin: de Gruyter, 1969.

Burkitt, F. C. *The Gospel History and Its Transmission*. 2nd ed. Edinburgh: Clark, 1907.

Bury, R. G. "Theory of Education in Plato's Laws." *Revue des Études grecques* 50 (1937): 304-320.

Byatt, A. "Josephus & Population Numbers in First Century Palestine." *PEQ* 105 (1973): 51-60.

Campenhausen, Hans von. "Faith and Culture in the New Testament." *Tradition and Life in the Church*. Philadelphia: Fortress, 1968, pp. 19-41 .

Carmignac, J. "HRBYM: les 'Nombreux' ou les 'notables'?" *RdeQ* 7 (1971): 575-86.

Casaril, Guy. *Rabbi Simeon bar Yochai et la Cabbale*. Maîtres spirituels, no. 26. Paris: Seuil, 1961.

Cerfaux, Lucien. "Les sources scriptuaires de Mt. 11:25-30," *ETL* 30 (1954): 740-46; 31 (1955): 331-42.

Chadwick, H., and Campenhausen, H. von. *Jerusalem and Rome*. Philadelphia: Fortress, 1966.

Christ, Felix. *Jesus Sophia*. ATANT, 57. Zurich: Zwingli, 1970.

Christie, W. M. "The Jamnia Period in Jewish History." *JTS* 26 (1925): 347-364.

Clark, Martin L. *Higher Education in the Ancient World*. Albuquerque: University of New Mexico, 1971.

Cody, Aelred. *A History of Old Testament Priesthood*. Rome: PBI, 1969.

Cohon, S. S. "The Place of Jesus in the Religious Life of His Day." *JBL* 48 (1929): 82-108.

Colpe, Carsten. *Die religionsgeschichtliche Schule*. FRLANT 78. Göttingen: Vandenhoeck & Ruprecht, 1961.

Conzelmann, Hans. "The Mother of Wisdom." *The Future of Our Religious Past*. Bultmann Festschrift. London: SCM, 1971.

Creed, John Martin. *The Gospel according to St. Luke*. London: Macmillan, 1930, 1965.

Cullmann, O. *The Christology of the New Testament*. Philadelphia: Westminster, 1963.

Cumont, F. V. *Astrology and Religion among the Greeks and Romans*. 2nd ed. New York: Dover, 1960.

Curtis, W. A. *Jesus Christ the Teacher*. Oxford: University Press, 1943.

Dalman, Gustav. *Jesus-Jeschua*. Leipzig: Hinrich, 1922.

——. *Die Worte Jesu*. I. 2nd ed. Leipzig: Hinrich, 1930.

Danby, H. *Studies in Judaism*. Jerusalem: St. George, 1922.

Daniélou, Jean. *Philon d'Alexandrie*. Paris: Fayard, 1956.

——. *The Theology of Jewish Christianity*. London: Darton, 1964.

Dalbert, P. *Die Theologie der hellenistische-jüdischen Missionsliteratur*. Theologische Forschung, 4. Hamburg: H. Reich, 1954.

Daube, David. "Alexandrian Methods of Interpretation and the Rabbis." *Festschriebe Hans Lewald*. Basel: Helbing & Lichtenhahn, 1953, pp. 27-44 (non vidi).

——. "*exousia* in Mk 1:22 & 27," *JTS* 39 (1938): 45-59.

——. *The New Testament and Rabbinic Judaism*. London: Athlone, 1956.

——. "Rabbinic Methods of Interpretation and Hellenistic Rhetoric." *HUCA* 22 (1949): 239-264.

——. "Responsibilities of master and disciples in the Gospels." *NTS* 19 (1972): 1-15.

——. "Zur frühtalmudischen Rechtspraxis." *ZAW* 50 (1932): 148-58.

Davies, W. D. *Christian Origins and Judaism*. Philadelphia: Westminster, 1962.

——. *Introduction to Pharisaism*. Philadelphia: Fortress, 1967.

——. "The Moral Teaching of the Early Church." *Use of the Old Testament in the New and Other Essays*. Ed. by J. M. Efird. Durham, N. C.: Duke University Press, 1972, pp. 310-332.

——. *Paul and Rabbinic Judaism*. London: SPCK, 1952.

——. "Reflections on Tradition: the Aboth Revisited." *Christian History and Interpretation: Studies Presented to John Knox*. Ed. by W. R. Farmer, C. F. D. Moule, and R. R. Niebuhr. Cambridge: University Press, 1967.

——. "The Relevance of the Moral Teaching of the Early Church." *Neotestamentica et Semitica*. Ed. by E. E. Ellis and M. Wilcox. Edinburgh: T. & T. Clark, 1969, pp. 30-49.

——. *Setting of the Sermon on the Mount*. Cambridge: University Press, 1964.

Delcor, M. "Cinq nouveaux psaumes esséniens?" *RQ* 1 (1958): 85-102.

——. "Repas cultuels esséniens." *RQ* 6 (1967): 401-25.

——. "Zum Psalter von Qumran." *BZ* 10 (1966): 15-29.

Denis, A. M. *Introduction aux Pseudépigraphes grecs d'Ancient Testament*. Leiden: Brill, 1970.

——. *Les thèmes de connaissance dans le document de Damas*. Studia hellenistica, 15. Louvain: Publications universitaires, 1967.

Derret, J. D. M. *Law in the New Testament*. London: Darton, Longman, & Todd, 1970.

Descamps, A. "Essai d'interprétation de Mt. 5:17-48. 'Formgeschichte' ou 'Redaktions-geschichte'?" *Studia evangelica*, vol. 1 ed. by K. Aland et al. TU, 73. Berlin: Akademie, 1959.

Dibelius, Martin. *From Tradition to Gospel*. 1919. New York: Scribners, 1934.

Dihle, Albrecht. *Die goldene Regel; eine Einführung in die Geschichte der antiken und frühchristlichen Vulgärethik*. Studienhefte zur Altertumswissenschaft, 7. Göttingen: Vandenhoeck & Ruprecht, 1962.

Dodd, C. H. *Gospel and Law*. New York: Columbia University Press, 1951.

——. "Jesus as Teacher and Prophet." *Mysterium Christi*. Ed. by Bell and Deissmann. London: Longmans, 1930.

——. *New Testament Studies*. Manchester: University Press, 1953.

Donahue, J. R. "Tax Collectors & Sinners." *CBQ* 33 (1971): 39-61.

Donaldson, James. "The Title Rabbi in the Gospels; Some Reflections on the Evidence of the Synoptics." *JQR*, n.s., 63 (1973): 287-291.

Duesberg, H., and Fransen, I. *Ecclesiastico*. Turin: Marietti, 1966.

Dugmore, C. W. *The Influence of the Synagogue upon the Divine Office*. London: Faith, 1964.

Dungan, David L. *The Sayings of Jesus in the Churches of Paul*. Philadelphia: Fortress, 1971.

Dupont, J. *Les Béatitudes*. 3 vols. Études bibliques. Paris: Gabalda, 1965-73.

Dürr, Lorenz. *Das Erziehungswesen im Alten Testament und im antiken Orient*. Mitteilungen der Vorderasiatisch-aegyptischen Gesellschaft, 36. Bd, 2. Heft. Leipzig: Hinrich, 1932.

——. *Die Wertung des göttlichen Wortes im alten Testament und im antiken Orient*. Mitteilungen des vorderasiatisch-aegyptischen Gesellschaft, 42 Band, 1 Heft. Leipzig: Hinrich, 1938.

Ebner, Eliezer. *Elementary Education in Ancient Israel during the Tannaitic Period (10-220 C.E.)*. New York: Block, 1956.

Ehrhardt, Arnold. "The birth of the synagogue and Rabbi Akiba." *The Frameowrk of the New Testament Stories*. Manchester: University Press, 1964. Originally in *Studia Theologia* 12 (1958): 86-111.

Eissfeldt, Otto. *The Old Testament, an Introduction*. New York: Harper, 1965.

Ellis, E. E. "Paul and his Co-Workers." *NTS* 12 (1971): 437-54.

——. *Paul's Use of the Old Testament*. Edinburgh: Oliver & Boyd, 1957.

Falk, Zeev W. *Introduction to Jewish Law of the Second Commonwealth*. Part I. Arbeiten zur Geschichte des antiken Judentums und des Urchristentums, 11. Leiden: Brill, 1972.

Fascher, Erich. "Jesus der Lehrer," *ThLZ* 79 (1954): 325-42.

Feldman, L. H. "The Identity of Pollio, the Pharisee, in Josephus." *JQR*, n.s., 49 (1958-59): 53-62.

Feuillet, Andre. *Le Christ Sagesse de Dieu dans les Épîtres pauliniennes*. Paris: Gabalda, 1966.

——. "Jésus et la Sagesse divine d'après les évangiles synoptiques." *RB* 62 (1955): 161-96.

Fiebig, P. *Jüdische Wundergeschichten des neutestamentlichen Zietalters*. Tübingen: Mohr, 1911.

——. *Rabbinische Wundergeschichten des neutestamentlichen Zeitalters*. Bonn: A. Marcus und E. Weber, 1911.

Finkel, Asher. *The Pharisees and the Teacher of Nazareth*. AGSU, 4. Leiden: Brill. 1964.

Finkelstein, Louis. *Akiba.* New York: JPS, 1936; New York: Atheneum, 1970.

——. "Introductory Study to Prike Abot." *JBL* 57 (1938): 13-50.

——. *Mabo le-Massektot Abot ve-Abot d'Rabbi Natan.* Texts & Studies of JTS, Vol. 16. New York: Jewish Theological Seminary, 1950.

——. "The Maxim of the Anshe Keneset ha-Gedolah." *JBL* 59 (1940): 455-469.

——. "The oldest midrash: prerabbinic ideals and teachings in the Passover Haggadah." *HTR* 31 (1938): 291-317.

——. "The Pharisees: Their Origin and Their Philosophy." *HTR* 22 (1929): 185-261.

——. *The Pharisees.* 2 vols. Philadelphia: JPS, 1940.

Fischel, H. A. "The Uses of Sorites (*climax, gradatio*) in the Tannaitic Period." *HUCA* 44 (1973): 119-151.

Fitzmyer, J. A. "The Languages of Palestine in the First Century A.D." *CBQ* 32 (1970): 501-31.

Flusser, David. *Jesus.* New York: Herder and Herder, 1969.

——. "Blessed Are the Poor in Spirit...." *IEJ* 10 (1960): 1-13.

Fox, Michael. "The Sign of the Covenant." *Revue biblique* 81 (1974): 557-596.

Freyne, Sean. *The Twelve: Disciples and Apostles.* London: Sheed and Ward, 1968.

Fuller, R. H. *The Foundations of New Testament Christology.* London: Collins-Fontana, 1969; first edition, 1965.

Funk, R. W. *Language, Hermeneutic, and Word of God.* New York: Harper and Row, 1966.

Gaechter, Paul. *Das Matthäus Evangelium.* Innsbruck: Tyrolia, 1963.

Gelin, Albert. *The Poor of Yahweh.* Collegeville, Minn.: Liturgical Press, 1964.

Gerhardsson, Birger. "Du Judéo-christianisme à Jésus par le Shema^c." *Judéo-christianisme* (Mélanges Daniélou). Paris: Recherches de science religieuse, 1972.

——. *Memory and Manuscript.* Acta Sem. Nt. Upsaliensis, 22; Lund: Gleerup, 1961.

——. *Tradition and Transmission in Early Christianity.* Coniectanea Ntica., 20; Lund: Gleerup, 1964.

Gese, Hartmut. *Lehre und Wirklichkeit in der alten Weisheit.* Studien zu den Sprüchen Salomos und zu dem Buche Hiob. Tübingen: Mohr, 1958.

Glatzer, N. N. *Hillel the Elder.* New York: Schocken, 1966.

Glombitza, Otto. "Die christologische Aussage des Lukas in seiner Gestaltung der drei Nachfolgeworte Lukas 9:57-62." *Nov. Test.* 13 (1971): 14-23.

——. "Die Titel *didaskalos* und *epistatēs* für Jesus bei Lukas." *ZNW* 49 (1958): 275-278.

Goldberg, Abraham. "Purpose and Method in Rabbi Judah ha Nasi's Compilation of the Mishnah." *Tarbiz* 28 (1959): 260-70.

——. *Untersuchungen über die Vorstellung von der Schekhinah in der frühen rabbinischen Literatur.* Studia judaica, no. 5. Berlin: de Gruyter, 1969.

Goldin, Judah. "The End of Ecclesiastes: Literal Exegesis and Its Transformation." *Biblical Motifs.* Ed. A. Altmann. Studies and Texts, 3; Cambridge: Harvard University Press, 1966, pp. 135-158.

——. "Hillel the Elder." *JR* 26 (1946): 263-277.

——. *The Living Talmud: The Wisdom of the Fathers.* Chicago: University of Chicago, 1957.

——. "A Philosophical Session in a Tannaite Academy." *Traditio* 21 (1965): 1-19.

——. "Several Sidelights of a Torah Education." *Ex orbe religionum* (Studia Geo. Widengren). I. Leiden: Brill, 1972, pp. 176-191.

——. "The Third Chapter of Abot de Rabbi Natan." *HTR* 58 (1965): 365-386.

——. "Three pillars of Simeon the Righteous." *PAAJR* 27 (1958): 43-58.

——. "The Two Versions of Abot de Rabbi Nathan." *HUCA* 19 (1945-6): 97-120.

Goodenough, E. R. *Jewish Symbols in the Greco-Roman World.* New York: Princeton University Press, 1953.

Graetz, H. *Geschichte der Juden.* 4th ed. Leipzig: Leiner, 1888.

Grant, R. M. "The Book of Wisdom at Alexandria." *After the New Testament.* Philadelphia: Fortress, 1967, pp. 70-82.

———. *The Secret Sayings of Jesus.* New York: Doubleday, 1960.

Grelot, P. *Sens chrétien de l'Ancien Testament.* Tournai: Desclée, 1962.

Griffiths, J. G. "Wisdom about Tomorrow." *HTR* 53 (1960): 219-221.

Grundmann, Walter. *Das Evangelium nach Matthäus.* Berlin: Evangelische Verlaganstalt, 1968.

Guillaumont, A., et al. *The Gospel according to Thomas.* New York: Harper, 1959.

Gundry, R. H. *The Use of the Old Testament in St. Matthew's Gospel.* Leiden: Brill, 1967.

Guttmann, Alexander. *Rabbinic Judaism in the Making. The Halakhah from Ezra to Judah.* Detroit: Wayne State University Press, 1970.

———. "Tractate Abot—Its Place in Rabbinic Literature." *JQR* n.s. 41 (1950); 181-193.

Haenchen, E. *Die Botschaft des Thomasevangelium.* Berlin: Töpelmann, 1961.

Hahn, Ferdinand. *The Titles of Jesus in Christology.* Translated by H. Knight & G. Ogg. New York: World, 1969. (Original edition, 1963).

Hanson, P. D. "Jewish Apocalyptic against Its Near Eastern Environment." *RB* 78 (1971): 31-58.

Harder, G. "Jesus und das Gesetz (Mt 5:17-20)." *Antijudaismus in Neuen Testament.* Ed. W. P. Eckert et al. Munich: Kaiser, 1967.

Harnack, Adolf. *The Saying of Jesus.* New York: Putnam, 1908.

Harrington, D. J. "Matthean Studies since J. Rohde." *Heythrop Journal* 16 (1975): 375-388.

Haspecker, Josef. *Gottesfurcht bei Jesus Sirach.* An. Bib., 30. Rome: Biblical Institute, 1967.

Helfgott, B. W. *The Doctrine of Election in Tannaitic Literature.* New York: King's Crown, 1954.

Helfmeyer, F. J. " 'Gott nachfolgen' in den Qumrantexten." *RdeQ* 7 (1969): 81-104.

———. *Die Nachfolge Gottes in A.T.* BBB 29. Bonn: Hanstein, 1968 .

Hengel, M. "Die Ursprünge der Christlichen Mission." *NTS* 18 (1971): 15-38.

———. *Judaism and Hellenism.* 2 vols. London: SCM, 1974.

———. *Nachfolge und Charisma.* BZNW 34. Berlin: Töpelmann, 1868.

Herford, R. T. *The Ethics of the Talmud.* New York: Schocken, 1962.

Hertz, J. H. "An Explanation of Abot VI.3." *JQR,* n.s., 10 (1919-20): 199-202.

Hill, David. *The Gospel of Matthew.* New Century Bible. Greenwood, S. C.: The Attic Press, 1972.

Himmelfarb, Milton. "Gentlemen and Scholars." *Commentary* 56 (Oct., 1973): 68-71.

Hoh, Joseph. "Der christliche *grammateus* (Mt 13:52)." *BZ* 17 (1926): 256-269.

Hruby, Kurt. "La synagogue dans la littérature rabbinique." *L'orient syrien* 9 (1964): 473-514.

Hummel, Reinhart. *Die Auseinandersetzung zwischen Kirche und Judentum im Mattäusevangelium.* BET, 33. Munich: Kaiser, 1966.

Hunter, A. M. "Crux criticorum—Matt. xi. 25-30—A Recent Appraisal." *NTS* 8 (1961-2): 241-249.

Hunteau-Dubois, L. "Les sursauts du nationalisme juif contre l'occupation romaine: de Massada à Bar Kokhba." *REJ* 127 (1968): 133-209.

Isaacs, Nathan. "Study as a Mode of Worship." *Commentary* 1 (June, 1946): 77-84.

Jaeger, Werner. "Paideia Christi." *ZNW* 50 (1959): 1-14.

Jensen, Joseph. *The Use of Tora by Isaiah: His Debate with the Wisdom Tradition.* CBQ Monograph Series, 3. Washington D.C.: CBA, 1973.

Jentsch, Werner. *Urchristliches Erziehungsdenken.* Gütersloh: Bertelsmann, 1951. *BFCT,* 45, 3 Hefte. Pp. 85-139.

Jeremias, Joachim. *Jerusalem in the Time of Jesus*. Translated by F. H. & C. H. Caves. Philadelphia: Fortress, 1969.
——. *New Testament Theology*. Vol. 1. *The Proclamation of Jesus*. Translated by John Bowden. New York: Scribners, 1971.
——. *The Prayers of Jesus*. SBT, n.s., 6. London: SCM, 1967.
Jocz, Jakob. "Jesus and the Law." *Judaica*, 26 (1970): 105-124.
Johnson, M. D. *The Purpose of the Biblical Genealogies*. SNTS, MS, 8. Cambridge: University Press, 1969.
Kaminka, A. "Hillel's Life and Work." *JQR*, n.s., 30 (1939-40): 107-122.
Käsemann, Ernst. *Essays on New Testament Themes*. SBT, 41. London: SCM, 1964.
Katsch, Abraham I. "Unpublished Geniza Fragments of Pirke Aboth in the Antonin Geniza Collection in Leningrad." *JQR* 61 (1970): 1-14.
Kayatz, Christa. *Studien zu Proverbien 1-9*. WMzANT 22. Neukirchen-Vluyn: Erziehungsverlag, 1966.
Kilpatrick, G. D. *The Origins of the Gospel according to St. Matthew*. Oxford: Clarendon, 1946.
Kirk, K. E., ed. *The Apostolic Ministry*. London: Hodder & Stoughton, 1946.
Klein, Gunter. *Die zwölf Apostel*. Göttingen: Vandenhoeck & Ruprecht, 1961.
Knox, W. L. "The Divine Wisdom." *JTS* 38 (1937): 230-237.
Koester, Helmut. "Nomos physeōs: the Concept of Natural Law in Greek Thought." *Religions in Antiquity*. Goodenough Fs., ed. J. Neusner. Supp. to *Numen*, 14. Leiden: Brill, 1968.
Kohn, Jacob. "An Explanation of Abot vi.3." *JQR*, n.s., 11 (1920-21): 83-85.
Koolmeister, R. "Selbstverleugnung, Kreuzaufnahme und Nachfolge." *Charisteria Johanni Kopp*. Stockholm: 1954, pp. 64-94.
Krauss, S. "Outdoor Teaching in Talmudic Times." *JJS* 1 (1948-49): 82-84.
——. *Talmudische Archäologie*. 3 vols. Frankfurt a.M.: Kaufmann, 1912.
Kuhl, Josef. *Die Sendung Jesu und der Kirche nach dem Johannesevangelium*. Studia Instituti Missiologici Societatis Verbi Divini, no. 11. Steyler Verlag/St. Augustin. Kaldenkirchen, 1967.
Kuhn, K. G. *Achtzehngebet und Vaterunser und der Reim*. WUzNT, 1. Tübingen: Mohr, 1950.
——. *Phylakterien aus Höhle 4 von Qumran*. Heidelberg: Winter, 1957.
Kümmel, W. G. "Jesus und der jüdische Traditionsgedanke." *ZNW* 33 (1934): 105-130.
Kuss, Otto. *Der Römerbrief*. Regensburg: Pustet, 1963.
Lagrange, M. J. *Évangile selon St. Matthieu*. Paris: Gabalda. 1927.
Laistner, M. L. W. *Christianity and Pagan Culture in the Later Roman Empire*. Ithaca: Cornell University Press, 1951.
Landau, L., ed. and trans. *Épître historique du R. Scherira Gaon*. Antwerp: Bary, 1904.
Leaney, A. R. C. *The Rule of Qumran and Its Meaning*. Philadelphia: Westminster, 1966.
Leclercq, Jean. *The Love of Learning and the Desire for God*. New York: Fordham University Press, 1961.
Légasse, S. "Scribes et disciples de Jésus." *RB* 68 (1968): 321-345; 481-506.
Légasse, Simon. *Jésus et l'enfant*. Études bibliques. Paris: Gabalda, 1969.
Levi, Isidore. "L'origine davidique de Hillel." *REJ* 31 (1895): 209 ff.
Lewis, J. P. "What Do We Mean by Jabneh?" *JBR* 32 (1964): 125-132.
Lewy, Hans. "Aristotle and the Jewish Sage according to Clearchus of Soli." *HTR* 31 (1938): 205-235.
Lieberman, Saul. "The Discipline in the So-Called Dead Sea Manual of Discipline." *JBL* 71 (1952): 199-206.

Limbeck, Meinrad. *Die Ordnung des Heils*. Untersuchungen zum Gesetzesverstandnis des Frühjudentums. Düsseldorf: Patmos, 1971.

Ljungman, Henrik. *Das Gesetz Erfüllen*, Mt 5:17 ff and 3:15 untersucht. Lund: Gleerup, 1954 .

Loeb, Isidore. "Notes sur le chapitre premier des Pirke Abot." *REJ* 19 (1889): 188-201.

Lohmeyer, Ernst, with Schmauch, Werner. *Das Evangelium des Matthäus*. Göttingen: Vandenhoeck & Ruprecht, 1956.

Lohr, C. H. "Oral Techniques in the Gospel of Matthew." *CBQ* 23 (1961): 403-435.

Lohse, Eduard. *Die Ordination im Spätjudentum und im Neuen Testament*. Göttingen: Vandenhoeck & Ruprecht, 1951.

Loisy, Alfred. *Les évangiles synoptiques*. 2 vols. Ceffonds: Chez l'auteur, 1907.

Lührmann, Dieter. "Ein Weisheitspsalm aus Qumran (11 Q Ps^a XVIII). *ZAW* 80 (1968): 87-98.

——. *Die Redaktion der Logienquelle*. WMzANT, 33. Neukirchen-Vluyn: Neukirchener Verlag, 1969.

McEleney, N. J. "Conversion, circumcision and the law." *NTS* 20 (1974): 319-341.

Mack, Burton Lee. *Logos und Sophia*. Untersuchungen zur Weisheisstheologie im hellenistischen Judentum. Studien zur Umwelt des N.T., 10. Göttingen: Vandenhoeck & Ruprecht, 1973.

Mack, R. *Der Zaddik in Talmud und Midrasch*. Leiden: Brill, 1957.

McKane, W. *Prophets and Wise Men*. London: SCM, 1966.

McKay, J. W. "Man's Love for God in Deuteronomy and the Father/Teacher-Son/Pupil Relationship." *VT* 22 (1972): 426-35.

McKenzie, J. L. "The Knowledge of God in Hosea." *JBL* 74 (1955): 22-27.

McNeile, Alan Hugh. *The Gospel according to St. Matthew*. London: Macmillan, 1915, 1961.

Maher, Michael. "Some Aspects of Torah in Judaism." *ITQ* 38 (1971): 310-325.

Maier, Gerhard. *Mensch und freier Wille*, nach den jüdischen Religionsparteien zwischen Ben Sira und Paulus. WUNT, 12. Tübingen: Mohr, 1971.

Manson, T. W. *The Church's Ministry*. London: Hodder and Stoughton, 1948.

——. "Sadducee and Pharisee." *BJRL* 22 (1938): 144-159.

——. *Sayings of Jesus*. London: SCM, 1937.

Mantel, Hugo. "The Nature of the Great Synagogue." *HTR* 60 (1967): 69-91.

——. "Ordination and Appointment in the Period of the Temple." *HTR* 57 (1964): 325-346.

——. *Studies in the History of the Sanhedrin*. Cambridge, Mass.: Harvard, 1965.

Marböck, Johann. *Weisheit im Wandel*. BBB 37. Bonn: Hanstein, 1971.

Marcus, Ralph. *Law in the Apocrypha*. New York: Columbia University Press, 1927.

——. "A Selected Bibliography of the Jews in the Hellenistic-Roman Period." *Proc. American Association for Jewish Research* 16 (1946-47): 97-182.

Marmorstein, A. "Les 'Épicuriens' dans la littérature talmudique." *REJ* 54 (1907): 181-193.

Marrou, H. I. *History of Education in Antiquity*. New York: Sheed & Ward, 1956.

Marti, Karl, & Beer, Georg. *Abot*. Giessen: Töpelmann, 1927.

Mays, J. L. *Hosea: A Commentary*. Philadelphia: Westminster, 1969.

Meeks, Wayne A. "The Image of the Androgyne." *History of Religions* 13 (1974): 165-208.

Mertens, H. *L'hymne de jubilation chez les Synoptiques* (*Mt. 11:25-30, Lk 10:21-22*). Gembloux: Gregoriana, 1957. (non vidi.)

Meye, R. P. *Jesus and the Twelve*. Grand Rapids: Eerdmann, 1968.

Meyer, Eduard. *Ursprung und Anfänge des Christentums*. Vol. 1. 1921. Darmstadt: Wissenschaftliche Buchgesellschaft, 1962.

Meyer, Rudolf. *Tradition und Neuschöpfung im antiken Judentum*, dargestellt an der Geschichte des Pharisäismus mit einem Beitrag von H.-F. Weiss: Der Pharisäismus im Lichte der Überlieferung des N. T. Sitzungsberichte der sächsischen Akademie der Wissenschaften zu Leipzig, Philol.-hist. Klasse, Bd 110, Heft 2. Berlin: Akademie, 1965.

Montefiore, C. G. *The Synoptic Gospels*. 2 vols. 2nd ed. London: Macmillan, 1927.

——, and Loewe, H., eds. *A Rabbinic Anthology*. New York: Meridian, 1963.

Moore, G. F. "The Am Ha-Areṣ (The People of the Land) and the Haberim (Associates)." Appendix E of Vol. I of *Beginnings of Christianity*. Ed. by K. Lake and F. J. Foakes-Jackson. London: Macmillan, 1920-33.

——. *Judaism in the First Centuries of the Christian Era: The Age of the Tannaim*. 3 vols. Cambridge, Mass.: Harvard University Press, 1927-32.

——. "Simeon the Righteous." *Jewish Studies in Memory of Israel Abrahams*. New York: Jewish Institute of Religion, 1927. Pp. 349-364.

Morgenstern, Julian. "The Hasidim—Who Were They?" *HUCA* 38 (1967): 59-74.

Murphy, R. E. "Assumptions and Problems in Old Testament Wisdom Research." *CBQ* 29 (1967): 407-418.

——. "A Consideration of the Classification, 'Wisdom Psalms.'" *Supplement VT*, 9. Leiden: Brill, 1963.

Murphy-O'Connor, Jerome, ed. *Paul and Qumran*. London: Chapman, 1968.

——. "The Essenes and Their History." *Revue Biblique* 81 (1974): 15-44.

Neusner, Jacob. *Development of a Legend*. Studies on the Traditions concerning Yohanan ben Zakkai. *SP-B*, 16. Leiden: Brill, 1970.

——. "The Fellowship (*haburah*) in the Second Jewish Commonwealth." *HTR* 53 (1960): 124-42.

——. *Fellowship in Judaism*. London: Vallentine, Mitchel, 1963.

——. "From Exegesis to Fable in Rabbinic Traditions about the Pharisees." *JJS* 25 (1974): 263-269.

——. *History and Torah*. New York: Schocken, 1965.

——. *A History of the Jews in Babylonia*. 5 vols. Leiden: Brill, 1965-70.

——. "The Ideal of Purity in Ancient Judaism." *JAAR* 43 (1975): 15-26.

——. "Josephus's Pharisees." *Ex orbe religionum* (Studia Geo. Widengren) I. Leiden: Brill, 1972.

——. *A Life of Yohanan ben Zakkai. Ca. 1-80 C.E.* 2nd, rev. ed. Leiden: Brill, 1970.

——, ed. *The Modern Study of the Mishnah*. Leiden: Brill, 1973. Studia Post-Biblica, no. 23.

——. "The Phenomenon of the Rabbi in Late Antiquity." *Numen* 16 (1969: 1-20; 17 (1970): 1-18.

——. "Priestly Views of Yohanan ben Zakkai." *Kairos*, N.F., 11 (1969): 303-312.

——. *The Rabbinic Traditions about the Pharisees before 70*. 3 vols. Leiden: Brill, 1971.

——. "Rabbis and Community in Third Century Babylonia." *Religions in Antiquity*. (Goodenough Fs.), ed. by J. Neusner (Supplements to *Numen*, 14) Leiden: Brill, 1968. Pp. 438-459.

——. "Some Early Traditions concerning Yohanan ben Zakkai." *Studies in Jewish Bibliography, History and Literature in Honor of I. E. Kirv*. New York: Ktav, 1971.

Newman, Jacob. *Halachic Sources. From the Beginning to the Ninth Century*. Leiden: Brill, 1969.

——. *Semikha*. Manchester: University Press, 1950.

Nichelsburg, Jr., G. W. E. *Resurrection, Immortality, and Eternal Life in Intertestamental Judaism*. HTS, 26. Cambridge, Mass.: Harvard, 1972.

Nilsson, M. P. *Die Hellenistische Schule*. 1955. (Non vidi.)

Nock, A. D. *Conversion*. Oxford: University Press, 1933.

Norden, Eduard. *Agnostos Theos*. 1912. Stuttgart: Teubner, 1956.

Norman, Friedrich. *Christos Didaskalos*. Die Vorstellung von Christus als Lehrer in der christlichen Literatur des ersten und zweiten Jahrhunderts. Münsterische Beiträge zur Theologie, 32. Münster i./W: Aschendorff, 1966.

Oesterley, W. O. E. *The Jews and Judaism during the Greek Period*. London: SPCK, 1941.

Östborn, G. *Tora in the Old Testament*. Lund: Gleerup, 1945.

Paschen, Wilfried. *Rein und Unrein*. SANT, 24. Munich: Kösel, 1970.

Perrin, N. *Rediscovering the Teaching of Jesus*. New York: Harper, 1967.

Pesch, W. *Der Lohngedanke in der Lehre Jesu*. Munich: K. Zink, 1955.

Philonenko, M. "L'origine essénienne des cinq psaumes syriaques de David." *Semitica* 9 (1958): 35-48.

Pines, S. "Judaeo-Christian Materials in an Arabic Jewish Treatise." Proc. American Academy for Jewish Research 35 (1967): 187-217.

Plummer, Alfred. *An Exegetical Commentary on the Gospel according to S. Matthew*. 1909. Grand Rapids: Eerdmans, 1953.

Podro, Joshua. *The Last Pharisee*. London: Vallentine, Mitchell, 1959.

Polzin, R. "Notes on the Dating of the Non-Massoretic Psalms of 11 Q Ps^a." *HTR* 60 (1967): 468-76.

Rabin, Chaim. *Qumran Studies*. Oxford: University Press, 1957.

Rad, Gerhard von. *Deuteronomy: A Commentary*. Philadelphia: Westminster, 1966.

——. *Old Testament Theology*. 2 vols. Edinburgh: Oliver and Boyd, 1963.

——. *Wisdom in Israel*. Nashville: Abingdon, 1972.

Rankin, O. S. "The Extent of the Influence of the Synagogue Service upon Christian Worship." *JJS* 1 (1948): 27-32.

——. *Israel's Wisdom Literature*. New York: Schocken, 1969; 1st ed. 1936.

Reese, J. M. *Hellenistic Influence on the Book of Wisdom and Its Consequences*. An Bib., 41. Rome: PBI, 1971.

Reicke, Bo. *The New Testament Era*. 500 B.C. to A.D. 100. Philadelphia: Fortress, 1968.

Reider, J. *The Book of Wisdom*. New York: Harper, 1957.

Ringgren, Helmer. *Word and Wisdom*. Lund: Gleerup, 1947.

Riesenfeld, Harald. *The Gospel Tradition*. Philadelphia: Fortress, 1970.

Rivkin, Ellis. "Pharisaism and the Crisis of the Individual in the Greco-Roman World." *JQR*, n.s., 61 (1970): 27-53.

Robinson, J. M. "Die Hodajot-Formel in Gebet und Hymnus des Frühchristentums." *Apophoreta* (Fs. Haenchen.) BZNW, 30. Berlin: Töpelmann, 1964, pp. 194-235.

——. "Logoi Sophon: on the Gattung of Q." *The Future of Our Religious Past*. Essays in Honor or Rudolf Bultmann. London: SCM, 1971, pp. 84-130.

Robinson, Theodore H. *The Gospel of Matthew*. New York: Harper, 1927.

Rordorf, W. "Un chapître d'éthique judéo-chrétienne: les deux voies." *Judéo-Christianisme*, Daniélou-Festschrift. Paris: Beauchesne, 1972.

Rössler, Dietrich. *Gesetz und Geschichte*. WMANT, 3. Neukirchen: Neukirchener Verlag, 1962.

Rowley, H. H. *Worship in Ancient Israel*. Philadelphia: Fortress, 1967.

Sabourin, Leopold. *Priesthood: A Comparative Study*. Supplements to *Numen*, 25. Leiden: Brill, 1973.

Saldarini, A. J. "The End of the Rabbinic Chain of Tradition." *JBL* 93 (1974): 97-106.

Sand, A. *Das Gesetz und die Propheten*. Biblische Untersuchungen, 11. Regensburg: Pustet, 1974.

Sanday, W., and Headlam, A. C. *Romans*. Edinburgh: Clark, 1902.

Sanders, J. A. *The Dead Sea Psalms Scroll*. Ithaca, New York: Cornell University Press, 1967.

Sandmel, Samuel. "Parallelomania." *JBL* 81 (1962): 1-13.

Schechter, Salomon. *Aboth de Rabbi Nathan*. Vienna: Lippe, 1887.

——. *Aspects of Rabbinic Theology*. New York: Schocken, 1961; 1st ed. 1909.

Schlatter, Adolf. *Der Evangelist Matthäus*. Stuttgart: Calwer, 1929, 1963.

Schoeps, Hans Joachim. *Aus frühchristlicher Zeit*. Tübingen: Mohr, 1950.

——. *Jewish Christianity*. Philadelphia: Fortress, 1969.

Sheridan, Mark. "Disciples and Discipleship in Mt and Lk." *BTB* 3 (1973): 235-55.

Schrenk, Gottlieb. "Rabbinische Charakterköpfe im urchristlichen Zeitalter." *Judaica* 1 (1945-46): 117-156.

Schulz, Siegfried. "Die Bedeutung der neuen Targumforschung für die synoptische Tradition." *Abraham Unser Vater*. (O. Michel Fs.), ed. O. Betz et al. AGSU, 5. Leiden: Brill, 1963.

Shanks, Hershel. "Is the Title 'Rabbi' Anachronistic in the Gospels?" *JQR*, n.s., 53 (1962-63): 337-349.

Schelkle, K. H. *Discipleship and Priesthood*. New York: Herder and Herder, 1965.

Schlatter, A. *Das Wunder in der Synagoge*. BFCT, 16, 5. Gutersloh: Mohn, 1912.

Schmid, Josef. *Das Evangelium nach Matthäus*. Regensburg: Pustet, 1959.

Schmithals, Walter. *The Apocalyptic Movement*. New York: Abingdon, 1975.

——. *The Office of Apostle in the Early Church*. Nashville: Abingdon, 1969.

Schniewind, Julius. *Das Evangelium nach Matthäus*. NTD. Göttingen: Vandenhoeck & Ruprecht, 1936; 1963.

Schultz, A. *Jünger des Herrn*. Munich: Kösel, 1964.

——. *Nachfolgen und Nachahmen*. SANT, 10. Munich: Kösel, 1962.

Schürer, Emil. *The History of the Jewish People in the Time of Jesus Christ*. 3 vols. Edinburgh: T. & T. Clark, 1885.

Schweizer, Eduard. *Lordship and Discipleship*. SBT, 28. London: SCM, 1960.

——. *Matthäus und seine Gemeinde*. Stuttgarter Bibelstudien, 71; Stuttgart: KWB, 1974.

Skehan, P. W. *Studies in Israelite Poetry and Wisdom*. CBQ Monograph Series, no. 1. Washington: Catholic Biblical Association of America, 1971.

——. "They Shall Not Be Found in Parables (Sir. 38:33)." *CBQ* 23 (1961): 40.

Smith, G. A. *The Book of the Twelve Prophets*. New York: Doubleday, 1929.

Smith, Morton. "Ezra." *Ex orbe religionum* (Studia Geo. Widengren), I. Leiden: Brill, 1972, pp. 141-143.

——. "Jesus' Attitude toward the Law." *Fourth World Congress of Jewish Studies*. Vol. 1. Jerusalem: World Union of Jewish Studies, 1967, pp. 241-4.

——. *Tannaitic Parallels to the Gospels*. JBL, MS, 6. Philadelphia: SBL, 1951; cor. repr. 1968.

Soggin, J. A. *Joshua: A Commentary*. Philadelphia: Westminster, 1972.

Sonne, I. "Remarks on 'Manual of Discipline,' Col. VI, 6-7." *VT* 7 (1957): 405-408.

Starcky, Jean. "Les quatre étapes du messianisme à Qumran." *RB* 70 (1963): 481-505.

Stemberger, Gunter. *Der Leib der Auferstehung*. An. Bib., 56. Rome: PBI, 1972.

Stendahl, Krister. *The Bible and the Role of Women*. Philadelphia: Fortress, 1966.

——. "The Called and the Chosen." A. Fridrichsen et al., *The Root of the Vine*. New York: Philosophical Library, 1953.

——. *School of St. Matthew*. Philadelphia: Fortress, 1968.

——, ed. *The Scrolls and the New Testament*. New York: Harper, 1957.

Strack, H. L. *Pirqe Aboth*. Leipzig: Hinrichs, 1915.

——, and Billerbeck, Paul. *Kommentar zum Neuen Testament aus Talmud und Midrasch*. 4 vols. Munich: Beck, 1922-1928.

Strauss, F. D. "Jesu Weheruf über Jerusalem und die *sophia tou theou*. Matthäus 23,

34-39, Luk. 11, 49-51. 13, 34 f. Ein Beitrag zur johanneischen Frage." *ZWT* 6 (1863): 84 ff.

Strecker, G. *Der Weg der Gerechtigkeit.* FRLANT, 82. Göttingen: Vandenhoeck und Ruprecht, 1966.

Strugnell, J. "Notes and Queries on the Ben Sira Scrolls." *Eretz-Israel* 9 (Albright Volume), 1969. Pp. 109-119.

——. "Notes on the Text and Transmission of the Apocryphal Psalms 151, 154 (= Syr. II) and 155 (= Syr. III)." *HTR* 59 (1966): 257-281.

Suggs, M. Jack. *Wisdom, Christology and Law in Matthew's Gospel.* Cambridge: Mass.: Harvard University Press, 1970.

Sutcliffe, E. F. "Sacred Meals at Qumran." *Heythrop Journal* 1 (1960): 48 ff.

Taylor, Charles. *Sayings of the Jeiwsh Fathers.* Cambridge 1897-1900; reprinted Amsterdam: Philo, 1970.

Taylor, Vincent. *The Gospel according to St. Mark.* London: Macmillan, 1966.

Teeple, H. M. "The Oral Tradition that Never Existed." *JBL* 89 (1970): 56-57.

Tinsley, E. J. *The Imitation of God in Christ.* London: SCM, 1960.

——. "Some Principles for Reconstructing a Doctrine of the Imitation of Christ." *Scot. J. T.* 25 (1972): 45-57.

Towner, W. S. "Form Criticism of Rabbinic Literature." *JJS* 24 (1973): 101-118.

——. The Rabbinic "Enumeration of Scriptural Examples." Studia Post-Biblica, no. 22. Leiden: Brill, 1973.

Toynbee, Arnold, ed. *The Crucible of Christianity.* London: Thames and Hudson, 1969.

Urbach, E. E. *Class-Status and Leadership in the World of the Palestinian Sages.* Proc., Israel Academy of Sciences and Humanities. Jerusalem, 1966.

——. "The Laws regarding Slavery." *Annual of Jewish Studies.* London: University Press, 1963 .

——. "The Rabbinical Laws of Idolatry in the Second and Third Centuries in the Light of Archaeological and Historical Facts." *Israel Exploration Journal* 9 (1959): 149-165, 229-245.

Vajda, Georges. "Une copie non identifiée du commentaire de Rabbi Israel ben Joseph sur *Abot.*" *REJ* 130 (1971): 99-102.

——. Review *REJ* 129 (1970): 101-110, of E. E. Urbach, *The Sages, their Concepts and Beliefs.* Jerusalem: Magnes, 1969.

Van Dulmen, Andrea. *Die Theologie des Gesetzes bei Paulus.* Stuttgart: Katholisches Bibelwerk, 1968.

Van Tilborg, Sjef. *The Jewish Leaders in Matthew.* Leiden: Brill, 1972.

Van Unnik, W. C., ed. *La littérature juive entre Tenach et Mischna: quelques problemes.* Journées bibliques de Louvain, 20, 1969. Leiden: Brill, 1974.

Vattioni, Francesco, ed. *Ecclesiastico.* (Hebrew, Greek, Latin, and Syriac.) Naples: Istituto Orientale, 1968.

Vaux, R. de. *Ancient Israel, Its Life and Institutions.* New York: McGraw-Hill, 1961.

Vermes, Geza. "The Decalogue and the Minim." *In Memoriam Paul Kahle.* BZAW, 103. Berlin: Töpelmann, 1968.

——. "Hanina ben Dosa." *JJS* 23 (1972): 28-50; 24 (1974): 51-64.

——. *Jesus the Jew.* New York: Macmillan, 1974.

——. "Pre-Mishnaic Jewish worship and the Phylacteries from the Dead Sea." *VT* 9 (1959): 65-72.

——. "The Torah Is a Light." *VT* 8 (1958): 436-438.

Vielhauer, Philip. "Anapausis." *Apophoreta* (Haenchen Fs.) BZNW, 30. Berlin: Töpelmann, 1964.

Vööbus, Arthur. *Celibacy, A Requirement for Admission to Baptism in the Early Syrian Church.* Stockholm: Papers of the Estonian Theological Society in Exile, no. 1, 1951.

Wach, Joachim. "Master and Disciple: Two Religiosociological Studies." *Journal of Religion.* 42 (1962): 1-21. Leipzig: 1924. Trans. by S. Heigelwach and Fred Streng.

Wacholder, B. Z. "A Qumran Attack on the Oral Exegesis?" *Rev. de Qumran* 5 (1966): 575-578.

Weber, Max. *Ancient Judaism.* Trans. and ed. by H. H. Gerth and Don Martindale. Glencoe, Ill.: Free Press, 1952.

Weinfeld, Moshe. *Deuteronomy and the Deuteronomic School.* Oxford: Clarendon, 1972.

Weiss, Johannes. "Das Logion Mt 11:25-30." *Heinrici Festschrift.* 1914 (non vidi).

Wellhausen, Julius. *Das Evangelium Matthaei.* Berlin: Reimer, 1914.

———. *Die Pharisäer und die Sadducäer.* Göttingen: Vandenhoeck and Ruprecht, 1967.

Wernberg-Möller, P. *The Manual of Discipline.* Studies on the Texts of the Desert of Judah, ed. by J. Van der Ploeg, vol. 1. Leiden: Brill, 1957.

Whybray, R. N. *The Intellectual Tradition in the Old Testament.* BZAW, 135. Berlin: de Gruyter, 1974.

———. *Wisdom in Proverbs.* SBT 45. London: SCM, 1965.

Williams, J. G. "The Prophetic 'Father': A Brief Explanation of the Term 'Sons of the Prophets,' " *JBL* 85 (1966): 344-348.

Wolff, H. W. *Amos the Prophet.* Philadelphia: Fortress, 1973.

———. " 'Wissen um Gott' bei Hosea als Urform von Theologie." *Ev. Theologie* 12 (1952/3): 533-54.

Wrege, H. T. *Überlieferungsgeschichte der Berg-Predigt.* Wiss. Untersuch. z. NT, 9. Tubingen: Mohr, 1968.

Wright, A. G. *The Literary Genre Midrash.* New York: Alba House, 1967.

INDEX OF REFERENCES

BIBLE

EARLY JUDAISM

QUMRAN

HELLENISTIC JUDAISM

RABBINIC
1. Mishnah

2. *Tosephta*

3. *Babylonian Talmud*

4. Palestinian Talmud

Pesachim
3:7 105, 106n
33a 21

Taanith
4:5 78

Yebamoth
1:6 50

5. *Targums*

Targum Canticles
5:10 100

Targum Jerus. Deuteronomy
32 100

6. *Midrashim*

Mekilta de Rabbi Ishmael
Exodus
17:9 100
18:12 100
20:21-23 69
31:13 22

Mekilta de R. Simeon b. Yohai
Exodus
19:17 107n
20:21 69

Sifra Leviticus
Intro. fol.
3a 22n

Sifre Deuteronomy
6:9 100
11:13 107n
11:12 102
sec. 34-35 32n
sec. 41, 48, 321 110n
sec. 343 17

Midrash on Psalms I
17, p. 23 151n

Midrash rabbah

Lev. R.
7:3 88

Ruth R.
1:17 104

Qoh R.
1:15 104

Cant. R.
2:14 106

Lam. R.
2 78
2:4 on 2:2 47n

Midrash Tannaim
1:7 107n

7. *Prayerbook*

Seder R. Amram Gaon, ed. Hedegard
18f 41n

183 121n

GREEK AND ROMAN LITERATURE

Aristotle
Eudem. Ethics
7, 15 87

Metaphysics I
1. 18 39

Nic. Ethics
10, 7 87

Diogenes Laertius
7:92ff 54

Herodotus
1, 32-34 38

Martial
Epig.
7:81, 6 80

Menander
Thais
(218) 52

INDEX OF NAMES